# BEN HELFGOTT

The Story of One of the Boys

## Also by Michael Freedland

*Al Jolson* (later and in the US, *Jolson*)
*Irving Berlin* (later, *Salute to Irving Berlin*)
*James Cagney* (in the US, *Cagney*)
*Fred Astaire*
*Sophie: The Story of Sophie Tucker*
*Jerome Kern*
*Errol Flynn* (in the US, *The Two Lives of Errol Flynn*)
*Gregory Peck*
*Maurice Chevalier*
*Peter O'Toole*
*The Warner Brothers*
*So Let's Hear the Applause: The Story of the Jewish Entertainer*
*Katharine Hepburn*
*The Goldwyn Touch*
*The Secret Life of Danny Kaye*
*Dustin*
*Leonard Bernstein*
*Kenneth Williams*
*Sean Connery*
*Andre Previn*
*Music Man*
*Bob Hope*
*Bing Crosby*
*All The Way: A Biography of Frank Sinatra*
*Michael Caine*
*Doris Day*
*Some Like It Cool: The Charmed Life of Jack Lemmon*
*Liza with a 'Z': The Traumas and Triumphs of Liza Minnelli*
*Witch Hunt in Hollywood*
*The Men Who Made Hollywood*
*Judy Garland: The Other Side of the Rainbow*
*Elvis Memories*
*Man on the Rock*

With Morecambe and Wise
*There's No Answer to That*

Memoirs
*Confessions of a Serial Biographer*

For Adele
who has brought back the sunshine

# BEN HELFGOTT

## The Story of One of the Boys

## Michael Freedland

VALLENTINE MITCHELL

LONDON • PORTLAND, OR

*First published in 2018 by Vallentine Mitchell*

Catalyst House,
720 Centennial Court,
Centennial Park, Elstree WD6 3SY, UK

920 NE 58th Avenue, Suite 300
Portland, Oregon
97213-3786 USA

**www.vmbooks.com**

British Library Cataloguing in Publication Data:
An entry can be found on request

ISBN 978 1 910383 15 5 (Cloth)
ISBN 978 1 910383 16 2 (Ebook)

Library of Congress Cataloging in Publication Data:
An entry can be found on request

Printed by Clays Ltd, Bungay, Suffolk

# Contents

# Acknowledgements

In some ways six million people contributed to this book, plus a smattering of Olympians.

But more directly, it was Ben Helfgott himself who is not just the inspiration for the following pages and the central character. He is, in some ways, its narrator, in the form of a hundred or more interview sessions with me. It is very much a family story, in a way a love story – between Ben and his father, Moishe, whose presence is always with him – and, consequently, with this story.

I also have to thank his wife Arza, their three sons, Maurice, Michael and Nathan and, very specifically, his sister Mala Tribich, who has illustrated the tale of her brother's life incredibly graphically.

Also, my thanks go to Angela Cohen, Alan Jay, Jeffrey Pinnick, Ruth-Anne Lenga, Aubrey Rose, Ruth Rosen and Ben's Piotrkow neighbour Harry Spiro. Special thanks also to my publisher, Stewart Cass, plainly his father's son. And especially to my editor Lisa Hyde, whose advice and work is so appreciated.

MICHAEL FREEDLAND
Bournemouth, 2017

# The Story

It's a popular twenty-first century term – multi-tasking. Usually, it's applied to a person of many talents: a carpenter who can mend drains or an engineer who in his spare time can knock up a new suit or write a treatise on ancient literature. One can't be sure that Ben Helfgott can do any of these things. On the other hand – and there is always another hand when you talk about Jewish people – he can and does and has done more than most other people could possibly achieve in a couple of lifetimes – at least.

Start analysing it and he is a man who has lived not two, but four different lives – his peaceful early childhood; his days just struggling one step ahead of death in a Polish ghetto or in a series of German concentration camps of one kind or another; coming to Britain after the war and, almost unbelievably, representing his new country twice in the Olympic Games. And then as a husband and father – not just to his own family, but to others who could be listed as Holocaust survivors.

There are all sorts of reasons for writing books. And for those reasons, there are biographies and histories and romances written on seemingly the same subject by thousands of different people. Don't ask how many books have been written about the assassination of John F. Kennedy. Or of Abraham Lincoln. Books about Queen Victoria. Or Josef Stalin. Or Adolf Hitler. Of those thousands, there are authors who sometimes had to struggle to find, as we journalists say, a new angle.

Ben's story presents no such problem. For one thing – and a particularly advantageous thing – this is the first study of a very unusual life. A life that would for many be a contradiction in terms. On the other hand – and here I go again – the person who first coined the statement that truth is stranger than fiction had never heard of Ben Helfgott and his story. It really is that contradiction in terms, a story of what might be thought the impossible. After all, what would the average man or woman in that street, which every commentator thinks he knows so intimately, say of the tale of a man who endured all the terrible experiences of the Holocaust as a citizen (so-called) of Poland who indeed did go on to become an Olympian – just a handful of years after leaving the infamous Nazi concentration camp of Buchenwald?

I am writing this as Ben celebrates his 88th birthday. Eighty-eight years into which he has crammed more than seems humanly possible. That, I suppose, is the reason for this book. But not just that. Seventy-two years after being released from the hell and humiliation of Nazi subjugation, he is still working for the dwindling number of his fellow survivors. In America, he attempts to ensure some kind of restitution for survivors and their heirs who lost everything in the Holocaust. In Britain, there are Jewish former camp inmates who, without the help of the '45 Aid Society which he founded, might be on the poverty line.

In many ways, I suppose this is a love story; a tale of devotion – not just to his wife with whom he remains smitten, not just as a father and grandfather of exceptional closeness, but devotion to a cause that he made his own and 'infected' others to do the same. You go through his background and it is difficult, if not impossible, to divide one section of his life from another. A psychiatrist would probably say that it was all those years of suffering that made him so devoted. But there was more to it than that. It's a spirit of gratitude, of wanting – and succeeding – to belong. It is often said that new citizens of a country are more patriotic than those who have that nation on their birth certificates. Just as converts to a religion are often more pious than others in the pew. Ben is the exemplar of that.

One shouldn't, however, get the impression that everybody loves him or thinks that he is beyond criticism. Perhaps anyone who is so devoted to causes is likely to cause controversy. Ben is not immune to that. How come that a man whose childhood was spent in Poland, a country that was at so many times in history washed in Jewish blood – in its own pogroms as well as in the iniquities of its German conquerors – is so keen on good relations with that very land to the extent that he is feted by them?

How can he speak so enthusiastically about his German friends? Maybe, controversy is inevitable. To those who follow in his footsteps or come to his house and watch him still lifting his weights – not exactly as heavy as the ones he lifted in the Olympics or in the various championships in which he took part and won – to them, there is a descriptive Yiddish word that sums him up. He is a mensch.

Translation: A man? Not exactly. As the American humorist Leo Rosten put it: 'A mensch is...well, it means ... a mensch!'

Also, an enigma? The answers are, hopefully, in the following pages.

# Foreword

The Holocaust was humanity's darkest moment. During those terrifying years, one third of the Jewish people were destroyed, whole communities were obliterated and it remains, to this day, a stain on the history of Europe.

The Hebrew Bible uses words about Noah that it uses about no one else. He was righteous, perfect in his generations, he walked with God, and yet, Noah after the flood could hardly live. At the end of his life, we see him drunk and dishevelled, a sad shadow of what he once was. Even Noah, the righteous man, could not bear the pain of seeing his world destroyed.

The Holocaust survivors I knew and know somehow found a greater strength than that. Many of them had lost their own families, and so they became one another's family and in doing so lifted each other to unbelievable heights. With an iron will, they looked towards the future, perhaps knowing that if they once looked back they would be turned like Lot's wife into a pillar of salt.

What I find most moving of all is their indomitable faith in life itself, and how they married, had children, grandchildren, and refused to let evil have the final word or the final victory.

The survivors became my heroes. For many, the pain was understandably too much and they remained silent for the rest of their lives. For others, it was only once they had built a life for themselves and others that they could recount their experiences and share their memories with the world so that people would know the horrors of the Holocaust happened not just through films or books, but through the words of those who were there.

Among the most inspirational of the survivors is Ben Helfgott. He has been a source of strength to both Elaine and myself, and we feel privileged to count him as a cherished friend. I am delighted that his story has now been captured in this book through the beautiful and powerful words of Michael Freedland.

Ben has long been one of the heroes of our community. His whole life after the Holocaust was a way of thanking God for life by enhancing the lives of others. He recognised that whilst it was impossible to change the past, out of the wreckage of destruction something could be redeemed.

For his fellow survivors, this was done through the establishment of the '45 Aid Society. For his fellow countrymen, it was achieved through his sporting success. For the next generation, it has been achieved through his decades of determination to share his story with thousands of schoolchildren, urging them to address the challenges in today's world by fighting hate with love, brutality with compassion, and death with an unconquerable dedication to life.

Ben's life is truly remarkable. He was someone who, as I have said before, witnessed the angel of death and yet became an angel of life.

May his powerful story continue to inspire us all.

Emeritus Chief Rabbi Lord (Jonathan) Sacks
November 2017

# 1

## Piotrkow

*'We walked into the woods'*
*– Ben Helfgott*

It was an idyllic scene. A summer's day in 2015. Children playing on a swathe of grass just a few metres from what in Britain would be called a motorway. But this is not Britain. It is Poland. The place Piotrkow, two and a half hours by car on that motorway from the capital, Warsaw.

Ben Helfgott and I are watching a couple of, perhaps, ten-year-olds on a see-saw. Others are kicking a ball around, while a dog looks on. Ben is smiling and talking to a couple of the youngsters in Polish. He is remembering his own childhood, recalling the time when he played those same games with children dressed rather differently. These kids are wearing jeans and T-shirts, just like youngsters anywhere else. Seventy-five years ago, the boys were in short trousers and jerseys, the girls in shapeless little dresses. But the two scenes could have been merged with each other, like in one of those movies where a sepia-coloured street scene suddenly turns into colour.

The motorway has replaced spare land. But the buildings at the other side of the verdant playground have not changed. Except that the Jewish-owned bakery of the Malenicki family in the remembered picture of the past is now a general store. There was the shop where the religious men went for their hats. And there on our journey was where Mr Horowicz, the husband of Ben's teacher, a man who sold suitcases, lived. Over there was the herring shop run by a Mr Zajaczkowski. Today, the area is dominated by a Zara store, selling the kind of clothes the women of that Jewish community would have marvelled at. Ben recalled a man named Janowski who had a big shop selling the best fruit. The search for places that rekindled memories continues all the way. There was one shop where a Jewish man used to sell cloths and other materials. We found two churches – on both sides of the main road. And there was a big hall where Piotrkow Poles used to go dancing. The 'frum' Jews would never have entered such a place. And a bank – a Millennium bank now, a Polish bank at the time we found ourselves remembering. 'We couldn't go walking like this when I lived here after the Germans came,' Ben said, I thought wistfully, seeing the stores on Slowackijo Street.

Piotrkow, its full name Piotrkow-Trybunalski, had been founded in 1317. In the 1930s the population was 55,000 of whom 15,000 were Jewish. The number of Jews in the ghetto in 1940 was 28,000 because they had been herded in from outlying places. By the time of the deportation there were 25,000 Jews in the ghetto and in 1942 within one week between 14 and 21 October 22,500 Jews were sent to Treblinka where they were murdered. The remaining two and a half thousand Jews were forced to move into the small ghetto.

Ask one of the few survivors of the Jewish part of Piotrkow, that faraway dot on the East European map, and chances are they will call it a shtetl – *their* shtetl. Some of them still talk about it as if they are discussing home – a home for which they have a deep connection as if there was a kind of umbilical cord there, a cord that, without the help of a midwife (a kind, indulgent population) strangled them. Like the cord that linked them in the womb, this is one to which they have no wish to give life again. A home they are glad to have left behind.

It was a pretty place in those far-off pre-war, pre-Holocaust days. Mala Tribich, Ben's younger sister, says: 'Yes, that is how I remember it. Very pretty, very lovely. I have lovely memories of the town because it had so many beautiful things – lovely squares, a great deal of greenery.'

And yet and yet, as so frequently happens, things come flooding back into her psyche. But at the same time she admits she doesn't have many memories of childhood Piotrkow. But when she talks about her three visits there in recent times, even just the telling of it, is always an emotional experience. 'Going there makes me feel really, really sad and emotional. It is painful, but at the same time very meaningful.'

First, one thing has to be stated. When the Helfgotts talk about their home town, it is always Piotrkow. But it was not where Beniek Helfgott was born on 22 November 1929. It was in the nearby town of Pabianice, not too far away from the place that Ben always thinks of as where it all began for him. They lived there because it was where his mother Sara's parents had their home. Those were Ben's and Mala's grandparents who were originally from a place called Sieradz, a town that will, for him, herald the beginning of everything terrible that was to happen. Their father's parents hailed from Widawa. But stir the mix and it is easy to see that everything in the Helfgott story is centred on Piotrkow.

The family, Sara, father Moishe and at first two children, relocated, as the current term has it, to Piotrkow to be close to the father's flour-milling business. Neither sibling can put a precise date on the move. Mala was born in Piotrkow – and since there is less than a year between them, obviously Ben was a baby when they made the move.

It was a great success, that mill. You could tell that by the way the family lived. As Mala recalls, 'We had a small flat and then, before long, we moved to a larger, nicer flat.' That was in the tree-lined Ulica 3 Maya (named for the third of May, the date on which Poland gained its post-World War One independence. Ben, as we shall see, is wont to produce historical titbits whenever they occur). The street's name would have impressed the historians of Piotrkow. But there was another indication of the family's place in local society. 'And we had a maid.' That was when Mala's fact-retrieval system came into play. 'I remember her name. It was Andzia. I think she may have come to us when my parents got married. She came from another town. I don't remember her very well, but I do remember her particularly when we moved from one place to another. I remember she travelled in the moving van. We didn't. But they put a little stool inside so that she could sit on it in comfort for the journey.'

Andzia is remembered as being very kind to Mala and her brother. 'She left us before the war began.' But while she was with the Helfgotts and wherever they went, she went, too. First, to the smaller flat and later to the larger one. 'We enjoyed quite a nice lifestyle for that period.'

Yet there were fairly frequent other moves. 'At one time my father was doing very well and we could afford something much nicer and bigger. Then perhaps things weren't so good, so they moved. It was the 1930s and things were very bad everywhere. When I think of why my parents moved, it was because the same thing happened to them.' But there was that 'nice lifestyle' that continued.

Mala and Ben were always well dressed. It was particularly obvious at the time of the Jewish holydays. 'We always had new clothes for Rosh Hashanah [the Jewish New Year] and Pesach [Passover].' There was soon another child who enjoyed that lifestyle by the time the moves began – Lusia (or Leah in Hebrew) was the baby of the house.

Mala and her sister were given the full female-child treatment just before festival time. 'My mother would choose the fabrics and, I remember, would then take them to the dressmaker. We didn't have ready-made clothes.' That was not what up-and-coming families did. There were few restrictions imposed. The dressmaker would run up a new dress and a coat to match. 'I particularly remember one with little checks in really nice colours.'

Their parents dressed perfectly, too. Sara had style – and always wore a hat. Her husband Moishe wore suits made for him by one of Piotrkow's band of tailors. 'They had lots of tailors in Piotrkow. The tailoring business thrived. He chose fine cloths in pinstripes with a matching tie. The hat that he wore was not what had already begun to be called a "Jewish hat" – an ordinary hat; you know, not a Chassidic type hat. We were well past that.' There were quite a few ultra-Orthodox ('Charedim') people in Piotrkow who were decidedly not past 'all that'. But, she told me, 'like our own immediate neighbours, we didn't stand out as Jewish in any way'.

As we shall see, a nice lifestyle didn't extend to the transport they used. There was no car in the family, so they hired – that wonderful word so familiar in Yiddish literature – a 'droshky', a horse and upholstered cart. Sometimes their father drove it himself. If they went far, they had the services of a driver, a 'balagulah'.

Certainly, by most standards of Piotrkow and the Jewish families living round and about, they had become rich and lived – to use one of Ben's favourite words – comfortably. One of the reasons, before the financial crash hit Poland, that the Helfgotts were doing so well was that their business was as up to date as was considered possible at the time when Ben was a boy. Today, you'd call it 'state of the art'. Ben's maternal grandfather, who first established his own business selling flour, would have been proud. Michael – the family name was Klein – made it possible for Sara's father to spend his time studying Torah and Talmud, learning not just about religious practices, but good business ethics, and how you had to keep a pet dove without damaging it. As used to be said by the American advertising agents, 'All life is there' in the Talmud. And it really was.

There was a family history that now, in the second decade of the twenty-first century, Ben cherishes. Unlike many Jewish families, he knows names, dates and places. 'I know that my mother's grandfather died at 86 and my father's grandfather lived to be 101. He was born in 1830 and died in 1931 a very rich man who owned a lot of land. Everybody knew him.'

On the other hand, Ben has no idea how his parents met. Their own mothers and fathers lived near each other (both sets very religious; the men had beards and wore skullcaps; the women long, dark dresses and wigs, the 'sheitel' hair pieces so revered in the writings of Sholom Aleichem who wrote the story that became 'Fiddler on the Roof' and Isaac Bashevis Singer, the Yiddish author who was to receive the Nobel Prize for literature). Sara's father was, Ben says, 'extremely Orthodox,' a 'chasid', following a rabbi known as the 'Alexander Rebbe'.

The chassidic movement, established in the eighteenth century by a Rabbi Eliezer (known as the 'Bal Shemtov' or 'The One of the Good Name') was divided into numerous sects all led by a particular rabbi, known as the 'rebbe' who laid down laws and customs that his flock had to observe to the letter – as though they were an extension to the Torah, the word of God, which some believed they actually were. They concentrated more on ritual than on study, enjoyed singing and dancing – sometimes in almost ecstatic trances which they saw as a tribute to the Lord. And so rich and poor, brilliant and backward, could come together to share the same devotions. To this day, many of their men dress in the clothes recognised as similar to the garments worn by gentile Polish nobility 200 years ago (they see no contradiction in their overwhelming belief that Jews have to dress 'Jewish'). They wear long dark coats and big fur hats on Sabbaths and holydays – all irrespective of the weather. Some sects wear trousers tucked into thigh-high stockings (despite the injunction against cross dressing; their women would rather die than wear trousers). Some wear white socks, some black – all 'tribal' identification codes. And in places like Stamford Hill in London and Crown Heights in Brooklyn, their young and old wives still have their sheitels, their dowdy dark-coloured dresses and, if they are young enough, their pushchairs for multiples of small children.

Ben needs little encouragement to talk about the family that were the Helfgotts of his early childhood. 'That more religious grandfather,' says Ben, 'lived in a different town. When he came to visit, he stood [in the kitchen] and watched my mother and how she prepared everything.' Not something to endear her father-in-law to her and vice versa. 'She didn't like it at all.' Particularly, there was a question of the milk she bought. The churns had to come from the dairy of a religious Jew to make sure they were strictly kosher. But the old man didn't trust her. Most of his day was spent in the synagogue, praying and studying the Talmud and other holy books. Even more upsetting for Sara was the feeling that Moishe's mother was constantly at war with her. 'I only really knew one grandmother, as my mother's mother died in 1935,' says Ben, 'and my mother did not talk to her. But I had no idea why she did not take us to visit her.' It was a big family. 'My mother had five sisters and three brothers.'

In relative terms (and, yes, we are talking about relatives) Sara's father was somewhat less religious than Moishe's. (In Jewish lore, the parents of one's children's spouse are known as the 'machatonim'; the other side's father is the 'mechuten' and the other mother is the 'machatenister', sometimes more accurately known as the Leader of the Opposition.) Ben's mother's dad did very well for himself selling his flour, no doubt milled by his son-in-law and his two partners. As Ben said, everybody knew him. Like the rich man that Tevya dreamed of being in 'Fiddler On The Roof', he was probably consulted by the citizens of the area, perhaps because, as the milkman in the song said, 'when you're rich, they think you really know'.

Like a lot of Jewish families, they were close, but also there were those members who split and went their own ways. Sara was one of eight children and she had cousins who, before the war, left for Belgium – where, with one exception, their fate was to be no happier than it would have been had they stayed in Poland. On the other hand, the Polish world seemed to be providing an environment that both Moishe and Sara could happily accept, even though, if they allowed themselves to think about it, anti-Semitism and the fear that a pogrom might be just a town away, was ever present. Ben says he knows for sure that the marriage was a good one.

Somehow, survivors of the Holocaust, more possibly than those who did not experience such traumas at first hand, tend to dwell on their ancestors. It is, I am sure, a subliminal thing – a wishful thought that it would be so good to be able to talk about murdered family members in such positive ways. They, maybe, liked to show that there were those people in their families who lived and died normally. As I say, wishful thinking, the kind that gives them a feeling of equality with luckier people. A psychiatrist might have fun with such thoughts, although there is little to laugh at about it at all. Ben Helfgott doesn't laugh. But he does enjoy talking about those ancestors who were born and died in the nineteenth century or for a few years beyond. Those for whom the Depression years of the 1930s were the most tragic that they would ever know are indeed thought of as the lucky ones.

His paternal family was exactly the same size as that of his mother. 'But an elder brother of my father died at about the age of 21 soon after the First World War during the influenza pandemic. My father had three other sisters. One of them died in childbirth. Just imagine how big our family could have been had it not been for the Nazis. You find that everywhere. People who lived in our part of the world nearly all ended up in the gas chambers.'

But the overwhelming fact is that the parents of these now elderly men and women didn't believe that things were going to change. That idea of pogroms, of anti-Semitism floating in the air like the birds in the trees around the square, was so much part of general living (for the most part, outside Piotrkow) that they were happy to accept it all as part of the status quo. Things had never really changed, as far as the populous was concerned – and indeed were a lot better since independence – and everybody seemed to think that any anti-Jewish activity wasn't likely to get worse. That was all part of the tragedy.

The tree-lined beauty of Ulica 3 Maya seemed to symbolise the fact that life had, in all probability, never been better. The family knew that their home and its surroundings put them in an enviable position. The greenery wasn't quite matched by the nearby river – which, really ceased to be a real river when it reached their part of town – but there was also the park to which the avenue that was their street led. As we have seen, a great many of Ben's memories are centred on that park. How many of the 15,000 Jews of Piotrkow had a chance to enjoy the park is perhaps a matter for speculation. Most of them had little time to do more than scrape a living – or pray. Never were prayers seen to be so important and, sadly, so useless.

In the town, there had been two 'shuls', as Jews call their synagogues. One was the older building to which the Helfgotts went on Shabbat, the Saturday sabbath, and the festivals of Rosh Hashanah, Yom Kippur, as well as on Succot (the autumn harvest festival), Passover and Shavuot, the commemoration of the giving of the Ten Commandments on Mount Sinai. It was known as the 'shtiebel', with a simple service unadorned by choral singing, without even a rabbi of its own.

The town's main synagogue was as Orthodox – or 'frum' as the word goes – as the schtiebel. But it was a beautiful building, newly renovated only two years before the Nazis moved in and changed and killed everything, including the Jewish heritage of a whole continent.

It was not because the family were so observant that they chose to worship at the schtiebel – as most of the congregants at such places were – but it was the nearest prayer house to their home. That word 'home' is highly significant. Synagogues are not churches with the very brickwork regarded as holy. In Hebrew, a synagogue is a Bet Kenneset, House of Assembly. The Helfgotts, like most Jews, regarded their homes as part of their religion, the place where candles were lit on Friday evenings, the food was strictly kosher and the men in them usually regarded going to synagogue as important, but possibly only because religious services required a *minyan*, a quorum of ten men.

Plainly, the Helfgotts were not extremely Orthodox. Yes, Sara did keep a kosher kitchen – it would have been a rarity had she not done so. But there were times when she cooked things that the rabbi would not have appreciated – certain Polish dishes 'like shinka [incredibly, ham] because she thought it would be good for me. My father smoked on Shabbat,' Ben recalled, something that religious people think of as close to a cardinal sin (that is, if Jews only had cardinals, which they don't). 'The best cigarettes, Mewa. He smoked between 20 and 30 of them a day.'

For a time, the very young Ben went to Hebrew school ('cheder') from five to nine every school day, at the local Yesoda Hatorah establishment. Now, this is where he parted company with the family. He at the time was strictly Orthodox, more so than his parents.

Not that most Jewish people were educated in the conventional sense. The synagogues and their Talmudical colleges provided an incredible religious learning experience. But secular education had not figured in the lives of Piotrkow's older Jewish citizens. 'They lived in a different world,' Ben now says. The different world was that they lived in a country they called Poland but was not run by Poles. It was officially part of Russia. And they didn't have compulsory education. A lot of them didn't speak anything but a Polish dialect of Yiddish. It was not until 1918 to 1920 before a Polish government made going to school compulsory. As was the learning of another language, Polish.

The new Act of the incoming Polish parliament made a big dent in the lives of Jews. People who were being brought up to know nothing but their family's breed of Judaism, which usually meant strict Orthodoxy, suddenly stopped being quite so 'frum'. Nearly all of them kept *kashrut*, the Jewish dietary laws. Many continued to observe the Sabbath, but not all did everything their parents and grandparents had expected them to do. Some, like the very young Ben, actually read secular books and newspapers.

Strangely, that main synagogue in the town is still completely intact. It is now a very impressive public library, which one can suppose would have been regarded by the sages of old as the next best thing to a house of prayer. Except that it has no Jewish books there, let alone prayer volumes. But it is easy to imagine where the Ark containing the scrolls of the Torah was situated and the purpose of the upstairs room when it housed the women's gallery. Its origins as a synagogue are not ignored.

It is remembered today as the beautiful building it was when the Nazis moved in to desecrate it. There are photographs of the days when bearded men would gather for worship – and one 'souvenir' that the custodians of the library have had the sensitivity to keep. It is the one un-repainted part of the upstairs room. Just a couple of square metres of wall that perhaps, by some message from above, stubbornly refuses to fade – the tablets of the Ten Commandments with a lion on each side. But part of it could never have been covered with paint – the holes in the wall, each with splintered edges: bullet holes, where people were shot as victims of a macabre firing squad. But that would come a little later.

On 1 November 1939, the Jewish citizenry were told to move to what had become the ghetto. Harry Spiro put it like this: 'Then there was the big shock – they designated a few streets in Piotrkow, which became the ghetto. That was when it started affecting me and the family and had us asking, even now, what made us do this? Why did we stay in Piotrkow? I could see my family go hungry and so was I. I saw people selling goods on the streets – which they had smuggled in. I did that too.' Easier said than done. 'I didn't realise how dangerous this was until after I had done it. When it became dangerous, they set the dogs on you. Oh yes, I was one of those the dogs wanted.'

It was very early on, just days before the start of what was to be World War Two, that Ben and his family really came close to knowing just how severe things were. As he himself tells it: 'We walked into the woods and people were shouting.' The shouts were deafening and appalling. No child of ten should ever have had to hear – or see – such things. It was no picnic for his parents either.

# 2

## War

*'We knew he was clever'*
*– Harry Spiro*

It was mystifying for the children to be suddenly thrust into a situation for which there had been no preparation. No-one told them what was going to happen – because no-one told the adults either.

And yet there was an element of excitement about it all at first. 'Excitement,' Ben agrees. 'Excitement – and fright. It was terrible when you knew that people were being killed.'

It was not that Ben himself actually saw people being murdered, but before long, it was as if he had. 'I saw people being taken to be killed.' It was an image that no-one could ever be expected to lose.

Piotrkow, that quiet town, appealed to Jews simply because it *was* quiet. The taverns were not, as in other places, on every street corner. It had its drunks, but they were not lying on every pavement or staggering along, shouting abuse at everyone or everything. But now it was a target – and not simply because so many Jews lived there.

The Germans knew there were Jews and knew, too, that they would probably have carte blanche to both verbally and physically assault them. But for the moment, it was the poorly-equipped Polish army that the Germans had in their sights. No-one doubted that the Poles stood little or no chance of beating the bombers and the invaders who would follow. But the Nazis needed to make sure. There were barracks close to the town. There was also a nearby hospital. German navigators aimed at the barracks and bombed the hospital. They cared not at all for the sick and elderly any more than they were going to care about Jews. All that was good reason to attack the area around Piotrkow. If the bombs went astray, they landed in Piotrkow itself. And killed Jews with everyone else who accidentally got in their way.

Warsaw was being flattened. In the scheme of things, you possibly can understand that. It was the capital city of a country to which Adolf Hitler had taken a fancy, to put it mildly. Lvov was a big trading centre. So OK, give them the benefit of the horrific doubt, if such things were doubtful. Warsaw, though, *was* the capital city, and when you conquer a capital city, in so many cases, you conquer a nation.

The biggest doubts surrounded Neville Chamberlain, putting his umbrella away in the stand outside the cabinet room at Ten Downing Street, as he phoned his French counterpart, Édouard Daladier. Both were trying to make up their minds about going to the rescue of this Eastern European place that had always existed, but had been an independent nation for just over two decades.

What, without a shadow of a doubt, that they didn't consider or worry about, was that the bombs dropped on little Piotrkow were going to lead to ending the lives of the 15,000 Jews living there – or that Lvov was a centre of Jewish learning. Or that Warsaw was home to more Jews who professed their faith, its culture and way of life than anywhere in the world outside of New York.

The bombs led to fires in Piotrkow which made the late summer weather seem even hotter. That day, the Helfgott family were out of town, visiting young Ben's grandparents and were ready to rush back to their comfortable home in the apartment block on Ulica 3 Maya. But Harry Spiro, now a retired tailor living in quiet residential Hertfordshire just a few miles from London, was there, a little boy mystified by what was happening. 'I remember hearing the planes overhead and then the terrible noise of the bombs.'

Like Ben, Piotrkow was the only town young Spiro knew – although he hadn't yet met his future close friend at that time. They lived in a different part of the town, not as nice a district as where the Helfgotts resided. But young Harry knew of Ben's reputation, much in the way that the leader of any gang is known by the other people living nearby. Ben's was not so much for his leadership qualities, but because everyone in the local Jewish world knew he was a very clever lad. 'We knew that he was very clever, much cleverer than I was. Ben's family was more intellectual than mine and he had an awareness of what world affairs meant, what is going to be happening tomorrow. I could only think of what Mum was doing and what she wanted me to do – that sort of thing. Not about the rest of the world.'

Unlike Ben's, the Spiros were a religious family. His father was a tailor who regarded going to the synagogue three times a day as being more important than earning a living for his wife, son and daughter. What he recalls is the time it took for the big changes that they anticipated to come. 'I was ten years old and I don't think I even knew what or where Germany was.' He got to know before long, but at first life was surprisingly unchanged. 'People were even talking to the German troops.' By then, he knew they were both soldiers and German. They went into the Jewish shops and bought things there, paying the right money for them. 'I saw them buying cigarettes and chocolates and walking about the streets. I was just a child, and I couldn't understand why people were complaining. There was not a lot of change. The first thing I remember is that we all had to wear white armbands with a Star of David.'

As far as he was concerned for the first two months, before the large ghetto was established, there was virtually no change. His father still went to the synagogue, the shul. Then, restrictions came into play. Just as it would for Ben and Mala, it happened: he could no longer go to school. 'Personally, I thought that was not too bad,' says Harry, 'because I didn't like school'.

It was another difference between Ben and Harry. 'Then, again, came another announcement that no Jews could be employed by anyone in any organisation. Whatever job or profession you had, it didn't affect my father because he was self-employed as a tailor. But you could sense people kept on asking questions about what was going to happen.'

Piotrkow was experiencing the first signs of Nazism that would spread like a virus throughout the country and before long across almost the whole of Europe. The word Holocaust wouldn't come into use for more than 20 years. Nobody as yet knew that the deprivations they were experiencing were the first shoots of the weeds that would poison and destroy their lives.

The first day of September 1939 was the day the Germans invaded Poland at the start of the Second World War. It had been a lovely, sunny late summer day although the calendar would say it was the first day of autumn. Poland can be as certain of having warm late summer days as it can guarantee winters so cold that not even furs and mufflers can stem the freezing of limbs and fingers and toes that no longer seem to have any relationship with each other.

Sieradz seemed like an ideal place to be with Sara's parents. The three Helfgott children had been spending their summer holidays in the small town, close enough to Piotrkow but far enough to be a tiny urban oasis in a sea of countryside. Ben played with a group of boys who had become friends within an astonishingly short time. They were racing each other. Ben, of course, was the leader, giving all the instructions. As far as they knew, life was completely normal – and rather lovely. Mala was having a great time, too.

Ben, with the memory bank of a well-stocked reference library, has vivid recall of what happened to change all that.

It was a Friday and Sara was preparing to bring the children back home. 'She left early in the morning because she needed to prepare food for Shabbos,' Ben recalls. 'Also, we had to return to Piotrkow because we were due back in school the following Monday.'

If only life could have been that simple. Sara chose her usual form of transport to make the journey. She went by bus on a trip that normally takes two hours. She arrived ten hours later. 'No sooner had we boarded the bus than we heard aircraft and the unmistakable sound of bombs falling. On the way home, there was bombing all around,' Ben recalls. 'Bombing and fires. When we came home, my mother made supper and we went to sleep. The following day our town was bombed at 12.30.'

Mala recalls it all only too well. As always it is the incidental detail that stays most in the mind. 'I remember going out into the street and there was a broken bottle and some kind of commotion. When the bombing started we took shelter in the basement. Whilst we were gathered there, a man injured by shrapnel was brought in to our shelter. He had extensive wounds and was covered in blood. This was our first experience with the realities of war. After the bombing there was panic and people tried to move east away from the invading army. My father secured a horse and carriage, the sort of transport most people in Poland used, and we too set off heading east.'

There was now a long line of refugees, walking. Just walking. Some carrying children. Old people halting for breath every now and again, propelling themselves along with their sticks. Other old and sick people were lying on beds hastily placed on to other people's horse-driven carts. They arrived in Sulejow, a pretty village 15 kilometres away with a population of 5,000. It was here that they met up with Moishe's brother Fischel, his wife Irene and their young daughter Hania. They too had decided to leave Piotrkow and go east.

'It was quiet and people were strolling through the streets,' Ben remembers. 'All looked peaceful. I soon started playing with the local boys enjoying the peace and calm of the beautiful sunny day. Then, quite suddenly, it all changed. There was a whistling sound.' It wouldn't take more than a matter of seconds before everyone realised that terrible whining was not coming from a man happily walking with his wife or sweetheart or from a dog owner calling to his pet. It was a noise that would be all too recognisable before long. The sound of bombs falling and a sense that the world had caught fire left no-one in any doubt. The bombs were incendiaries, a weapon that did its work so efficiently that minds boggled as fires swept through the little place and its 5,000 inhabitants huddled in their homes. Whole families were being consumed by flames.

The Helfgotts followed people making for the open door of a brick house. It was a Jewish house with a *mazuzah*, the tube containing a tiny scroll bearing the Shema, on the doorpost. 'Listen, Israel, the Lord our God, the Lord is One.' People were packed into the house, crying, pleading. Someone recited that same Shema as on the scroll nailed to the doorpost. Suddenly, everyone joined in, reciting the same prayer, the declaration of the unity of God taught to children as soon as they can speak – and recited, should a minimum of strength be there, on the deathbed most of those Jews would be denied. To this day – and probably to his eternal regret – Ben doesn't know either how they came to the house or to whom it belonged. All he remembers now is that he ventured out of the place and was in the street when German planes started strafing. 'Suddenly, there was no-one else around. Bombs started falling around.' The luckiest – almost miraculous – part of the story is that his mother saw him, ran outside and grabbed him. 'She pulled me into the house.'

'When the bombing stopped, the door opened. People started pushing and everything around us was burning. Everybody started running into the woods,' Ben recalls. 'As we were running, the bombing started again and people were being shot from the air. I can never forget it.' He won't forget joining the other hapless temporary occupants of this house going into the nearby woods, sheltering among the tall trees, not knowing where they would go next.

It was one of those moments and one of those places to which most Jews who were to experience the Holocaust can relate. In that place, at that moment, it could seem that the whole world was Jewish. With no bombs apparently left to fall and the fires spreading like the virus it really was, people left the house and ran to the nearby forest. A strange thing to do, since forests catch fire as easily as the striking of a match. But who can tell what a people will do in desperation? Hope, a forlorn demonstration of optimism which no-one felt. No-one could possibly realize this was the start of what became the Second World War. The enormity of the Holocaust, so much of it centred in their country, couldn't be contemplated. But the Jews knew they would be the first to suffer should the tanks and infantry make their way towards them.

If the whole world was going to catch fire, they were going to be the kindling wood. Of course, they never knew where they were going. 'People were running away. Running like chickens with their heads chopped off.' It was strange territory. So not only did they not know where they were headed. They didn't know where they were. All they could hope for was that the huge trees which seemed to be looking down on them as mystified as these new refugees were, would offer them some form of protection.

About 800 people were killed. As for their family, it was Sara who was keeping them together in this new kind of wilderness. 'We would never have fled unless we were together.' Eventually at nightfall, the distant sound of bombing stopped and they were ready to continue the journey again. In the dark they found the horse and cart, except that the horse was dead and the cart had been smashed into matchwood.

It had been the sort of transport most people in Jewish Poland used. There were no buses or trams in the rural areas like the one where they were now. Now, there was no means of getting back to Piotrkow except by what the British poor knew as 'Shanks's pony' – in other words, using their own boot leather and walking. 'My father led us out of the village on foot though he did manage to hire a new horse and cart.' The horse and cart was as good as a Rolls-Royce for moments like this. A craftsman's work on a hand-built chassis couldn't have got them anywhere any quicker. Ben remembers: 'We couldn't go any further than the people in front.' In years to come, motorists would experience delays caused by what came to be known as traffic jams. They would know where they were heading. In this case, most of the other people had no real idea.

'We travelled from village to village until the Germans caught up with us and my parents made the decision to return to Piotrkow. We moved in the opposite direction from the one taken by the other refugees. Passing Sulejow on the way home we saw strong evidence of the destruction that had taken place there. What we found there took me years and years to get out of my mind. Just arms and legs and decapitated heads. We had to walk through dead bodies lying on the ground. And body parts – a leg here, an arm there. I had never seen or imagined anything like it.' As he says, 'It was the worst day of my life.' There would be others, but not perhaps so firmly etched on his mind. Of course it was the first time he had seen dead bodies. 'And the smell of dead humans. The burnt body parts along the streets. I have never forgotten the sickly sweet smell of human carnage. It has haunted me all my life.'

To Ben it was a 'blooding' into the horrors of war all around him and a precursor of what was to come. What he saw that day was a holocaust all of its own. Ben says, 'When we lived in the ghetto and terrible events took place, my mother used to say that if we had survived Sulejow, we would survive anything.'

At the end of a long, hot frightening day, munching on the few bits of food Sara had managed to scrape together in such a hurry for a journey that, for the more religious among those fleeing, resembled the children of Israel's flight from Egypt when there had been no time for the dough they carried to rise, the difference was that in the Bible the refugees had been fleeing from slavery; now they were travelling to it.

On their return to Piotrkow Ben says, 'We were very fortunate. Our house was still there and our belongings intact. We heard that in our absence the Germans had burnt the Sefer Torahs and holy books in the synagogue and 30 Jews, including a rabbi, all of whom lived near the synagogue, had been shot.'

Twelve other Jewish leaders were arrested and a ransom demanded. Because the savings of the Jewish people had been confiscated, it was difficult to raise the money but somehow it was and they were released.

As it turned out, there were only a couple of bombs dropped on Piotrkow. But they were enough. Those bombs that fell on the town, nevertheless, signified the start of the Second World War, besides introducing its Jewish population to what would all too quickly become not just a holocaust – but THE Holocaust.

On 5 September 1939 at 4pm the Germans entered Piotrkow and conquered the city after only two hours of street fighting. Twenty Jews were shot. Ben remembers when they returned to Piotrkow 'a curfew was enforced and at the end of September we were ordered to move to the ghetto by 1 November. This was to be the first ghetto in Poland.'

It was all changing. So very quickly. They knew in their hearts that nothing was going to be the same. They might have tried to kid themselves that the Germans would have no interest in their little town, but they knew that was not going to be. Yet no-one really did think that a Holocaust was on the way. Even so, things were already pretty bad for Jews.

Even the Germans had not yet thought how they were going to administer their 'Final Solution' (a phrase they had not yet used in public). But everyone knew they didn't like Jews very much. Stories had leaked out to the local synagogue that some of their co-religionists were being rounded up in Warsaw, to go where, nobody knew. Ever since the 'anschluss', in which Germany had taken over their Austrian neighbours, elderly middle-class Jews had been 'cleaning' streets with toothbrushes and in Czechoslovakia, invaded in 1938, a little later than Vienna and surrounding places, things weren't all that good for their people. As for in Germany itself, a few more lucky Jews had been released from Dachau with stories of horrendous treatment of themselves and their fellow inmates. All with the 'legal' cover presented by the Nuremberg Laws which established the idea of Jews being 'untermenschen'.

Jews were no longer allowed into the professions, children couldn't go to their old schools, to say nothing of them and their parents being banned from sitting on park benches. Their shops and stores were boycotted. Kristallnacht, less than a year before, had given licence for synagogues and other Jewish properties to be destroyed, while the police and fire services looked on. Could this come to Piotrkow? The family knew it could and probably would.

Even as a child, Beniek Helfgott, as he was known in those days (his Hebrew name was Dov – meaning 'Bear', highly appropriate for a boy who had all the charm of a Teddy bear, but the strength of a fully-grown grizzly) was not one to show fright, let alone panic. But that day everyone panicked, he recalled.

The bombs led to fires in Piotrkow. However, at first few people realised when the aircraft first entered the local air space what they were all about.

Harry Spiro recalls: 'I vividly remember Polish people in the town saying they were Polish planes. I thought that's nice, but, then, I had never seen a plane before.' Mala puts it like this: 'For children, nothing much was happening anyway because we were protected from knowing what was going on. We could only judge from what we saw.'

After five days of airplanes strafing, bombing and frightening, the troops came into Piotrkow. The men in their green uniforms and 'coal scuttle' helmets came by foot, on horses that were better looked after than any human being (particularly any Jew) and in open cars as much to scare the inhabitants of this peaceful place as to gain some kind of strategic advantage. There was already no Polish army to stop them. The Allies who had declared war on Adolf Hitler to 'save Poland' were doing nothing of the kind, just looking after their own backyards in what for the next few months would be known as the 'Phoney War' but not by Polish Jews. Who could blame them? They hadn't thought it through. Maybe the Germans would take fright simply by their declaration of war and go back home.

Had Britain and France seriously thought that they could really save Poland by invading the country themselves? Or did they not care? Finally, they were showing they had principles but were going to leave it at that. There were also the Russians to worry about. Between them and the Nazis, they had carved the country in two. The infamous Molotov-Ribbentrop Pact had changed the map of Europe and the only people who really bothered about the effects were those who lived there. The Jews more than anyone.

As far as the Poles were concerned, they were in a kind of a stupor. Nobody had thought of establishing some sort of resistance movement. To some Poles, of course, it had considerable advantages. Nazis on their territory had to mean one thing – they could get rid of those same bloody Jews who were giving Hitler so much trouble. It is doubtful if the Polish army would have done anything to help the Jews, even if they were fully armed and imbued with kindness for their neighbours. As it was, they themselves were finished the moment that the Russians moved into the part of Poland that had been 'assigned' to them under the Pact. Polish officers were massacred – and non-commissioned ranks were also taken out to the streets and sprayed with machine-gun bullets.

There are hundreds, probably thousands, of stories about Russian atrocities and of conditions in the gulags to which Polish citizens – Jews and gentiles – were taken. But being controlled by Soviets was, at least at first, going to be preferable to being murdered by the Nazis. The Russian zone was about 200 kilometres from Piotrkow, too far for most Jews to try to escape there, and under the terms of the Pact they would never have been allowed in. But Ben recalls some 15 year-olds (and a few who were older) who did go there, only for most of them to come back.

Ben, if given the chance and really old enough to weigh up the options, would have tried to go. 'Conditions were absolutely better in the Russian sector than they were in the German part of Poland. For one thing, I could have gone to school there. I used to be the first into the [school] building in the morning and the last to leave. I missed it greatly. But had I told my mother I wanted to go off there, she would have gone crazy. I told one boy and he said he'd go with me, but we didn't. I don't know what would have happened had I left, but I was very keen to do it.'

It wouldn't arise less than two years later when, under Operation Barbarossa, the Germans invaded the Soviet Union in June 1941.

By 25 September the war was over in Poland. That is, the shooting war.

# 3

## Raids

*'I couldn't get over it'*
*– Mala Tribich*

Mala, meanwhile, was being hidden by a Christian family in the fairly nearby city of Czechochowa. 'It was really very near the German border, nearer even than Piotrkow. Almost *on* the border,' is how she puts it today. 'As a result, there were a lot of Germans living there.' In fact, it was a German family who hid both Mala and her little cousin Idzia. So it was due to Germans that she survived being killed by other Germans – or was it? 'Sometimes, we were hidden. Sometimes, we weren't.'

Any vestige of the old life was gone when the Nazi Germans moved into Piotrkow. Any thought of producing a Jewish newspaper for Piotrkow was immediately recognised as impossible. The synagogues were gone, but the churches were more active than ever – particularly the Catholic edifice to which many of the Nazi soldiers would go on Sundays. And, before long, there were no schools for Jewish children.

There were ways in which Ben and his parents tried to replace the patently very good Polish-style education to which he was subjected. For one thing, thanks to his mother's present, he was now an enthusiastic stamp collector. 'Through those stamps, I learnt geography. I knew all the capitals – and to this day I have not forgotten any of them.' (Except, of course, that so many of the capitals have changed, much like the countries themselves.)

By then, it was the letter inside, and not that which was on the envelope, that counted. People were desperately awaiting whatever news there was of families miles away, in different countries. They were not allowed radio sets, so in those earliest days of the war, they were asking among themselves: 'Are the Nazis in Belgium, in France? Would the Jews in England be suffering as we were?' They really had no way of knowing how things were in these other nations.

It used to be so different. As a child, it was the stamps that caught Ben's attention whenever an overseas letter arrived. Friends – even the local postman – gave him the stamps from the letters they received; in the Polish

Jewish community there were always letters from relatives who had gone to America, in particular, and other parts of the world where, presciently, they thought life was going to be better. After proving his interest like that, he started to actually buy stamps. Once again: 'My father always gave me the money. My mother wasn't very pleased about that.'

It was now all just a matter of memory. He had been as good at school as he was at his games. 'I was the best in my class. Right from the start. Not just from the first. I didn't go into the first class, but was in the second, the third and the fourth – always the youngest in the class.'

Ben had one competitor for the position of top of the class. A girl who was always just one mark behind him (except in behaviour – there, the positions were reversed). Her name was Ruta Horowicz, who like Ben survived the Holocaust then she went to live in Israel where she died in 2014. (They had kept up a continuous correspondence and whenever Ben was in the country they would meet. 'I don't have anyone from Piotrkow to meet there now,' he says mournfully. But he has scores of friends there from as many original nationalities as the child Ben ever knew of.)

It was a complicated business, nationality. Ben's father Moishe was born in Poland which meant he was Russian, but when the family moved to another part of the country, he became German. By the time he met Sara, he was Polish. That itself formed part of the Jewish story. The Jews of Piotrkow were about to learn about another. The children were no exception.

No longer allowed to go to school was at this stage the hardest part of his new life for Ben. It had been such an exciting thing for him to do. The pattern for Jewish boys (in particular, boys) took shape very quickly once that compulsory education law had been enacted. It became a combination of secular studies (never on the agenda before Polish independence) and a pretty extensive religious learning programme, which provided almost as much as had been available before. After the lunch break at his day school, there had to be three hours at cheder. It was like school and run on the same basis as school – with first, second and third classes. Now there would be no school. Of any kind.

Even more than his fascination with stamps and geography was his love of history – it was not taught in schools until pupils were 11 years old – which Ben was in 1940, a year after the Nazis moved in. So he found ways of getting hold of books to teach himself the Polish story. As we have seen, to this day, he will go through the important dates in the history of the country. And he dashes off statistics like a college professor. He knows dates the way British schoolboys learn when William the Conqueror landed at Hastings: 'Poland had 40 kings until 1791 when the country was divided into three parts – the biggest was the area taken over by Russia.'

For years, American Jews, in particular, talked about their ancestors coming from Russia. In many cases, that served as a sort of collective noun for the so-called Pale of Settlement, which included Poland. As Ben adds: 'The population of Poland before the First World War was 36 million. Out of the 36 million, 12 million were ethnic, six million Ukrainians, 3.5 million Jews, 1 million Lithuanians and 500,000 people from other countries.' He goes on to develop the theme with more figures – including the fact that when that war ended there were 300,000 Jews fewer. After the Second World War and the Holocaust, 90 per cent of the Jews in Poland had been exterminated like an assault on a plague of ants. Had there been no Holocaust, he reckons there would be 30 million Jews in the world today, rather than the twenty-first century total of perhaps 14 million.

Yet, nothing will allow him to blame Poland as such for what had happened to his people. Even his feelings about the Germans which, as we have also noted, are not the conventional views of that race among his fellow survivors. His close friend Aubrey Rose sees nothing odd about that. 'I don't believe that it is strange that a man like Ben treats the people he is with at the moment as human beings. The Germans and Poles he may have contact with are not those who were guilty of the most abominable event in human history. He treats people for what they are, rather than for their background. For he is not talking about their past history and their own past.'

But, actually, he *is* talking about Poland in particular and about his reactions today. Like it or not, among Jews – even among those who had never got close to a gas chamber – that fact is controversial. His feelings, of course, are ingrained within him. And nurtured by the Holocaust. 'When I was born, the country had been independent for more than ten years. I loved Poland and loved the language very much because I learned to read very early.'

He is not modest about his own early achievements. 'I was very much advanced because I started reading very early. I was very familiar with lots of books – all the top Polish writers – and I was interested in what was going on in politics. I would listen everywhere I was and to everybody.' Before long, it wouldn't be easy for either those conversations to go on or for Ben to listen to them.

Until the occupation, religion, too, had played a big part in everything he did. 'At the beginning of 1939 – because I was doing a lot of reading of Polish books – I found them very interesting and exciting. It was a different world and somehow I became not so keen now to pray. I was brought up to do good and be honest and help others and I believed in God – and everything God told me to do. I prayed every day. I knew my prayers 100 per cent. I knew them and I never missed any. When I walked, I always thought God was watching me and when I thought about something, God knew what I was thinking.'

That would change until neither God nor the worship of Him meant anything to this youngster who before long was seeing things no child should even know about. The arrival of the Nazis in nearby towns destroyed his faith. 'I cut it out,' he said. I wondered if that applied to his parents, too. 'Yes, I think so. I myself cut it out completely.'

Ben allowed himself to wonder how in other ways his own life would alter. Would he still be able to play football? Would his friends still want to be with him? As he says: 'From the first day I can remember and then when I was five, I was very competitive. I always challenged everybody to see who could run faster.'

The 34 year-old Moishe would have been athletic, too, had there been the facilities available to him. 'He could ride a horse well,' his son remembered. Not his own horse, but in those days and in places like Piotrkow, there were always horses around, ready to be ridden. The idea that those horses would, before long, be killed for meat didn't enter the minds of a nice Jewish family.

While, today, Ben Helfgott sees only good in his neighbours in Piotrkow and, mostly, with the Poles in general, his sister Mala is more circumspect about their relationships. And, inwardly, it has a lot to do with her earliest childhood which she has to convince herself she actually remembers. She does think kindly of today's Poles. 'I have changed over the years. It changes with the circumstances. Ben is always happy to be with Polish people and working with them. I am like that, but not to the same degree. Yet there is something about that period that you know about. I don't even know how to express it. It draws me. It holds something for me.'

Of course it does have a lot to do with their childhoods. Those memories again. It is as if a screen is placed between the two periods, the good and the bad. There doesn't appear to be any reference between them.

Years ago, when Ben and I first walked through the streets of Piotrkow together for my radio programme, he told me: 'When I am here, I feel like I am walking with my parents.'

A psychiatrist would probably say that Mala sees things more in black and white than her brother, seems more conscious of some of the atrocities committed in her native land – the ones on the other side of the screen. 'I remember there was a television programme in which Jews were shown to be thrown by Poles out of windows and then cast into the local lake. They were bludgeoning them to death. They were pursuing Jews. That was enough to make you feel anti-Polish. As I watched that, I said, "I'm never going to have anything to do with Poland ever again". I just couldn't get over it.'

It made Mala, for one, think again philosophically about those relations between the two populations in Poland. 'The educated Poles can keep their anti-Semitism under wraps because they are not abusive. Only the yobbos are abusive. They had a lot of yobbos in Poland in my childhood and not so many educated people. When you talk to the educated ones, they are very pleasant, polite and kind and when you go to visit them they'll give you anything. You can never leave without a present – even if you went unexpectedly like, for instance, when I went back with my cousin Hania. She couldn't remember anything about Piotrkow, where she was also born.'

The truth is, of course, that even before the occupation anti-Semitism was officially part of Polish policy.

All that Mala says she can remember is a balcony in the tenement block where the family would live for a few months after the Germans arrived. There was the time that a man hanged himself, leaving a note ending 'I promise not to do it again'. His body was hauled out on to an upstairs landing. 'He lay there for a week. The Germans wouldn't allow him to be moved – so for a week we had to pass his decomposing body. I had never seen a dead body before and it was horrible.' Another example of the Nazi exercise in humiliation.

Her mother was still alive then. 'My mother didn't survive, so my memories just stop.' As we shall see, a little probing brings back more than she had imagined. And she adds: 'There is nobody for me to reminisce with. I mean, there was Ben, but we never do that.'

Today, she forgives him for not telling but, more strangely and tellingly, finds it more difficult to forgive herself for not asking. 'We were always busy with our lives. We were not going to sit about and talk about Poland. If it came up, yes, but otherwise we had families. We had spouses, children, to worry about. On the other hand, when you have time on your hands you start to reminisce, but we didn't and even now we don't.' Plainly, however, the story is subliminally there…

Truth to tell, conditions at the very start of the war in Piotrkow were not exactly like those in other parts of Poland or as they were in Latvia or Lithuania where the locals happily joined in the German shooting party. 'That was a terrible time.' But the Nazis eventually did get cracking. Two of Ben's uncles were killed in those early days. '[Up to then] all of my family saved themselves.' It wouldn't last. His 72 year-old grandfather was sent to the death camp at Treblinka.

But within days, the emphasis of the marauding occupiers was on finding the Jews in the town. Not that they were in hiding. They stayed at home. And their own traditions gave them away. There were synagogue registers and records of charitable contributions to destroy their freedoms. The *mazuzot* tubes bearing scriptural passages on the doorposts of probably every single Jewish home betrayed them. The names and where they were written became vital to both the Jews and the men who almost instantly became their captors. Whether the Germans were yet certain of what, or how, they were going to do with 'their' Jews, it was obvious that they were not going to allow them to live a 'normal' life. Firstly, the Nazi passion for ordered bureaucracy left no doubt that everything they discovered had to be recorded. So down on paper was the information ready for future – and not so far in the future – use. With no problems as to who the Jews were, the only decision to be made was what to do with them. That decision would be finalised soon enough.

Every member of what regarded itself as a community had to be registered. Then they had to be moved. The word commonly used for this in the twenty-first century is to be 'relocated'. It was the kind of word used by the Gestapo when the Helfgotts and every other Jew had to leave their comfortable apartment on Ulica 3 Maya and move into a single room in another block that had been allocated for Jewish use. It was the start of the ghetto.

# 4

## Ghetto

*'I love Poland'*
*– Ben Helfgott*

Not all the Nazis were venomous.

'There was always someone who was kind,' Ben says, an almost surprising look back at his own horrific story. 'We knew who to fear and who you didn't have to.' That was information that had to be taken seriously. The consequences of not doing so were not to be thought of lightly. That is, if you had the opportunity to even think about them.

'To be honest about it, if there hadn't been such people, the good ones, we wouldn't be here today.' But he doesn't include any Nazis in uniform when saying that. He reserves his memory of kindnesses from non-Jews in Piotrkow for Poles. But he doesn't pretend that all the citizens of the town qualified to be listed under that word 'kindness' either. Germans certainly did not. 'You learn it very quickly because if they took your life – as they could any minute – then it wasn't worth anything.'

The family and all their Jewish friends and neighbours knew that and so much else that 1 November morning in 1939. The announcements came via orders (you couldn't call them advertisements) on the walls of houses or various public places, along with posters for new films in the cinema. Orders they certainly were. Nobody was going to use conventional advertising to inform passers by that the only alternative they had to showing up was going to be the hangman's noose or, more likely, the firing squad.

It was an historic moment. Piotrkow had the distinction of being the first place in Poland to have an official ghetto. Non-Jews living in a hopelessly overcrowded area only a shortish walk from the Helfgott home were told to leave their own houses and apartments for what was in many cases far better accommodation and for which they paid nothing. The Jews, on the other hand, had paid every zloty of rent due. There had to be somewhere to put those nasty Jews, who would now move into *their* homes. It was a good swap – for the gentiles.

On the other hand, all Slavs, not just the Poles, were also regarded as second-class persons in a world that the Germans would have wished did not exist. Pride of place (literally) would go to the ethnic Germans living in and around the town (even Poles had to let German speakers occupy the places where their families had sometimes lived for generations). The Nazis probably were afraid they would join the Jews and be sleeping on the pavements and scaring the horses (the Warsaw Ghetto, soon to be the biggest of them all, where the sight of dead bodies and dying children lying in the street was a common occurrence, had not yet been set up). The Slavs, too, were all *untermenshen*, but not quite as *unter* as the Jews who had to be accommodated somewhere, like it or not.

The Jews were ordered to an area but not to the particular place where they could direct their bodies alongside whatever could be loaded into a suitcase. In a way, this was class distinction. Rich people had better luggage than their poorer co-religionists, and so could carry more of their belongings. Where to go was the big problem. The other difficulty was one of surprise – terrible, shocking surprise. Not only were they, rich and poor, directed to (very) inferior accommodation, when they got there, they found they would often be sharing a single room with complete strangers.

Moishe Helfgott was a clever resourceful man used to running a successful business. To Ben none of that is enough to describe him. 'He was also a courageous man. My father had a way of getting on with people.' He was also something of a wheeler-dealer, who, for the sake of his family, usually knew which wheel to deal or whose back to scratch. This, above all any other moments, was a time to call in favours. He had helped a gentile man who, like Moishe himself, had influence. Then there was a man heavily in debt who went to him for help. 'My father sorted it out for him. He was very generous, too.'

There were countless examples of that sort of thing, helping hands that make his son more than 75 years later feel unabashed pride. He likes to talk about his father and his exploits. And to stress that he was clever enough not to be an easy touch. 'He was travelling a lot before the war. Once there were two boys who asked him if he could somehow take them to Piotrkow, where they had an uncle. So he did – and brought them home. I was just seven or eight years old when they came to our flat. I was asleep. Then it turned out that they didn't have an uncle in Piotrkow at all. So he took them to the station and put them on a train that took them back to where they came from.'

There was also a local judge who, in addition to knowing his way around and knowing Moishe in particular, was a distant relative. He was the brother of an uncle of Ben's who was married to one of Sara's sisters. The judge's home was out of town – a place to which he would never return. Instead, he now managed to get a flat on the edge of the ghetto. But his wife and child were away and while that was so, he only occupied one room. The other parts of the apartment block which he now had to call home he made available to the Helfgott family.

They had a living room and a bedroom – where the family beds were, in addition to a table and chairs. As Ben says today: 'We could never have got a place like that otherwise. We had a kitchen and the most important thing is we had water in the apartment, in the living room.'

After the comparative luxury of their own home, this might be considered to be impossibly uncomfortable. A horrible existence seemed to be their fate. 'Actually, it was not horrible at all,' Ben recalls. 'It was a nice building.'

But, philosophically, it didn't stay nice. It was clear that this was merely a way-station to something much worse. Even so, there were others who discovered this, for certain, a little while before the Helfgotts did.

Perhaps if more Jews had gentile friends things might have been better for them. There had, it has to be said, been very little contact between the Jews and their Polish neighbours before the occupation.

Another one of the group of refugees who, as we shall see much later in this story, became known as The Boys, the outstanding late British Rabbi Hugo Gryn, recalling his days before being sent to Auschwitz regretted that there had been no such association with the non-Jewish population of his town in Czechoslovakia. 'I'm sorry because when it came to it, there was no-one to speak for us.'

But Ben today tells no stories about the indigenous population going out of their front doors to jeer at the Jews as they were rounded up and taken to the railway station on their journeys to hell (the popular phrase is 'to hell and back', but for most of them there was to be no coming 'back').

It is debatable whether the Helfgotts had this problem. 'We lived among Polish people. In our [former] apartment building, while I was there, about 45 per cent among the tenants were Jews. The rest, Poles.' It had taken hundreds of years for the family and its ancestors to become so well integrated.

But even he, with all his feelings for Poland and its people, has made no visits to the myriad Polish communities in Britain – in towns where they have their own shops and have established other businesses. But he does speak to some of these expats. 'I talk to them about my experiences and I have changed their minds many times.' But he adds sorrowfully: 'My family – my mother and my sister – would have been alive [if previous generations] had behaved differently. What happened to me happened to so many others.'

Inevitably, such thoughts constantly occur – again despite his seemingly enviable relations with the Poland of the twenty-first century. He repeats how he enjoyed playing with Polish children. But in the same sentence he will say: 'My father came home once and – I had never seen him like that before – after a group of Poles got hold of him...' The sentence was not immediately finished.

They tried to beat him up. But they didn't succeed. Moishe had a secret weapon – a pistol. Amazing as it might sound, he had a current licence to carry a gun. 'If he didn't have that gun, they would have killed him.'

Resignedly Ben, for whom it seemed so many Poles could do no wrong, admits: 'There will always be people like that. Every place has got these people.' As was proved by events in the few Polish towns where they were Jews again after the war, it didn't need a Holocaust for Jewish adults and children to be murdered.

Six weeks after the Nazis arrived in Piotrkow, the first residents of the ghetto received letters telling them to report to a place which for many had always had good associations, the start of journeys to visit close relatives or perhaps even to go on holidays – the local railway station. They never knew where they were going, other than being told they were being 'resettled'. The word 'Treblinka' was mentioned. They knew *where* that was. It wasn't very far from Piotrkow. But they had no idea *what* it was.

Ben's family were spared this initial 'transport'. But it wasn't long before the annoyance they felt at being *ordered* to leave their homes for a place in which they had no interest in being 'resettled' was quickly giving way to fear. The cattle cars in which people like themselves before long travelled without food, air or sanitation, didn't augur well. The screaming of guards and the barking of dogs held by the men in uniform had them shaking with fear.

The agony had really begun as they lined up at the station and had their names checked by a petty official. It was from a list that they soon enough got to know was a death warrant.

# 5

## Hiding

*'She was a beautiful girl'*
*– Ben Helfgott*

It was a strange ghetto – with those few Germans hanging around for much of the time, yet at others never to be seen. People had been stripped of most of their valuables, but there was a tiny amount of money around. 'On the whole, people didn't have money. But if you did, you were allowed to keep it.' Strangely, too, during the three years that the remnants of the Helfgott family were living there, there were almost no stories of the fights over cash which one might have expected.

After a time living at number 4 Plac Trybunalski, their 'home' in the ghetto, was not nice, in no way pleasant, but compared with the arrangements in other places – to say nothing of the camps – it was tolerable. For those who were transported to Treblinka, it was a paradise to which they would have given anything for the chance of returning.

It was 1942 when things really changed yet again in Piotrkow. Changed drastically. Changed terribly. It was when the deportations started in earnest. 'You can never imagine what we went through,' says Ben now. 'Every day, we could hear that in one town after the other, Jews were being deported. Everybody was saying: "When will be our turn? Where will we be going?"'

The Germans had their own way of answering – if they deigned to answer an inferior person's questions. They realised that by just saying they were going to somewhere where they would find a new life – one where they had been 'resettled' – was not enough. Now they had new answers: 'The Germans said they would be sending them to a place where the Russians had hidden a lot of gold.' A nice anti-Semitic touch there, as if everything else was nothing. 'They were hearing that Jews were being gassed. Every day, we never knew whether it was going to be our last. We were all helpless. We didn't know what to do.'

The family were luckier than most, even so. It was all because of the piece of paper that Moishe carried with him at all times – the written permission, the licence in effect – that showed he had sanction to leave the ghetto's borders. He still didn't have an official pass. But he showed what he had to the guards and they let him through. They didn't know what the official papers should have looked like and, as his son now says, there would have been no means of checking. Of course, the now ageing and creased papers were forgeries (of what no-one knew). He was, the papers said, to go into the nearby villages and buy animal skins. He never did that. He sold flour.

For a brief time the family was beginning to break up. Ben's eight-year-old younger sister Lusia was living with a Polish family who introduced her as their niece. She didn't stay there long. 'She was a sweet beautiful little blonde girl who didn't look Jewish. She spoke Polish better than the other chillden,' Ben recalled, rather more emotionally than usual. The real reason for her going back to Piotrkow was that her Polish 'aunt' and 'uncle' were asked by their neighbours 'how much did you pay for her?' The people who had been looking after her said. 'She is such a lovely girl and we wish we could look after her, but we are afraid. It is only a matter of time before someone gives us away.' She was returned to the ghetto after the deportation to be with the family. One of the other side effects of Polish anti-Semitism.

Moishe was with his family during this period of 'exile' but Ben was not. He had a job in the local glass factory. He did go to see them – an amazingly brave thing to do when Jews were banned from travelling, but Ben, rather like his father, never let rules, even ones that could threaten his life, interfere with things he either wanted or needed to do. Moishe came back with his son leaving Sara and her sister in the care of the Polish family. 'The woman soon afterwards had an affair with a man who was working for the Nazis. The woman started harassing my mother and demanding money. She told her: ' Other people know you are here. So you will have to "buy" us.' In other words, she demanded a bribe. 'My mother said "I haven't got any money".'

Soon after Ben and his father returned to the ghetto, Sara decided to go back with her sister. She saw everything she had with her being stolen in front of her eyes. Ben remembers her saying: 'They took everything, including my ring. And then they said "If I find you here tomorrow, I'll pass you on to the Gestapo".' So Sara and Gucia came back to living in the ghetto, although for many people 'living' was just about all they were able to do. But, as the old saying went (and still goes) it was better than the alternative. From that point on, it was a question of how they could avoid that alternative.

Mala, together with her young cousin Idzia, the daughter of Sara's brother, had been with yet another Polish family. She too returned to the ghetto to be with Ben, his parents and younger sister Lusia. Idzia, the ten and a half year-old daughter of Dora and Joseph Klein, did not return. Her fate remains unknown.

It was in desperation that their parents had sent them there. As Mala tells it: 'We stayed with people who were recommended – people who would hide two Jewish girls for money.' They weren't friends. They weren't even Polish – but ethnic Germans which at that time, remarkably enough, seemed to be a better option, even if any Polish people were ready to make the offer. 'I remember these people came into the ghetto and they made the arrangement – for which they were very well paid. We were told we would be absolutely safe. They were considered safer than the Poles because as Germans they enjoyed privileges that the Poles didn't. They could travel. They had more food They were the lords.' And they were treacherous. 'They got rid of Idzia.' How, no-one ever knew.

'My aunt told me after the war that they were so worried about Idzia getting back safely. There was this man and this woman, his sister-in-law, not his wife. As they were leaving, my aunt said she gave her a gold ring with a diamond – just to make sure, a little extra – just to make sure they would look after her.' Mala remembers now that she, a 12 year-old, persuaded her father and uncle that she didn't mind going. 'I said it was all right to take me to these people. They are hiding valuables.' They came to her uncle's and aunt's home – such as it was – with a suitcase. 'They took a suitcase full of goods and they left with Idzia and the suitcase.' They were taken on the train separately a week apart. 'They didn't treat us badly or anything. I mean, they were OK, but we were very scared and very vulnerable. We were very homesick and Idzia was so homesick that she wanted to go back. She didn't want to stay, but they said they couldn't take her back because the deportations are still happening.'

That was meant as a kind of reassurance. It was not enough to convince a couple of little Jewish girls. The woman told them that they had very good friends in Piotrkow who were looking after her parents' 'valuables'. Believe that, of course, and, if you were young enough, you'd believe anything. The family also believed that Idzia was safe. They wouldn't know until after Mala got home a short time later. 'They took her and I thought how lucky she was. When the time came for me to go back, arrangements were made. They said, "We are going to take you back home now to your father. We are going to meet in the flour mill" – which before the war belonged to my father, but where he was now a worker. When we arrived, there was my father and also Idzia's father, Josef Klein. He looked at her and he went white and said, "Where is my daughter?" And the man said, "We took her to your friends, the Mackowiaks".'

The Mackowiaks were not Jewish, but they were friends of Ben's and Mala's uncle and aunt. They were not able to take the girls themselves because of the current deportations, but she recommended the couple in Czechochowa. 'My uncle said they knew she was not there. "Where is she?" he asked. He was just pacing up and down, saying, "What have you done with my child?" That's the end of the story. Nobody knows what they did with her.' Alas, that really was the end of the story – and almost all of the family, the remainder of whom still remember, wonder and grieve. 'You know when I think about it now, I feel even more deeply after all those years.'

All that was a demonstration of the desperation every Jew was experiencing. A desperation that led to a trust that no loving parent would, in normal circumstances (and what was normal then?) possibly consider.

The little girl's fate was never discovered (or rather how she died, as she so assuredly did). No-one knows, either, what happened to the couple who, one supposes, ought to be called the kidnappers, if not the murderers, which they possibly, if not probably, were. As Mala tells it: 'They left – with the goods and with the little girl. But where they went, no-one knows – except that eventually, they were back in Czechochowa.' It was not a time when the police could be brought in and the criminals brought to trial. The Nazis would in no way want to know, and if they did, it would have merely been a new excuse to murder another Jewish family.

Mala says today: 'I myself didn't ask to go home. I suppose if I did, I could have led them to some things. My aunt said to me: "How could anybody get rid of a child for the sake of some goods? I would have given them everything I suppose to save her".'

As she now tells it, her own 'escape' was indeed miraculous: 'I was sent a message from Piotrkow asking if I was all right. The messenger got to deliver it. But he didn't escape afterwards.'

Mala has a theory about what happened to her little cousin. Although neither she nor anyone else can be sure. 'I think Idzia might have had a paper on her with certain addresses on it. I haven't, however, had that confirmed by anyone.' Knowing how things were in those dreadful times, one guess is as good as any other and this one was probably better than most.

Harry Spiro was one of the ones who benefited by the false mathematics of the German Piotrkow high command. At the same time, he became a 'lucky victim'. Twenty-one men who had been given permission, after all, to stay in their ghetto homes were now sent to join the other 550 or so people who were starving, praying, relieving themselves and dying in the synagogue, the place where they had spent their lives going for solace and quietude on countless Sabbaths and holydays. But before that happened there was the infamous selection process. This was one with a slight difference. The 550 stayed there for ten days. 'It was terrible. A lot of them were people who had been in hiding. The conditions were horrific. After two days, the action director came in.' He was the man who actually held lives in his hands. He had decided that 20 people were needed to work in the German-managed (taken over from the original Polish owners) glass factory, where Ben worked. He made his selection of men and boys who he thought could stand the pressures of the work – one of whom was Spiro. As we shall see, it turned out to be a momentous decision. A decision which plainly was as much whim as serious choice. 'He phoned up the SS people, told them he knew of men who could be useful and were now in the synagogue and asked that we should be released.' Twenty-one went.

Spiro knew how lucky he was. The synagogue selections were as vicious as any recorded in the history books – those about men like the infamous doctor Mengele at Auschwitz who by a flick of his hand chose who would live and who would go up in smoke from the crematoria minutes later. But those who survived the deportations from Piotrkow all have their own stories to tell.

'There are two things I cannot forget,' Harry told me. 'One was the guy in the synagogue, standing with a baby in his arms. He could have been saved, but he begged to be allowed to take the baby with him. The SS man said No and he went back to where he had stood – and, of course, both perished. Now, more than 70 years down the line, I ask myself if he made the right choice.'

To say this was a terrible time is to underplay the sheer misery brought by the horrors of that day in the synagogue at Piotrkow – men, women and children from the Jewish community parading in an upstairs room, those at the front, facing the painting of the Ten Commandments – including the one declaring Thou shalt not kill – before being murdered.

The invaders delighted in seeing the Piotrkow prison filling up. The place that had been used for local petty criminals, drunks and assorted thieves mostly, was now echoing with the sounds of terror, coming from Jewish men and women whose crime was mostly just being on a certain list that designated them for a new existence, which generally was no existence at all.

It was the time of terrible tragedy in the lives – or rather the remaining lives – of the Helfgott clan. The worst thing that could happen to a family was just around the corner. But there were Sara's brother Josef Klein and Moishe's brother, Fischel, among those who paraded into the Jewish cemetery at Piotrkow in March 1943 and, as they walked, one by one, through the iron gates, were shot in the back of the neck. It was typical Nazi barbarism and their love of irony that they chose the cemetery for these murders – a similar, but far more sinister, form of cruel irony that Hitler adopted when he ordered that the same railway car that had been used by the French to sign the 1918 armistice with Germany should serve as the spot for the taking of the French surrender in 1940.

They probably laughed at the thought of how much valuable petrol was being saved by killing the men in the same place where they had always expected to be buried (when, as they all had prayed, they would die in their beds.) The mass grave is situated exactly opposite the entry to the cemetery into which they had been marched.

As Ben recalled: 'At one time, they killed in one go 12 families – including five doctors with their loved ones. Simply no-one was safe. I came home from work one day and saw two men who were not taken away. Everybody knew why. They were [Jewish] policemen. They had been shot and their bodies left for all to see and act as a deterrent should anyone be tempted to help.'

# 6

## Police Jews

*'Others kept shouting "Murderer"'*
*– Ben Helfgott*

The German organisation and efficiency was obvious. Jews had to be controlled. But why waste manpower on sorting out Jewish people and Jewish property? Let the Jews do it themselves. Before long, they had set up a Jewish police force – usually made up of the sort of men no Jewish mother would want to have marry their daughters. But some, as Ben told me, were not like that. 'After the war, there were trials. Someone gave evidence and said that one of the Jewish policemen had killed his parents. And then someone else came forward and said that he had *saved* his parents.'

Certainly, some did try to prove they had hearts – of a sort. As Ben recalls: 'Yes, some of the policemen wanted to save their own parents. But that didn't always work. Sometimes, the Germans discovered [their motives].' That is when the Germans came out in their truest of true colours. 'They told the Jewish police that if they did not bring their parents to the Nazis, they and their children would be shot alongside them.'

This happened to one of Ben's friends, Henry Kazanowski – one of the children included in that threat. His father belonged to a different kind of so-called law enforcement organisation, the 'Sanitary Police'. This was a group of Jews set up in 1941 after a typhoid outbreak to try to curb the epidemic.

It turned out to be one of the sad and all too familiar stories of what would be known as the Holocaust. Henry's grandparents were told by their son what was happening. They said, 'We are old and you are young. We will go [to a concentration camp]'. If that was their wish it was granted. But Henry's father, their son, denounced them incredible as it might seem. The sanitary inspector decided that it was the only way to save the life of his wife and son as well as his own. Henry's grandparents were murdered and his parents and he survived.

Why would previously nice Jewish boys want to do this job? 'It was to save their skins – of course,' says Ben. 'They were not all cruel. Some were very nice. But when it came to the deportations a little later on, they realised that they had a job to do.' And if they didn't, they would end up in the same gas chambers and ovens as the rest of their co-religionists.

'Absolutely, that was what happened,' Ben recalled. 'When we were deported, they were nobodies, just like us. But at first, they were protected and they were bragging about it. Once they ceased for any reason to be useful to the Nazis, to have no more use, they were sent to the camps just like we were. The Germans sent them away outside the town.'

It wasn't just the Jews in police uniforms who were collaborators. The story of two brothers stands out. Years later, soon after the war, Ben, once more older than his years, approached the younger of these brothers, Abram, in Germany. 'I said to him "somebody is here, who said he knows you." Others gathered around as I put it to him that he and his brother had been cruel to his fellow Jews. I think I was very good on this occasion but the others kept shouting the word "Murderer" at him.' One might ask what else could they do? The brothers were so well known. 'He gave away so many people.' Their victims – or the relatives of their victims – had seen them watch Germans either kill or deport Jews they had given away and just stand and do nothing. 'Straight away, the men beat him up.'

The Jewish police were the obvious ones, the men treated as traitors because of the uniforms they wore and the way they treated people, making them appear little different from the Germans. They were among the unwelcome people who walked the streets of both the large and what became the small ghetto after most of the inhabitants had been deported. They wore ill-fitting suits and caps with a blue band above the peak and a badge consisting of the Magen David, the Star (as it is called, although the first word actually means 'shield') of David. Right from the earliest days, that same star – blue in Poland; mostly in other countries being ravaged by the Nazis, yellow, a colour with distinct historical connotations – that had to be sewed on all their clothes, at least the clothes they had managed to save when the 'relocation', as the Nazis called the trips to the gas chambers, took place.

The Jewish police, largely, *were* cruel and enjoyed being so. They thought that volunteering for the force would not only allow them to escape the fate of the other Jews, but it brought them great power. Yes, it did – for the time being; until there were no more Jews to control. They were like batteries – essential to keep things moving and then to be thrown away. For the moment, however, the Nazis were happy to leave them to do their dirty work. And work came not much dirtier.

After the war, they, too, received retribution, not all of which was generally publicised. 'A number died very quickly,' was how Ben put it. We'll see more of the cause and the retribution as this story moves on.

# 7

## Death and Deportation

*'Most had already gone'*
*– Ben Helfgott*

At first there had been reasons for optimism, no more so than when Sara 'escaped' from deportation along with Lusia. Mother and younger daughter had been taken away in one of the regular round-ups.

'We had already had one very big deportation,' Mala recalled for me. 'Most people had already gone. But those who remained after Hania's father was shot were nearly all arrested – including my mother and one of my Klein uncles. Strangely, they were later let go.' As will soon become apparent, it was not to mean freedom for either of them. The Germans said that Sara was needed for work. 'She was told, "Everybody who is here now will be legal and they should not be afraid. They should also give their names [to assure this would happen]".'

'I don't know why they were released,' Mala told me. 'But then we don't know why they were arrested either. They [the Germans] didn't need excuses to arrest people.' Of course, merely causing trouble was sufficient reason. The ones who survived breathed again – for a short time.

But they went into hiding. It was an attempt to beat the Germans that was never going to work. A woman with Sara had been told that if she revealed the whereabouts of another family, she would be released – and she could take her friend with her.

For a time, that was the end of one dreadful chapter. But what about Moishe since he had had the 'discussion' with the Polish taskmaster? And his mother? He hadn't seen either for some time. Where were they? Ben's idea of where his parents might be could easily have been accurate. It was the house of a Polish friend of his father – whom he had last seen there the day before.

Getting out of the factory during that shift was far from an easy proposition. Had he done so and been caught, the kind of punishment likely to be meted out didn't bear consideration. Sacked and so form an addition to the number of deportees was highly possible. Death? Well, that was the inevitable outcome, although at that time, exactly how inevitable he couldn't imagine.

'I went into the building where the wife was. "What are you doing here?" she asked. 'I have come to find out where my parents are', The answer was not what anyone, let alone a desperate child, could easily accept. It told him nothing. 'Well, your parents were here until yesterday. The Germans have started killing people around here, so my husband took them somewhere.'

'Somewhere', of course, translated as 'nowhere'. There were no other answers from the woman. But ten minutes later, her husband came into the house. 'That alone was an experience that combined fear with hope, but mostly fear. "Yes", said the man, "I'll take you to them." So I began to sit down. "No you can't sit here. You come when it is dark." It was the afternoon and the days were getting shorter. I started to walk and as I began to do so, I heard Polish voices. So I ran. I was always a good runner, but not for long distances – 60, 70 metres, the most.' That day he could have run an Olympic marathon. His mind was racing as fast as his feet. He wasn't sure whether the first Polish voice he heard was that of the man who had promised to take him to his parents, but that hope had turned into that fear.

The question about his family was losing priority to that of his own fate. The big park where until just a few months before he had run, jumped and played hide 'n' seek seemed to offer the best shelter. It was about half a mile away, a place that always offered him a welcome. To say that he knew every stone isn't only just an exaggeration. When he had been there before the war, it was as if it were his own kingdom. Knew every stone? He might have thought that he knew every blade of grass. In those days, the gutsy Ben 'just loved the life I lived. It was marvellous.' Now he had to rethink that life for as long as it lasted. 'I knew they were looking for me. Then they went away.' Ben really did know his 'kingdom'. Probably better than the searchers.

He could recall the times when he saw boys having a fight and would break them up – even if they were considerably older than he himself. Now, seeing fights were signals to run away.

The man who had offered him hope, on the other hand, was as good as his word. And so, perhaps surprisingly, was the one who had told him to come back. It was an offer that could have landed him in front of either a set of gallows or a firing squad. Now, dark as it previously been light, he followed the only one who offered him any hope. After about half an hour following the moment when Ben was finally sure that the men who were attempting to chase him out of his park lair were gone, he went back to the place where he was told the Helfgotts were hiding, Sara, Moishe and an aunt. They saw each other, they laughed, they cried, they hugged. 'You cannot imagine what a meeting it was. It was unbelievable.'

Moishe said he would return to the factory where he worked with his son. But they had to wait until 10 o'clock before they could be sure it was safe. The decision had taken a great deal of forethought. And there was one very good reason for the course of action they had decided upon: there was no electricity in the evenings in the factory. 'It was dark, so no-one could see from the street. When the [previous] shift people came out, we moved in together. Once I was in, my father went back to the ghetto.'

It happened because of the status of the ghetto and of people like Moishe. Ben found out how his father was, so unusually, able to go in and out of the prison which the place in fact really was – a prison where Jews had to walk in the road if they saw a German approach and raise their blue or black caps every time a man in Nazi uniform passed by. The Passover dictum, 'We were slaves, now we are free men', had to be turned on its head. Moishe was not the kind of person to accept serfdom. The fact that this was an open ghetto did not mean that anyone, not even Mr Helfgott, could move with ease whenever he wanted. He could go where his wallet allowed. The guards looked the other way, but only after they told him, 'Come on. You want to go out, you pay up.' He had another advantage. He was a local who had worked locally. 'That made him "legal". Those who had just moved into the town or who stopped working, these were the ones who were now hiding – and the Germans went from house to house, looking for these Jews and the people who had been hiding them.'

But then 'IT' happened. 'IT' was the worst event possible. Ten days after the false alarm, on 20 December 1942, when the German occupiers were celebrating Christmas (a time when the Jewish police were, naturally, proving useful) one of those Jewish policemen called and took Sara away with Lusia.

In truth, this wasn't altogether expected – at first, anyway. 'It was all quiet for about two weeks,' says Ben. But then came the moment to start getting worried. Seriously concerned. 'The Germans announced that everyone who had been in hiding should now register – and become what they described as "legalised". He doesn't know if his mother registered or mentioned other members of the family, All that was certain was that Sara and her younger daughter were taken away to the synagogue – and then with the other 550 or so others there, transported to the Rakow woods around Piotrkow and shot.

Before all that happened, there had been a feeling of a kind of security. The family had been left alone. As Mala told me: 'We had no idea they were going to come for us. In that room there was a dresser and behind that was a sort of recess into which people would hide when policemen came round. But on this occasion, there was no-one hiding because there was no fear that anyone would come. We were in that room when the police knocked on the door and came in.'

But what about Mala herself? Being taken away could have been Mala's fate, too. But when the feared Jewish police arrived in their city suits and blue caps, Sara had the intuition to tell her to stay in her bed and cover herself well, up to her neck. 'You are ill,' she said. As far as the Jewish police were concerned, she was very ill.

Mala didn't look ill and she certainly didn't feel sick, but in a way she was being saved by the problems of living in the humble apartment in the ghetto. 'There were two beds in that room, a large bed and another smaller one at the side. I was in the bed simply because the room was very crowded and this was how I could nicely be tucked up out of the way.'

Sara managed to get out just a few words, between sobs and shaking in fright, to tell the men who had invaded whatever little privacy that they might have had that Mala was ill. Tadek Glogowski, a policeman in his early twenties always previously thought of as coming from a 'good' Jewish family, went into the tiny room and as he pushed mother and younger daughter towards the truck with its deathly cargo, asked about the other girl. 'She's ill,' said Sara. 'Ok' said the policeman who was not known for any sense of human understanding. Glogowski left Mala alone, as she lay crying under the covers. It was a remarkable thing for him to do.

Some would call it luck. But try telling that to a nine-year-old child who sees her mother and 'baby' sister taken away. Children grew up quickly in the ghetto. It was not difficult for her to accept that the two who had been so much part of her young life would not be seen again.

One supposes that when they saw Glogowski was in charge, they and their neighbours in the building were overwhelmed with fear. That reputation as a 'baddie' went with him and he was high on the list of men of whom to be really scared. But also how odd was his story. Ben recalls: 'His father was a wonderful, wonderful man – a former schoolteacher whom everyone respected.' Glogowski was to write about his treacherous work after surviving the war. He did not mention that day in the Helfgott room. 'I didn't mention it,' he was to tell Mala when amazingly they came face-to-face long after the war, 'because I didn't think you would want me to.'

It would have been a dreadful thing for her and Ben to read. It was, after all, a story that had only one side and it wasn't the one belonging to Glogowski, who couldn't have put himself in the position of a child who last saw her mother and sister being carted off to their deaths. Neither would he have known the emotional moment when Sara told her surviving daughter 'Just stay and don't go anywhere.' Whether he stayed to watch the murders is not sure. Did he witness the men and the women undress for the last time in their lives? Did he watch the men dig the pits into which their newly-dead bodies would fall – a litany copied in every place in which the tentacles of the Holocaust extended? How about the man who shouted out, 'Just run away. Don't allow them to shoot you'? Did he see 50 others of the victims being saved when word got to the firing squads that that number of prisoners was required for work? Or perhaps he was the one responsible for taking those lucky ones and telling them that once the work was done, their fate would be the same of the ones who were shot? That was, of course, a promise to be kept. Actually three men from the pits did escape. They hid among the trees and then waited for dark before starting to run.

What happened to the three is one of the mysteries of the war in Piotrkow. 'But within an hour all those left behind in the ghetto knew about it.' Ben found out by listening to his father's conversation. 'My ears were always tuned to what he was saying or hearing.' The so-called bush telegraph buzzed instantly. 'In the evening, everyone in the ghetto knew what had happened. The following morning, as I was sleeping in my bunk, my father was up early. I saw him and I didn't have to be told what had happened.' One man who had witnessed the sordid events came back to the ghetto with the information. The question everybody involved later wanted to know was what had happened to him himself. No-one is absolutely certain. 'I don't think he survived,' says Ben today. That was just part of the incredible relationship between the two generations. He now says that Moishe was responsible for his own survival. 'Without him, I would never have survived. No, I cannot imagine what it would have been without him. My father took risks with his smuggling and if he were caught, they would have shot him instantly.'

Among the 550 were Ben's mother Sara and his younger sister Lusia. They were incarcerated in the synagogue. After two weeks, on the 20 December 1942, they were taken to the Rakow forest. Ben's father had secured a release for Sara but was unable to do the same for Lusia. Sara refused to leave Lusia and so knowingly went to her death with her eight-year-old daughter.

As Ben says: 'It was a new experience. No-one knew what was likely to happen. After the people were shot, everyone in Piotrkow and everywhere else knew.' The Nazis instructed the Jewish police to name and find fellow Jews. Most did. Some didn't. 'They didn't want to give anyone away and were shot by the Germans.'

Sara cried as she and Lusia were taken away. Well, of course, she did. She was only in her late thirties and the circumstances were too horrific to contemplate. She said that she had a terrible pain, but it made no difference.

Mala saw it happen, but, as we know, was left behind. 'I cried and I was upset,' she recalls, probably talking for herself and her brother Ben. 'But it didn't have the full impact on me.' Such are the vagaries of war and the effect it could have on very personal tragedies. And their father had jobs by then – a temporary passport to continuing life. 'I remember,' Mala told me, 'I remember seeing Ben first when he came home from work. I saw him when I was standing on a wooden balcony outside the room where we lived in the ghetto. Ben arrived and I said to him, "They have taken Mother and Lusia". And when I said it, I started crying again. Rather loudly, I remember. I remember him saying to me, "Be quiet. Don't make so much noise." Maybe I made a fuss that was almost embarrassing. I don't remember. But I did cry quite loud because I remember [the policeman] saying to me, "Don't make so much noise".'

Ben himself didn't make any noise when he heard the too-dreadful news. 'He was like a strong man and wasn't about to cry. Maybe he did, but I don't remember that. I am sure that he probably was crying – weeping without making a noise, crying in his heart.'

Ben now reflects on that day – he always has done. 'This was the most terrible time.' There were different stages of bad, but this was the worst time of all. 'I lost my mother and my sister, a beautiful blonde-haired girl of eight.'

One hundred people at a time were taken and shoved into the lorries in this one round-up. In a way, it should not have happened. Their deaths could just possibly have been avoided – for a time, anyway.

'You see, there were so many stages from the time of the round-up until the executions. People were taken from one place to another.' People who were not told to take the various journeys were the lucky ones. A few young Jews were all too seriously and successfully playing at policemen and rounding-up people. As we have seen, they form part of the background to the Holocaust, some as bad as the Germans, some not as bad as the French police who scooped up the Jewish population of Paris and elsewhere. But the French police were not Jews. The fact that Jews were responsible for sending their own people to the gas chambers or, as in the case of the two Helfgott victims, to the woods where they fell to the slaughter of the bullets, defies normal thought. But then, few thoughts could be considered normal at this time.

'The Jewish police, like Glogowski, were mainly young men who didn't care what they were doing,' says Ben. 'All they wanted first of all was that they did a "good job" and could be left behind. Some of them were 21 years old and before the war they simply had a better life. They were men who came from a good family – especially in my town. We had somebody whose father was a teacher, a very nice man, but his son didn't want to be Jewish. When the Germans came, he was pleased to be a collaborator. He took people away.' That was Glogowski.

Mala finds it difficult to blame these men who would, had they themselves not been sent to a death camp, been crippled by conscience, for this was, to people not put in that position, the ultimate in collaboration with the Nazis and the worst kind of treason. 'They did it because they had to,' she says now. To Ben, it was simply part of the picture. 'There were always some Jews who tried to be working with the Germans – and I knew there were Jews who left Poland at the time who said that the Poles were the worst collaborators. Some of them didn't look Polish and didn't act as if they were trying to work with the Germans or the Russians.'

There were those who prayed – most Jews prayed at that time, even those who had never been in a synagogue – for a return of the kind of regime of the one in the inter-war years, led by Marshal Josef Pilsudski, who as far as friendship with their community was concerned was the best relationship they had ever experienced (he died of cancer in 1935). 'After that, the Polish politicians had learned from Hitler. These were the worst years. But during the war some Poles helped the Germans – and some didn't. It was a little like the Jewish policemen.'

Mala talks about her faulty memory. But, the day when her mother and sister were about to be murdered would be remembered by a person even half her age at that time. There are those who always claim they had spiritual revelations after traumatic events. It only happened once after what has to be the most terrible day in her life. 'Actually, I hesitate to say this because it sounds so unbelievable. But I had a dream early that morning. I know it was early morning because I woke up after that dream. My mother appeared in that dream. But she only appeared at the foot of my bed. She was naked. She was not with my sister. All alone, naked – and then she disappeared.'

There was to be one more occasion when a dream manifested itself in a similar way. But it had nothing to do with either her mother or sister – although a psychologist might think otherwise. In conversation with me, Mala's mind strays to other events in her life during the Holocaust years. For her, there would just one manifestation of the sort. 'My best friend when we were in Ravensbruk [the women's concentration camp, more of which later] appeared in my dream, wearing black stockings. I remember the black stockings. The next day I heard that she had died.'

For the moment, luck seemed to be the operative factor in her life. There was a time when Mala herself was about to be stacked on to a lorry on the way to deportation. That was when she saw an SS officer and, by some kind of intuition, saved herself. For reasons that will stump most people for the sheer courage – or even chutzpah – of what she did, she accomplished something few Jews attempted. She ran up to the Nazi – often an act 'justifying' a swipe of a whip or, more likely, a bullet from the pistol in his holster. But in her case, it didn't happen. Not only did he not assault her, he listened. Not only did he listen, he agreed to her request: 'My brother is working in the glass factory, can I join him?" she asked. If that question was remarkable, his answer deserves to be preserved in the history of the Holocaust.

Perhaps he was swayed by the innocence of a pretty little girl. Maybe he was just kind. He agreed. Mala tells it like this: 'I didn't experience the main deportation, which must have been horrific. But the small one I was in, with my cousin and all these so-called illegals, was terrible. The lorries were coming and we were put in those lorries. I was at the end of the line. There were soldiers who were surrounding us. In front of me was a woman with a baby in her arms. I don't know what she did or said, but she was suddenly hit over the head with a rifle butt and the baby was screaming. The woman was crying as the blood was pouring from her head and there was my little cousin of five seeing it all.'

Today, she looks back on that dreadful time, thinking things that might not have occurred when, as a child of eleven, all that was in her mind was the scene before her eyes.

'There was this one officer who was in charge but he wasn't doing anything, just watching those in the column, standing in the corner watching what was going on. I don't know what gave me the idea or the courage, but I stepped out of line and went up to him and said, '"I have been separated from my father and brother. Can I go back to them?"'

'Before I said that, I could see he was a little shocked at being approached but he smiled. He really had a kindly face. I still remember that face. But what I really regret is I never found out his name. Ben told me that he actually visited the place, to go to the woodwork factory where we eventually both worked.'

The memories of the family tragedy transcend everything from that period. 'There was just talk and people crying, it wasn't such a big thing. People were always dying. There was no Shiva [the Jewish rite of mourning for parents and close relatives]. The times were so unusual.'

Desperate times can lead to totally irrational reactions. Ben has said: 'I had around me – strange as it might sound – a belief in invincibility, that nothing could happen to me. There were many times I was, absolutely terrified, but I had a great belief in my father. He would not allow any situation to get the better of him. So many people collapsed as they just didn't know what to do. But my father somehow always seemed to have a presence of mind, courage and resourcefulness.'

Whether Ben and his father realised how, despite it all, they were still so much luckier than the other Jews from Piotrkow – to say nothing of poor Sara and Lusia – lucky in that they had each other. It helped that both father and son later worked in the same Dietterich-Fischer woodwork factory. The little girls, Mala and her cousin Hania, would later work there too. It is engrained into Ben's memory like a sliver of the glass on which he was at first working floating through his bloodstream. Glass in a vein can be fatal. So could this job have been. But in the case of the Helfgottts, it was not.

The 650 Jews there worked side-by side-with several hundred Polish labourers as well as some ethnic Germans who believed they were experiencing the Second Coming there in Piotrkow. Jews were being metaphorically crucified and then resurrected to be their fellow workers. 'Some of them were all right. Others were really nasty and on the first day, they hit me and that was terrible.'

He was not one of the people who earned any money in the factory. But he says it was not slave labour. 'It wasn't because it was labour without which I would have been deported.'

The glass factory was owned by German and Belgian families with a German director. 'He was quite happy to have Jews working for him. That was why he employed me with other young boys.'

There was a reason why it was not regarded as slave labour. He could have had the choice of going there or not – without, perhaps, at the time before the wholesale deportations, knowing with any certainty of an alternative. But then it all changed and Moishe was the one who realised there was no real choice.

'My father didn't want me to go to work. But when it came to 1942, Jews were already being sent to the gas chambers and the conversation among people in the ghetto was that the time was getting nearer and nearer to when we would all be taken to them too. It became more and more difficult to get a job because there was such a shortage of employment opportunities. Everybody wanted work. Then one day I came across a group of Jewish boys who said they had got jobs in a glass factory. [One of them ] was very excited when he said that.' With reason. That job was a passport to a kind of freedom. 'I said I wanted a job in that glass factory and they said I'd never get in. When I came home, I told my father. He himself already had a job.' It wasn't a job, the former wealthy flour mill proprietor was now an entrepreneur – with that pass to work. The Germans didn't know officially what that work was: the flour he smuggled into the ghetto was a major contribution to the fact that the people living in those cramped surroundings were not starving. But Ben says: 'My father was not carrying sacks of flour on his back.'

Ben still rejects the suggestion that he was ever a slave labourer. Even if he was not one, he would have made a perfect example of the people who were described as such. Whatever he was told to do, he did – and did it well. 'My job for a time in the wood factory was to carry heavy bags up steps.

People looked at me. They kept saying, "How can you do that?"' Indeed, the bags were so heavy a weightlifting champion (shades of things to come) would have found them difficult to negotiate.

That was despite the appeal from one of the executives of the firm – who, in his way and on a smaller scale, was trying to play the Oskar Schindler game. The protests he made, requesting his employees stayed put, were centred on the fact that the boys were essential to the running of the factory. It bore no resemblance to the true facts and the occupiers probably knew that. They said no and most of the boys met the same end as the people who had been taken to the synagogue before them. They were lost to the factory and they themselves lost their lives.

On the other hand, because of the proprietor playing Schindler, some of the young boys who seemed destined to be shot in the synagogue, including Harry Spiro, were released to become one of those 'essential' workers – although in truth they were really nothing of the kind.

Ben knew he was, despite all, fortunate. He was lucky to have a job. He was fortunate that that job meant he had somewhere to sleep, even if it were just in a stable. By now, the ghetto grew until it was reduced by the deportations that would come to Piotrkow. What later became known as the 'big ghetto' was replaced by the 'small ghetto'. The Helfgott home, such as it was, was now in Stara Warszwawska.

'Can you imagine it?' these days Ben asks, knowing the answers only too well. Only one who has actually gone through the terrors of those days in those circumstances could possibly do so. 'After the deportations, the days were different, the worst days. The streets were empty. People were afraid to leave what had become their homes. The Germans were continuing to round up people. They were killing men, women and children to the point that there was no life – for anyone. The few women who managed to save themselves were going to be sent to work in a factory in the town of Skarzysko.'

The Jewish policemen continued with their work of active collaboration – including the one who hustled Sara and Lusia to their deaths. If Glogowski hadn't known before, he knew now. He could easily have been the one to impart the terrible news to the others in the town. However, whereas fellow Jews (and it is in many ways difficult to talk about 'fellow Jews', for it was almost as though he wasn't considered as such and he would have loved to have distanced himself from his origin once he put on his cap with its misuse of the Magen David) the people who quaked and wept when they heard about the murders, he heard or witnessed it all with an air of superiority and satisfaction.

Ben recalls: 'Apparently, he met my father once and he said, "I have left your older daughter behind. If anyone tries to take her, mention my name."'

Which, one could think (or might not) was nice of him. Plainly, until it came time to being treated like any other Jew under German domination, he considered himself to be superior to every other 'citizen' of the ghetto. ('When the deportations began', says Mala, 'the Germans told him, "you get on that lorry, too". "What me?" he asked. "Yes you. Take off those boots and get on that lorry", and he was deported to a concentration camp'.) He was proud of his role. Unlike his comrades, he was smartly dressed. 'He had boots', recalled Mala, 'up to the knees, just like the ones the Germans wore, with the spine at the back. He was always turned out well and pleased with himself and in such a high position. He thought he was very important, with a highly polished button [that showed his rank]'.

So he went to the camp and swapped his smart uniform for a striped 'pyjama suit'. 'Wherever he went,' Mala adds, 'he was with the Germans. But then suddenly he was just someone in the barracks. When the war was finished, he didn't return to Piotrkow.'

Poland was Communist by then and Mala and her brother know that suddenly he became a Communist. Wherever he went, he was on what he regarded as the right side. He got a job on a ship and spent months at a time at sea. Then he came back – and someone spotted him drinking coffee in a restaurant in Lodz. It was to be a fateful cup for him to imbibe. The man called the police and Glogowski was arrested and tried. At Glogowski's trial after the war, Ben's aunt Dora Klein offered to give evidence. It turned out to be partly for the defence. Mala says: 'She told the court that he had *personally* saved her niece's life. But she also said that he was also *personally* responsible for leading her sister-in-law and her niece to their deaths. Saying that he saved my life was treated as a sort of redeeming feature. She said she wanted to do it. I don't know if her intention was to say he was not all bad and that there was a little bit of good in him.'

Whether it was or not, Glogowski was sentenced to a long jail sentence and was eventually released under a mass amnesty. There were some policemen who quite seriously did the job because they believed they stood a slight chance of helping Jews. One particular occasion when, quite possibly, one of the men might have achieved his aim, only for his hopes to be dashed by a group of Nazis, was immediately the talk of what was left of the ghetto.

The Jewish police were rounding up more and more people. As the events moved on, it becomes more and more clear how much they form part of the background to the Holocaust, some as bad as the Germans. The fact that Jews were responsible for sending their own people to the gas chambers or, as in the case of the two Helfgott victims, to the woods where they fell to the slaughter of the bullets is beyond consideration – or mere reproach.

Ben and his father had indeed been fortunate in other ways – principally, the luck of not being involved in the round-ups. It was simply because of the Nazi policy at the time fitted into their needs. The Germans needed workers. Workers needed to stay alive – the only 'wages' they were allowed. And, plainly they were considered really essential – unlike the boys who had been rustled into the trucks, despite the factory boss's appeals. As he now says: 'If someone was working, they allowed him or her to stay at work. If they fell in the gutter, the Nazis broke into their homes and took away everything in them. Anything that was any good was sent off to Germany.' And, of course, this organised thieving was not limited to the property of corpses.

But why should nice, clean, beautifully dressed Nazis spoil their uniforms – or their consciences? Like the taskmasters in Egypt and their slaves building the pyramids – incredible how the comparison keeps recurring – the Jews were ordered to root out the treasures, such as they were and clear up the mess. There were still valuables – or what someone in authority decided were valuable and, whatever happened to them, no Jew was allowed to keep them. It was as if, having decided for propaganda purposes, that all Jews were rich, the Germans needed to make sure that, while they lived, they would do so in abject poverty.

Ben saw the result of one such clean up: 'One day, a young man of about 20, tried to take down a chandelier from his apartment and dropped it. A soldier got out his pistol and shot him. Dead. That was what was happening- they were shooting people all the time. My father managed to get food – and did not wait to start defending us.'

A number of the Poles were collaborating. It is one of the established facts of the war. 'They didn't get involved in the wholesale murders. Yes, they may have betrayed us and given them away, but they didn't kill anyone. It wasn't like the situation in Lithuania, which was terrible, beyond thinking when the local population often took charge of the killings. But two of my aunts were the first victims of the Nazis in Piotrkow. My grandfather was not one of them,. He did not live to see the Holocaust or even the beginning of the war. He lived until he was 72 in Sieradz.' He ran his flour business and also had the flower shop – so different from the sort of places where Jews would later experience. Not that population sizes mattered to the Germans. If there were Jews anywhere – millions of them in Warsaw, a handful or just a single individual – they were easy *kosher* meat.

The persecutions took in three generations of Ben's family. His father's father was murdered. The maternal grandfather was sent to Treblinka. 'He lived in a different town, a part of Poland that was close to Germany. He was obviously of the belief that that was not a good place to be and took off for Piotrkow. Immediately, he went into the ghetto – and he had his own place.'

If that was a prestigious position, it ended with the 'transports'. 'When it came to the deportations, he was the only one of my family who was also living in my town who was sent during the seven days when they were deporting the Jews to Treblinka.'

His other grandfather's fate they could only be guessed at. 'He was never seen by the family again. Members of my other family – all were killed in the gas chambers.'

After the deportations, the Nazis decided not to be satisfied with merely packing humans in cattle trucks or killing the ones who hadn't yet been told to assemble at the railway station.

'For about three or four months, they were regularly killing people there. It was like in the French Revolution when aristos were taken to the guillotine.' The Germans had no need of going to the trouble of putting men, women or children into flimsy wooden carts, as happened near the Place de Bastille. Much easier was it to simply take out a gun and get rid of them piecemeal.

The strange thing about the Piotrkow ghetto was that the German guards were not ever present. You didn't see them parading along the streets the way they did in Warsaw or other places under the Nazi heel.

For a child to daily witness the slaughter was bad enough, to run away from the slaughterers was beyond imagination. Every so often a Nazi official would descend on Piotrkow. His arrival would send panic through the ghetto. Not so much out of fright for the man himself, but for his companion – a huge Alsatian dog, trained it seemed to be thirsty for Jewish blood. The big black dog was the subject of conversation after conversation in the ghetto – not least among the children. I suppose you could say that the beauty of being in the ghetto was that the Germans rarely came inside. But the man with the dog was a regular unwelcome visitor.

Says Ben: 'When he came, he ran after people. One man was being chased by the dog and caught him in a couple of seconds. It went for the man's testicles. In two minutes everybody around had disappeared. The Nazi knew people would be watching him and that was always a reason to go for them. He was amazed and delighted when he saw how people were running away, so as not to be caught. 'I was always aware how this bastard, extremely good looking, could stop a man. I can still see the man's face and that of the growling dog.'

That was on Ben's own first encounter with the beast (there could never have been a second one). 'I can remember the man's footsteps and the sound of the dog panting with him.' That was the time Ben ran for his life – over fences and across walls. He made it and the dog probably never forgave him.

Ben probably surprised himself as much as the SS man. 'I had become very good friends with another boy. One day, I was going to his building when I saw right in front of me was this bastard, speaking to a Jewish policeman who was very friendly with him. The policeman knew me and asked what I was doing there. I said I lived there. Then he looked at my short trousers. "Why are you wearing these?" he asked. He wanted to know how old I was. I said 12. He said, "Prove it". All the boy wanted to do was get away. All the dog wanted was another feed of Jewish flesh and blood. Ben managed to escape.

What he didn't escape was the fear of that moment, a fear which still drives through his body. 'Ever since then I have been put off dogs.' Ben is not the sort who will, even now, accept that he was afraid of anything except dogs, although he will confess that anxiety, shall we say, began when he was five years old. On that occasion, he was walking with his mother who stopped to talk to a friend. That woman had a dog which started chasing him. No-one then could imagine the significance of coming face to face with that animal.

The snarling German dog affected the lives of all the Jewish Piotrkow children, not just the Helfgotts, to say nothing of any parents who were still alive. The ones who were able to run fastest, like Ben himself, had a better chance of survival than those who were, to use the Biblical phrase, 'halt and lame'.

Ben now depended for friends on the ones who wanted to play with him in games that they were sure to lose. As for his sister Mala, she found life getting complicated. Clearly, there were gentile parents who were not keen – to say the least – to let their offspring play with a Jewish child. It was a real cultural shock for a girl like Mala for instance who said she hadn't, in those never-to-be-repeated pre-war days, experienced anything resembling anti-Semitic behaviour.

'I had never looked Jewish, but then a lot of people didn't.' (It is always amazing how Jews who don't look Jewish are quickly identified as such by people who are about to enjoy a pogrom.) But there was another explanation for the fact that she was to experience that shock. 'I was very young, so [I didn't realise] there were people who didn't understand what they were saying and what it was all about. But I do remember being called names like "Dirty Jew". That sort of thing.'

It had never happened at school, which, after a lot of thought, she began to think might have been a Jewish institution after all. 'All my friends seem to have been Jewish.' It became a completely irrelevant fact.

When Ben's aunt Irene (Moishe's brother Fischel's wife) was one of the people rounded up, her daughter Hania was left alone so came to live with Moishe, Ben and Mala,

They didn't stay together long. Soon, the ghetto was liquidated and a new life and a probable new death awaited them. Even the small ghetto had served its purpose as far as the conquerors were concerned. As Harry Spiro told me: 'The Germans rounded up the 500-odd people from the small ghetto because they could see there were 500 too many who had permission to stay there – so they decided to get rid of them by ending the ghetto's existence. The trouble for the Germans was that this was going to be too many for the Jewish police to handle. They had to think of something else.' Mala remembered it well: 'When it *was* finally liquidated, they took all the "illegals" outside the ghetto – there weren't that many by now. There was this column where my cousin and I were standing. But, as you know, it didn't quite go as planned.'

Never more would people talk about the huge number of Jews in this comparatively small town – formally 10 per cent of the population there.

'When we went to the end of July 1943, they finally ended it all.' It was a new definition of a final solution. But it wasn't as final as all that, which goes a great way to explain why Ben is still alive and able to put everything from this period on record.

Those who were not so lucky were carted off in trucks to plants 80 to 100 kilometres away. But, clearly, as Ben remembers some were luckier than others.

1. Ben's father, Moishe Yakov Helfgott.

2. Ben's mother, Sara Helfgott.

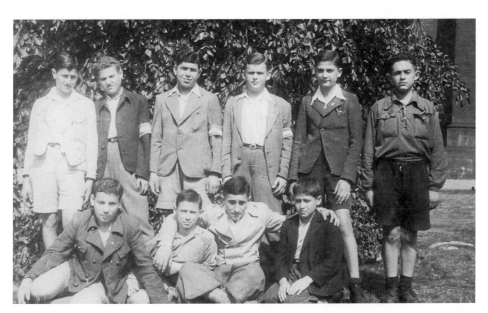

3. Prague 1945, with Ben fourth from left on the back row.

4. Synagogue in Piotrkow in which Sara and Lusia, Ben's mother and sister, were incarcerated with 550 others before all were shot in the Rakow forest on 20 December 1942.

5. Ben in England, 1946.

6. Ben is the flag-bearer at the Maccabiah Games, 1950.

istow Grammar School, 1947. Ben is on the extreme right
back row.

8. Ben with Oscar Joseph, President of the
'45Aid Society and Mrs Muriel Montefiore,
wife of Leonard Montefiore, the chairman of
CBF (the organisation that brought The Boys
to England).

9. Ben with Primrose Club leader
Yogi Mayer.

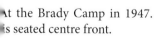

At the Brady Camp in 1947.
is seated centre front.

11. Southampton University College Athletic Club. Ben is second left on the front row.

12. At the Commonwealth Games in 1958. Ben won bronze medal.

Olympic Games, Melbourne 1956.

Ben in training, 1955.

15. Melbourne 1956, with his Aunt Irene and cousin Ann (Hania).

16. Ben's children (from left to right) Michael, Nathan and Maurice, 1980.

17. Honorary Doctorate, at last, from the University of Southampton, 2006.

18. Receiving his MBE from the Queen, 2000.

19. After receiving the Cavalier Cross of the Merit of the Republic of Poland, June 2000, with Arza and The Sons (from left: Michael, Maurice and Nathan).

20. Receiving the Commander Cross of the Order of Merit of the Republic of Poland from Ambassador Matuszewski in 2005.

21. Opening of the Imperial War Museum Holocaust Exhibition in June 2000, with the then Archbishop of Canterbury George Carey and the then Chief Rabbi Lord Sacks.

# 8

## Factories

*'We were very homesick'*
*– Mala Tribich*

There were 1,000 people working in the same woodwork factory, Dietterich-Fischer or Di-Fi, as the Helfgotts and in addition 800 or so distributed among other plants. 'The ones who were slave labourers [unlike Ben and Mala] were sent away to various other camps,' says Ben. 'But they didn't kill them.'

Then comes the factor which was so important in Ben's life: 'The only people who were saved [at this point from any kind of deportation] were the 650 of us working in the glass factory where I was and in the other part of the factory.'

Ben was taken there to work on 12 August 1942 – and stayed there until the end of July in 1943. That may have been seen to be a silver lining in the storm clouds. But let's look at Piotrkow. Of the 2,500 Jewish people left from the original population of 15,000 all but 10 per cent of them were soon to be gassed. So the chance of unpaid work in the factory was a great opportunity – or so they thought – of having their lives saved.

And yet, before long, all 80 of the Jews working in that establishment were taken away. But Moishe wasn't. So why? Ben now recalls: 'At that time, we were all living together, my father, Mala and I and our five year-old cousin who Mala was looking after. The women who were still alive used to call her "the little mother", because she was with her all the time.'

The fact that Ben Helfgott has survived into old age had a great deal to do with the man who believed the only thing he wanted to do was to watch over the family he worshipped, his father Moishe. While he was on the scene, it correctly seemed to the young boy that all would, eventually, be right with the world.

It was on the same day that Ben started work in the glass factory. 'They [the camp officials] came to our home at 11 on the Saturday morning. They said they needed 450 people to do a specific job and when they had finished this job, they would let them go back. I walked out of the house to go to work. After a week, I was still wearing the same clothes as when I left home. I never went back there.'

So, two thirds into 1942, it was all settled. Ben tells the story, but showing none of the emotion he plainly felt. It has been a very long time, but if you told him he had fallen asleep all those years ago, and just woken up, he could still insist that it could have been yesterday.

The precise Ben Helfgott had worked it all out. With the factory job, he was at least for a time spared either the trip to Treblinka or another shooting in the forest. He had not, however, thought it completely through and how close he was to disaster. 'I started at the factory two months and two days before the deportations began.' It would have been too easy for him simply to say it was nine days before the lorries came to round up as many of Piotrkow's Jews as they could carry. I was the only one in the family who had an actual job.'

When it happened, he was labouring in a factory that made practically everything which needed glass, bottles, drinking glasses. It was a good business in those days – and stayed so until well into the twenty-first century when its own glass doors were closed, courtesy of a bankruptcy order.

The work wasn't as hard as he imagined it would be, but it was tough enough – a fact that became evident when he got home after the first day's work. Or, rather, first night. He was put on the night shift. He couldn't sleep that day. It meant a complete change to his life pattern. If life was what it was. But it proved to be a life *saver*. If his work seemed only moderately hard, I wondered if it had anything to do with the fact that he was still so young.

He knew that working at night was the best thing that could happen to him – save perhaps being given a passport and told to take his family to America or England. 'I was very lucky. If I had been on a day shift, I would have been found and deported with everyone else. On the other hand, if I had been on the day shift my father would have taken me out.' There was no question of his being relieved of this monotonous and, in its own way, heavy work with heavy punishments meted out because he was a Jew. 'Young Poles kicked me. On one occasion they rained blows on my head.'

As it was, he had to try to carry on.

The work may not have been hard, but it was regularly monotonous and even he didn't spend all his time just thinking about how lucky he was to have this job. What was more, he was constantly on the move. 'My job was to sit and blow the glass and put it in a wooden mould and then roll it – because it was white hot, coming straight from the ovens. My shift ended at 6 o'clock in the morning, by which time I couldn't keep my eyes open. On occasions I failed to put the mould in water to cool it. So I was kicked.' It happened more than once and more than once he was kicked. 'They were swearing at me all the time.' Not the sort of thing a boy from what his parents always considered to be a 'refined' Jewish family was used to.

'It was terrible. I came home, but in those early days, before she and my sister were shot, I didn't tell my mother anything. She wanted to feed me, but I was too tired to eat anything. I just wanted to sleep.' It was a situation that could not be totally hidden. 'My mother said she was not going to allow me to go back. I said, "No. I'm going to see it through".'

There was a British song at the time called 'Keep Smiling Through', made famous by the 'Sweetheart of the Forces', the singer Vera Lynn. It was sung in air-raid shelters by people full of the optimism of those who were suffering the ravages of a war that cost them the lives of loved ones and the loss of houses bombed in the German Luftwaffe air raids – a different kind of suffering from those barely living at all in the Holocaust. To say that Ben was smiling as he saw this through is perhaps an exaggeration. But his father made life rather more humane. He bribed the man in charge of his son's shift- by giving him the money he had earned from bringing in the flour. The foreman saw to it that, from this moment, any work that he did was much easier. Sometimes he didn't have to work at all. 'Very often', Ben recalled for me, 'I wouldn't work for a whole day'.

Moishe, by now, had developed his smuggling 'business' to the proverbial fine art and sometimes the produce he brought in to Piotrkow was beautiful enough to be regarded as art in its own right. This was one side of what was now Piotrkow life for its citizens.

There was flour along with potatoes and other vegetables, the work of the hands of peasants who otherwise couldn't do anything with the things they were growing. The growing fields were all near the flour mill, all carried on the same horse and cart driven by the Polish farmer who had acted as his delivery man, again from the money he had earned from smuggling the flour. The foreman in Ben's shift was the contact who organised all this – and received the bribe. Moishe told him that his son was being treated very badly. The foreman was not pleased. 'The following day', Ben remembered, 'I passed this man and he called me over, He said, "I met your father yesterday. He is a nice man." The foreman was a Pole named Janota.

Annually, at about this time, he used to come to my father's Polish friend to borrow a horse and cart to transport produce from his allotment. Janota didn't realise that his name rang a bell with Moishe. Ben had told him that he was being badly treated by the master 'glass-blower'. That was Janota.

'My father's Polish friend, who had heard all about that, refused to lend him the horse and cart.' Ben maintains that it was through his own persuasion that the transport was handed over for the day. In return, he'd of course helped smooth the boy's time in the factory. This episode and the consequences of it remained a deep and permanent influence on Ben as he has always tried to see the other person's point of view, recognising the need for reconciliation by turning the other cheek.

The glass factory was close to the railway station at which the wagons were loaded with their desperate human cargo. 'Five weeks later, on the very last day of the deportations,' says Ben, 'the seventh day, there was still one wagon empty and they came into the factory to grab whoever was there. They grabbed me, got hold of me, but I protested, saying that I was a Pole. I knew I didn't look Jewish and my Polish language was perfect, so clear that I could do better than many Polish boys. It was Janota who came to my rescue claiming that indeed I was a Pole. Again, I could thank my father. If he were the type of person who wanted to take revenge, I wouldn't be here now. He made it up with that man in the factory and I lived to tell the tale.'

It was indeed a tale to tell. Ben says it was also a lesson he has never forgotten. Perhaps it was the root of taking out any anxieties on the weights which before very long would form the fulcrum of his life.

For the moment, and just for the moment, he was staying put. Somehow life had to go on – although it became manifestly clear that 'going on' was a relative phrase. They would go on for as long as their Nazi oppressors would allow them to do so. Time, so precious in relative 'freedom' –which meant, at that moment at least, not being taken away to the woods and the virtual human 'shooting gallery' where they would be the targets. It also absented them from getting on a truck taking them to the next 'transport' to Treblinka. At first, he still had a home of sorts to go to. And, when he wasn't working or sleeping, he went to the cinema. His father, still wheeling and dealing, had a free pass. Sometimes, when he was with friends, they played cards.

It is not surprising that the young Helfgott, so good at arithmetic as at everything else, was a good card player – which he remains to this day. Now, the game is bridge. In Piotrkow, it was something rather less sophisticated. But the cards were the same, half were red, half black. Kings were still kings, queens still queens. No-one, however, had much interest in jokers. It wasn't time for many jokes. 'And just like playing bridge, you have to keep playing. You need the repetition. ' Strangely, there was still time for repeating games.

That the eleven-year-old Mala escaped the deportations and the murders was another one of those miracles that somehow find their way to certain people. Although all that would follow, let alone her family tragedies, probably didn't seem to be especially miraculous at the time. At that moment, other Jewish citizens of Piotrkow were being loaded into trucks.

For the family, one of the only two surviving females, as she put it, of their immediate family, Mala became a sort of refugee and guardian of her other cousin Hania. At 12 years old. 'I remember my father going to collect her from wherever it was she was. My aunt had been taken away and her husband, my father's brother, had already been shot.' The story of what happened to those so close to her is one of the items in her retrieval system that can never be eradicated.

Naturally, for Ben, the fate of his murdered family is thus also in his brain and never to be eradicated.

'I was now in the small ghetto at Piotrkow. One day, my father came back home and looked for my mother. I remember hearing how my mother and sister had been murdered. Then they rounded up the aunt, Hania's mother.

She was taken away screaming, "Who will look after my little girl?" She had this five year-old child and the next thing I remembered was my father going to collect her. I don't remember the address to which he went. But it was somewhere in the small ghetto and there were a few others. But she was left alone and my father brought her to our home.'

The 'home' in which the Helfgotts lived was now just a single room shared with another family who, inevitably, had their own troubles. Neither of the siblings recalls the reaction of this other family when the number of residents of this room was suddenly swelled – the reverse of the usual situation in a ghetto. 'I remember that room so well. I can see where our bed was.'

Mala speaks of 'our bed' as she might have spoken of 'our couch' or 'our sink'. The bed was shared by the family. But it was slightly, very slightly, better than this now seems. 'Our father was out working during the day and Ben was always on a night shift.'

There was sanitation there – of a kind. 'There was a toilet somewhere in the building. The conditions were horrendous.' In this instance, she had no wish to summon up any recollections. What she will say is that 'it wasn't like our own home had been'. The Germans didn't want to waste good real estate by establishing the ghetto in anything but the poorest part of town. Pruszkogo was not a street in which the Helfgotts had ever seen themselves living. They were not used to sharing space with another family. But it was better than a lot of other ghetto residents had.

It was all so very different. Before the war, an uncle had come to live in Piotrkow. He had a house in which Moishe, Sara and their three children also lived. If it weren't for the constant fear of anti-Semitic legislation under the Polish government or the ever-creeping fear of neighbouring Germany, although very few people really believed it could present a problem to worry about too much – this would be an idyllic life. Certainly, a life with problems with which, for the moment at least, they were not going to worry their children. That absolutely was not going to be easy. How do you hide facts like these when every waking moment is tied up with frightening thoughts of an unforeseen future? Of course, it was fortunate that they *were* unforeseen.

Think of the effects of barely living in conditions in which they were now placed and one would imagine it would be subject to continuous evaluation by Ben and his sister. But neither of them remembers conversations like that. It is not that they try to pretend these things never happened to them. It just doesn't happen. Maybe it is as if some psychological barrier has subconsciously been built around the subject with a label saying 'Don't touch'. 'I find this is not unusual at all,' says Mala. But she doesn't go along with the thought that the silence is deliberate. 'Other siblings I know say the same thing. Sometimes, I want to ask Ben about something that happened. I want to check with him. But then the time has gone by.' One day, they might get around to it.

# 9

## The Ghetto Closes

*'My mother pushed me out of the house'*
*– Harry Spiro*

Almost as frightening as were the deportations themselves, principally to Treblinka, was the waiting for the call to either go to the station or from soldiers or the Jewish police knocking on the door and hauling the poor Jews into the trucks. 'We didn't know when the deportations were going to take place and when they would involve our family,' Ben says. 'For months, they were deporting Jews from different places. It is impossible to get people to understand just how horrific it all was.'

After his mother and younger sister were taken away, Ben was really almost totally independent. There were no restrictions on the employment of child labour under the Nazi masters of Piotrkow. Even on the work children were made to do on the night shifts. Ben was grateful for that – because it meant he could go to a wedding. It was that of his aunt Gucia, the 25 year-old sister of his mother on 7 October 1942. (One thing Ben never forgets is a date.) This was a week before the deportations began but, of course, no-one knew it.

That day, Ben was marched with other Jewish workers to the factory and then at the end of the day back to the ghetto. Moishe and his son called at the aunt's room so that they could attend the ceremony, complete with the 'chuppah' marriage canopy. A brief happy moment among the horrors.

The now seemingly incredible fact was that, while working in the glass factory, the end was close by. But it was an outpost of comparative civilisation, so close to the 'transports' to Treblinka, which were run with an industrial efficiency that boggled the minds of people who never experienced it. That was a different kind of factory, where the end product was summed up in one terrifying word, 'Death'. As we have seen, Harry Spiro's mother had told him that should a factory job arise, it just had to be taken. Ben considered what he was to do – and so did his parents – but really was offered no choice, either by the Germans who needed his labour to manufacture glass products – with medicine bottles a speciality – or his family, who saw that anything was going to be better than joining a truckload of deportees.

The signature fact about his time in the ghetto was that, like his father and when there was no vicious dogs around, he could walk around the area perfectly at liberty. How much of this was due to the indulgence or even negligence of the Nazi soldiers deputed to guard the entrances to the Jewish enclave-cum-prison is a matter for speculation. Another, in his memory and in his life, was the time on one of those walks that he had to wade his way through ankle-deep piles of feathers.

The occupiers had suspected that pillows were an ideal hiding place for valuables or arms. They searched every room for every cushion. They didn't exactly do it with delicacy. The pillow hunters were not Germans, but Ukranians, who, as a race have rarely had a good thought for Jews and had instituted some of the worst pogroms in history. Now they were having a proverbial field day. Their dreams had come true. They could do exactly what they wanted, kill, maim and assault Jews and no-one would protest. The feathers almost became an emblem for them and what they did. 'It was as if the ghetto in Piotrkow had had a snow storm,' Ben recalls. The connection with storms was only that it had been caused by men who might well have been storm-troopers, caring not for Jews or anyone else.

They didn't have much trouble finding the places where the pillows had been comfortably resting on beds, bunks or just floors. The Helfgotts's tenement apartment (if you could call it that) was searched along with everyone else's home. Their 'residence' was a single room, outside of which was a small corridor and a toilet and a small kitchen area. Luxury for some people living close to them, but even their hovels were considerably better than the alternative of a concentration camp barrack room.

As Ben recalls, 'I was grateful not to have been found there – and even more so when I realised that my family was away in hiding.' But that was before the walk among the feathers. 'When I came back there was a feeling which you just can't imagine.'

It was just another example of how complete the German domination of this part of town actually was. Like the dead bodies in the street, the feathers were there to stay – or at least as long as any poor Jew was ordered to get rid of the garbage, human or otherwise. In other matters, the German efficiency dictated that everything had to be done, almost literally at the speed of a bullet. Both the feathers and the bodies were there to increase the misery of the ghetto residents. 'It was a terrible time. I just couldn't wish anyone to go through it', is how Ben tells it: 'I was working at the time on the nightshift – which was between 10 pm and 6 am.' Jews were not allowed to walk after

8pm because of the curfew. Frequently, workers, all Piotrkow residents, were marched to the factory together to begin their shifts. That was another march from hell, picking their way through it all.

There was another reason why Ben managed to find his way in and out of the ghetto. His 'home' was close to the edge of the place, which was a distinct advantage. It was much easier to virtually take a few steps than walk through the length of a ghetto. Truth to tell, it was a combination of bravery and sheer chutzpah. Yet it was the kind of bravery and chutzpah that was not oblivious in all that was happening around him when he went on his perambulations.

At first, Ben was not yet living alone. 'My father was outside the ghetto, my mother and her sister were there. We started work in my shift at 10 pm and then left at 6 am when the morning shift started. One day, we started for home and someone came running and shouted: "Stop. You can't go back because the deportations have started."' His mother and little sister hadn't yet become victims of the massacre in the woods. The little boy of 12 who, in normal terms, would soon have been celebrating his barmitzvah, could only think about the fate of his mother. 'I knew my mother was still in the ghetto. That was when I knew that the deportations had started. They were to last over a period of eight days. On the third day and every day afterwards, people started coming to work in the factory. We got a place to stay there. A terrible place. Oh God...' It was with the horses.

The factory had been established in 1888 by German and Belgian businessmen. Now it was busy helping the Nazi war effort. 'After being there for two days, three people came who actually lived in the same building as we did. I asked them whether they had seen anybody from our family and they said, "No". Days later, we got a message from a Pole who told me, "I've got a message for you that everything is OK. You shouldn't worry."'

Easier said than done. But worry he did. He worried, this boy from Piotrkow with no home to go to, about things a child of that age ought never to consider. Like, was he going to die from an illness that he hoped was actually not quite as serious as he feared? He had been sleeping for nights in the stables and on straw and had developed a cold in his kidneys. 'I didn't realise that, while I slept, I had made the straw wet.' He wasn't sleeping alone, but with the son of one of the sanitary policemen.

Always there were questions from both people in the know and those who yearned to know. From both sides the same query was posed: "Where are your parents?" The answer was he didn't know. His mother and sister were in hiding. He knew that his father had escaped, in the course of what had seemed a normal day.

That question was posed by the mother of his sleeping companion, a kindly woman who was married with a five year-old child. 'You must come with me,' the woman told him. He now remembers that the first thing he did was use the toilet. The evidence of the kidney cold was embarrassingly obvious. The woman gave him a temporary home with unusual sleeping accommodation. For the first time in his young life, being small and wiry was a huge advantage. He slept, cramped it's true, in the child's cot while the right occupant shared the parents' bed in the same room. 'Nobody who didn't experience it could understand how people lived in those days', he says, reflecting on a time anyone who had not had his brushes with deprivation could contemplate. But it was much better than in the concentration camp later on.

As Ben says: 'I went through every stage that you could possibly go through.' Of course, at the time, he couldn't imagine what life in one of those camps could possibly be like. For the moment, sleeping in that cot in that one room was clearly sufficient. 'A week had passed, then a few days more and I thought, "I've had enough". I thought I had an idea where my parents might be.' It was also the week when he started on the afternoon shift at the glass factory.

A month later the deportations from Piotrkow began. It was to be the last day at the glass factory. For the moment Ben was not among the deportees from the plant about to be put on to a cattle wagon to be taken to Treblinka. But then he was being hustled on the way to the station after all. He began the walk to what he assumed was going to be the end, when he felt pressure on his shoulder – and a shout, 'Pole! Pole!'

'It was,' Ben recalls, 'the man who had beaten me – and was now saving my life by saying to the Nazi in charge that I shouldn't be taken because I was a Pole, not a Jew.' As he now comments: 'I learned a lesson from my father that day. Never try to take revenge. Without him, by October 1942, I would have been gone.'

The unemployed were the unluckiest of the lot. The shops they ran were closed. The factories that supplied the goods they used to sell were either closed or taken over, usually by people of German blood, such as in the Hortensia glass factory. For a time, Moishe would smuggle flour out of what used to be his business. One of the men working there had previously been an employee. That was a help. It had not been a help for Sara. The best insurance against death by Nazis was to have a job. Sara had grown up being told that going out to work was not for ladies. 'Very few women worked and children went where their parents went,' Ben says now. 'But they really were very few. Many just got married. They didn't stand a chance.'

Once the Piotrkow Jews had been deported from their homes, the few remaining townspeople began assessing the virtually new overnight situation.

Few people then or even now can truly grasp how it felt to be citizens of a country with all its rights taken away in exchange for persecution and death. Of course, that had always been stretching a point or two when, laden into the fabric of a nation, many of whose occupants had drunk in anti-Semitism with their mothers' milk. Having committed no crime, done nothing to hurt anybody, the Jews were hunted as if they were foxes or wild boar. The difference was that the animals were treated with certain respect by the hunters – gallant creatures with their own kind of beauty who would try to defend themselves. The Jews were not allowed any such respect. A week after the deportation, Sara and Lusia had joined all the others in a mass, unmarked grave. 'I went back to the ghetto,' says Ben. 'It was a terrible time. Everybody was gone, most of my family, most of my friends. You cannot imagine what it was for that to happen. You cannot imagine.' He never went back to the ghetto tenement again. 'I walked out from my home and only had what I was wearing.'

The big ghetto was now closed. There were not enough Jews to fill it. So the small ghetto was established for a time as the Jews' home. So small it wasn't even worthy of the name, as if there could be anything worthy about a Nazi style ghetto. As Ben now remembers: 'It had only 2,500 people in a quarter of the street one side going round to the next part which was surrounded by barbed wire. They gave us a tiny place.' Ben now found himself on his own.

Working in the factory was to turn the boy into a man. The kid who some might have thought of as precocious, grown up before his time, was now a worker doing a man's job (if perhaps a little easier than others). He was also a boy with a man's brain. A boy deprived of a childhood, but given powers of reason others of his age certainly didn't have. He didn't need to be told that if there were any ways of escaping the deportations or anything else that had hit his fellow Jews in Piotrkow, this could just be it. But it was always going to be a question of how. He knew without being told by the father who was now working in the wood factory that there were other certainties in their lives. They offered a glimmer of hope. Ben says he was on the whole well treated by the German proprietors of the factory, although there were the odd fights which he recognises as being as inevitable.

Harry Spiro had a similar experience. The 13 year-old was to thank his mother for pointing out what the Helfgotts already knew. He told me: 'My mother pushed me out of the house to work in a factory and I did not want to. I was crying and her word to me was that hopefully one of us will survive.' He was the only one who achieved the ambition in that family. Ben, one of the few in his who did. The interesting thing is that this was the same glass plant in which his fellow Piotrkow resident was working. For the first time Ben was under the same roof as the youngster who would become his best friend. But even then they didn't meet. They were on different shifts.

Spiro's job was considered well done by his German boss and worthy of promotion. He was in charge of a section that produced small glass bottles. There were three grades of jobs considered superior to the work of the labourers employed there: those of master, under master and a third-class official who doesn't appear to have had a specific name.

Neither Ben nor he had anything to do with the most skilled job of all – actually blowing the glass, still done by hand (or, rather, for those more pedantic people round and about, by mouth). 'No, we had to cut off pieces of glass and put it in a mould.' The master's task came after the glass left the ovens. Spiro recalled: 'You got the glass from the ovens on a long wand, as it was called, and then passed it to the master who checked it and cut off what he needed. We put it into the mould and then they blew it. This was a very skilled job.'

# 10

## Wooden Tents

*'You were not allowed to go out into the street'*
*– Ben Helfgott*

Bugaj is a suburb, somewhere off a main road in one of the less salubrious suburban areas a few kilometres from Piotrkow. It is important to Ben, even though when he and I went there, the only thing that held his interest was a large grass mound. Ben hardly ever allows a visit to his home town without going there – except that until the trip he and I made in 2015, a building had stood there. A building that played a huge part in his life during the ghetto years. It served as the reason he no longer was able to go back 'home' to the tenement room. It marked yet another change in his life.

Of those visits to his roots which he still regularly makes, Ben says: 'These journeys evoked mixed feelings, but usually pain and anguish and at times anger that, in most places, there was hardly any trace that Jews have ever lived there. A stranger could not have had an inkling of the richness and diversity of cultural life, the tradition of religious and secular scholarship.' He can't help thinking of the hell of being a child in Piotrkow during the occupation. And remembering his family.

Bugaj was the place where Ben had his second slave labouring job, even though he refutes the term. Slave labourers were beaten and worked to death. He wasn't, not at the plant where he was now employed (of course, still without any form of wages) along with Mala in what he calls the 'woodwork factory'. They were, they say, making tents.

Tents? Wooden tents? I suggested that these were more likely to be huts, but the word from the two siblings is that they were called tents, made by a furniture factory whose products were called Bugaj. 'No. They were tents. They were tents.' There was also a plywood factory adjoining the 'tent' makers. Moishe, too, had been sent to what was sometimes also called a furniture manufacturer.

'Next to the factory was our camp,' Ben recalled. 'You were not now allowed to go outside the camp into the street. Not that there was anywhere to go.' Unless he was going to try to escape, which, plainly, was not what he intended to do, no matter how pleasant the thought. 'Outside the factory, there were just fields, all green. There was nobody there. When we got there, there were about 1,000 Jews. So they had to build a camp for us, next to the factory, all surrounded by barbed wire. When we left the camp, the only place we could go to was the factory. There were always two guards watching us. One day, I looked and I saw one of the guards who I knew a year before.'

As he said: "We were living in the camp and working in the factory, although at first when I was working there, I was still living in the ghetto and then, after we went to the other place this is where my father was.'

He was lucky (sort of) that he made friends at the factory, like a young man with whom he was working. 'He was about 18 or 19 and didn't seem to have any trouble with the two guards who were always around. The young man spoke in an ethnic German accent. Every time I saw him, I would go up and talk to him.'

'One day I wanted to finish quickly. So I worked twice as hard as everybody else. And they wanted to come and finish quickly, too. But everyone else was annoyed with me. Yet I couldn't complain. I was actually very good at my work, in spite of everything. When I finished, I went to the foreman and he didn't believe that the work had been done so quickly. He was about to hit me with the stick when I ran away. As I was running, I was caught by two men who were acting as guards. I started talking to one of them, whom I thought was my friend.' Not very friendly, as it turned out. 'He grabbed his rifle and hit me over the head with the butt. I said, "Why are you hitting me?" I just couldn't understand how he could do this to me. All my young life I had been told to be fair. I have never hit anyone, so I couldn't understand how this could have happened. It felt as if my head was smashed. Blood was running down my face.' But his head was not all that injured – because he could get up on to his feet and talk, bewildered, but talk nevertheless. 'I was stunned because I liked this man and thought he was a friend. The other man he was with told me to run away. But I couldn't run. I walked, sat down and started crying. Not in pain, although that was terrible, but because I couldn't believe that a man I considered my friend could do this to me.

'I promised myself that I would survive. I swore I would come back and get my retribution. I would find him and remind him that he had done this thing to me. I would say, "I'm now challenging you to come and fight me."' It was the thoughts of a boy not yet 15, who always believed in being fair.

Ben was almost 15 years old when things began to change. The year was 1944 and there was an order that 12 of the boys working in the Bugaj plant were indeed having to move from one plant of the factory to another – a traumatic experience when every move seemed to have an ominous purpose. Perhaps it was an exaggerated fear, but it seemed to spell danger. It was, in fact, symptomatic of what was going on there in the atmosphere of a place where fear was represented by everything which in other circumstances would have seemed quite normal. But this move has remained in his mind ever since. For reasons that even he could not have foreseen.

'I was working very hard – twice as much as any of the other boys because I wanted to leave. I wanted to get on with reading a book on Welsh history in Polish.' Which says something for the 14 year-old polymath (Ben now says he was wanting to read H.G. Wells' *Short History of the World*).

'That day we finished work and were ready to leave, but we were told we were moving from one place to another. They were changing something. The foreman gave us our instructions and I asked him [doubtless, one of those occasions when chutzpah took over from what served as normal conversation] what will happen when we finished. He said: "come to me and I will give you a check and then you can go".

'When we finished, the foreman gave me the check.' But that was just at the end of what seemed to be an endless exercise in intimidation. 'The foreman was a man of about 40 and, on the surface, seemed a very nice man. But only seemed so. Actually, he was horrible. He always carried a big stick and I was always running away from him because I knew he was going to hit me with the stick.'

Ben and his fellow workers at the factory slept in bunks (Ben and his father shared the same bunk) at the factory. There was one small toilet outside the block where 500 people slept. 'It was so tiny that when you needed to go you had to stand up, you couldn't sit. It was terrible and when you needed to go in the night – particularly for the older people – that was hell. I was young and didn't have to go at night. Because the toilet was so small, you heard everything. You heard them farting.'

They slept and were fed there. Terrible, poor food, and yet it sustained them sufficiently for them to do their work. 'We could have been there for another ten years and survived.' But they all realised that it was better than being in a death camp. No-one was bothering with them. Apart from the foreman, that is.

'Because we worked with Poles, my father didn't stop finding ways of bringing in food. The Poles didn't give it to us, but we paid them.'

Plainly, that they got any of the food at all was because of Moishe's ingenuity, as active and imaginative now as in the days when he was running the prosperous flour mill and Polish peasants looked up to this still-young Jew. 'In the woodwork factory he got himself a job in a part where they were bringing in the wood and taking out the work that had been done. It was heavy work, but he managed to get out on the transports taking the products, so that he could meet his contacts. When he came back, he smuggled in the food, so we didn't go hungry.' It was like a bird bringing worms to their fledglings.

Mala finds it difficult to explain the end product of the work that she herself had to do. 'They must have been sort of round tents. My job was to sit at a table putting [triangular] sections of the roof together and nail together those strips into plywood. It wasn't very hard work. I was standing there with a hammer and nails, but some people's work was very hard because they had to do it from the raw material right to the finished product, from big trunks of trees that became the tents. They used to deliver the tree trunks with the bark and they had to be stripped and then they had to be cut before they went into the machines. I know one man lost his arm below the elbow. As he was putting the wood into the machine, his arm went with it. It was awful.'

In a way, Ben benefited (the alliteration is not deliberate) from his experience in the Bugaj factory, thinking about it, as this was indeed the first training he received in weightlifting. 'I had to carry heavy bags of wood up steps. People looked at me and asked, "How can you do this?" They didn't understand that a boy of my age could manage such weights.' Those who survived would before very long know only too well. 'I did it not to show off, but because I felt I could do it. I did that for two hours at a time – which gave me time to go round to talk to others in the camp. I knew everybody there and where they were working.'

Although Mala was working in the same place as Ben they didn't see each other. He and his father were living with the men. The women were always housed separately. Whether this was for decency's sake or for fear that sexual relations could reduce the work count has never really been explained.

Ben and his father may have been in the same factory, but they, too, were separated during working hours. Moishe's job, lugging heavy weights, was very different from Ben's, which poses a question: was Ben being shown consideration since he was at 14 still a child or were they conscious of just what they could physically get out of him?

Suffice it to say, the work imposed at Bugaj was not exactly like that suffered by workhouse children in Britain, the ones sent up chimneys or employed pulling trucks of coal in the mines of Yorkshire or Wales. 'My job was to take work to the women in the factory, so that they could finish the work – and I did it in about ten minutes.' The women, he says, were kind to him – an unusual situation, whichever way you look at it.

If the work wasn't backbreaking, nor was it remotely like a concentration camp. Yes, Ben today denies it was slave labour, although it is difficult to think of its being anything else. As we have seen, there was sleeping accommodation on bunks (in two blocks holding 450 'employees' of the factory each, hundreds of whom were Jews) which he and his father shared, and the food could have been worse. Still more remarkably, there was also medical attention available – as Ben discovered when he came down with an appendicitis attack. The diagnosis was made and suddenly his world, to say nothing of his appendix, took an unexpected turn.

It was 28 November 1944 and he was writhing in agony and still expecting, after two days from the first signs of an attack, to be taken to hospital. 'I was in terrible pain, lying on my back while everyone else was at work. Suddenly my father came rushing in and said, "You have to get up. They are going to take us away"'. In that terrible pain, he joined the others as they marched to the nearest railway station. They both knew what this meant – they were being deported, a word that had the ominous ring of execution about it but was part of the lexicon of the Jews of Poland. By now, the Warsaw ghetto had been obliterated and the population sent to Treblinka and in days – some on the same day, almost the same hour, most of them to the gas chambers and crematoria. But when the Germans talked of work camps, there was still a tinge of optimism, a whisper of hope, that it might be just that. All that the Helfgotts, father and son, knew was that 17 months of comparative ease in the woodwork factory had come to an end.

Now, the women were separated from the men. They were going to the female-only camp at Ravensbruck. The men didn't know where their destination was.

They were forced into cattle trucks, like every other Jew bound for the death camps. 'Eighty to ninety people were squashed together', he remembers. Their destination was neither of the better (or, rather, worse) known places of murder, not Auschwitz or Treblinka, but the town of Czechochowa, of which Moishe and Ben had terrible memories. They didn't know if this was their final stop, however.

Among those in the wagon was a doctor who saw – it would have been difficult not to see – Ben's agony. 'He was a certain Dr Wenzinger, an older man who was the best doctor in the town. He was brilliant and he gave me instructions. I should not eat anything and I should drink practically nothing.' The doctor later died in the camp which was to be Ben's ultimate destination on this 'trip', a place that was fulfilling the Nazi intention of just letting people die without going to the trouble and expense of executing them (gas and bullets were expensive).

The train had stopped in Czechochowa for two hours, seemingly with nothing happening. Some 1,360 men were taken off to go to work in various factories in the town. The women had gone to their factory jobs. But 300 were left on the train for an horrendous four-day-long journey to where, at that stage, no-one knew.

For four days he huddled with the others taken to the wagons. Finally, early in the morning on the fifth day, 2 December 1944, the train pulled into the station. There have been movies describing the cattle trucks and the deathly experience of the prisoners (for that, indeed, was what they were). But it wasn't just the journey, it was the, literally, indescribable fear of the unknown. No matter how much they had heard since going into the Piotrkow ghetto (and they heard a lot) there was still the hope that these were just rumours. The real fear was simply not knowing where they were going. After those four days they found out. It was Buchenwald.

# 11

## Buchenwald and Beyond

*'There was nothing on my mind but bread, bread, bread'*
*– Ben Helfgott*

The omens had not been good. The arrival at the camp has been demonstrated on millions of feet of film, as many hours perhaps of electronic screenings. But the feelings of those shunted into those cars can only be imagined – and probably varied from prospective prisoner to prospective inmate.

The rush out on to the station platform to the shouts of 'Raus' was the second moment of fear and shock. But what about the time when it all started, when they knew there was no alternative but to take a journey to no-one knew where and to a new sort of life that could just as easily have ended on that very trip?

You have to shudder at the thought. But, unless memory serves him badly – and that never happens to Ben Helfgott and how could he possibly forget? – it was not as traumatic as it could have been. 'We were ordered to go to the station and that was that. We went onto the train and there were no hysterics. There were mostly men, young and old. On the train, we were squashed. I was in pain all the time when we were on the journey and, as the doctor ordered, I didn't eat anything.'

They were standing all the time, giving new meaning to the mantra, 'Standing Room Only'. It was so crowded, but there was at least the 'comfort' of being able to lean on each other. 'The good thing was that this was winter, very cold, although we didn't feel cold. You couldn't with all those bodies around you.' Certainly, there wasn't the unbearable heat of a summer's day exaggerated by those same bodies.

The story is that there was a bucket, in lieu of a lavatory, in each car. Not in the one in which the Helfgotts, father and son, were travelling (a word distorted by the circumstances). So the smells were unbearable. But Ben maintains he wasn't aware of them. You could say that living in a ghetto and sleeping in a stable could have made him inured to them. But he says there was another reason: 'When you are hungry and you feel the way you feel, you don't smell anything.'

When they arrived, they experienced nothing like anything they could have imagined. The first thing they saw that night was a parade of emaciated inmates. Some of them thought they were about to be killed. Stories of gas chambers had leaked out by then, but the Germans were, on the whole, incredibly successful in letting information travel to the ghettos as more than just rumours.

Few knew where they were, geographically speaking. It was one of the largest camps in the Nazi empire (it had 130 satellite horror centres), situated on the slopes of the Ettersberg mountain close to the German city of Weimar, the seat of government between the abdication of the Kaiser and the accession of Hitler. Its name, which meant 'Birch Wood', had been given to the camp by Heinrich Himmler in 1937.

There were no gas chambers at Buchenwald, although those rumours persisted – and those who knew anything looked on in fear as they approached the showers to which they were immediately sent. There could have been reason for this – certainly not to make the recent train travellers feel better after the stifling conditions in the cattle cars. The Germans could have been concerned about the spread of disease – again not out of concern for the new prisoners; it would have brought havoc to the usual Nazi efficiency running the institution – to say nothing of having the guards and administrators facing the possibility of catching typhoid or some other 'plague'. And, yes, another reason for giving the guards a chance to see the women undressed. They were always on the look-out for jewels being smuggled in body orifices. Seeing the prisoners in their ragged clothes also presented the temptation to see if they had brought guns or knives into the camp – which almost never happened.

Ben recalls: 'In the morning when we went into the shower again, the guards searched us, looking into our bottoms. That was when we got fresh clothing. Not the usual blue and white striped "pyjamas". Nothing fitted, so we were swapping clothes with each other and getting terribly confused. It was like an old slapstick Hollywood comedy – people were running around with the clothing. A pair of trousers was too long, a jacket was too short. I suppose it was very good for us because it took our minds off everything else going on around us. We must have looked as though we were clowns in a circus.'

Not that many visitors or guards with a sense of humour would have appreciated what was going on. But the clothes were not the now expected striped 'pyjama'. Surprisingly, they were perfectly clean. Ben has an explanation for that. 'They had to be clean because we needed them for work. We even had a new shirt. They all had belonged to other people (the shirts, jackets and trousers the inmates had worn when they jumped from the cattle cars), but had been washed and cleaned ready for new owners.'

They didn't list the clothes he was wearing and from which he would never change while in captivity. About that, he says: 'My pants were torn. My socks had holes and my shirt was also shattered. I tried to wash it one Sunday. It was so wet that I couldn't put it back on. So I went to bed without it. It was freezing that night and I was eaten by bugs and lice. They fell on my face. There were also bats.' They were the kind that Dracula would have appreciated – along with the blood of their victims. Those bats were plainly Nazis.

The clothes remained his from the time of his arrival in Buchenwald on 2 December 1944 until his arrival in Theresienstadt on 21 April 1945. 'They didn't fit us when we first put them on. As time went on, they fitted even less.'

The inmates were in no mood to laugh while it happened – and when they endeavoured to rest on the banks of shelves in which they slept in their huts (each one housed about 200 people) at night, they were too tired to joke about it, one to the other.

The initiation ceremony had an unexpected effect: the pain from the appendicitis had gone. In fact, it would not return until years later when he had an operation in a London hospital. But, for the moment, that is another story.

As stays in the camps went, his occupancy there was brief. Just seven days from 2-9 December. It was long enough to be engraved firmly in his memory. He recalls things that happened to other people during what he has described as 'the start of the worst five months of my life'. There was a guard who, after the liberation, was asked what he did in the camp. 'I helped people,' he said. 'Not true,' says Ben. 'He was terrible. After liberation, they beat him and took him away.' Where, no-one admitted to knowing.

The Germans took no risk about that being forgotten – either by themselves or by Ben himself. In 2004, on a visit to Buchenwald Archives with his son, Ben was issued with a replica of an identity card which he still keeps in his Harrow house. His name is spelled out – in a way, unusual; inmates had to remember a number, by which they would always be addressed (or rather, shouted) – Helfgott, Beniak. His father's name is on the card, too: Helfgott, Moszek. His nationality: Pole/Jude. His weight is given as 163 kilos, surely a pointless exaggeration. If he escaped, a search party taking the card information as their only source, would never have recognised him. He was all skin and bones. His build: 'middle'; eyes: grey, face: oval, hair: brown, languages: Polish, German. Ben's number in Buchenwald was 94790 and that of his father was 94813.

Food was always the same and never deserving the name – soup smelling of excreta and a single crust of stale bread. 'From December 1944 until I was moved out four months later, there was nothing on my mind but bread,

bread, bread. Can you imagine, day after day, week after week? There were kitchens in the camp. It was for the Germans working there. We were not allowed to go into them.'

There was a strange regimen there when it came to food. Some inmates carried money – so they bought extra 'rations'. As Ben puts it: 'You've got to realise that when we were working in Poland, that no-one died there. Some people were hungry but we worked with Polish prisoners and they would sell us food – and the ones without money would get the rations of those who didn't need it.' It wouldn't last for long. 'On the whole, there was no comparison in that early stage at the camp with what was going to happen to us afterwards.'

Ben was then put to work at a quarry. 'We had to carry stones from the quarry to another place.' He says that without question, this was the worst place to which he was taken during the six years of war and Holocaust.

The philosophy behind having a camp like Buchenwald was simple: so many armaments factories had been destroyed, so ironically, Jews were there to help the war effort of their persecutors. 'There were still 40,000 to 50,000 Jews working for the Nazis from all over Europe and now they were sent to Germany – and places like Buchenwald. Probably, only half of the workers in Buchenwald survived – because conditions there were so inhuman. 'We worked 12 hours a day – six to six. They gave us coffee (made from acorns) but it was never hot.'

The Jews were the labourers doing what used to be called in war-time Britain, 'helping the war effort'. That was the main reason for having Jews there. On the other hand, there was as much humiliation on the Nazi agenda as physical punishment for being born Jewish. 'Not just no decent food, no fresh clothing, not even paper to wipe your behind. I think now to myself, "How did this happen?"' Sadly, most inmates knew precisely how that happened. He was there for more than four months. They were whipped, again like the slaves in Egypt.

Some of the inmates cried because of their living conditions – particularly the food. But those brief eating breaks were always opportunities to know what was going on – and how their fellow prisoners were treated. 'It came at 12 noon. People who had been there longer than I had, five or six months, would almost jump to the cauldrons. They were fighting to get to the front. They no longer looked like humans. We ate it because we were so hungry, but there was no goodness in it, just made of rotten potatoes. And it was just terrible. I never found even one piece of potato; it was just the same day after day, week after week, month after month.'

There was more 'food' in the evening, although again the word barely applied to what they were getting. 'We had the soup and when we came back from work, we all got a quarter pound of bread. It was not very nice bread and wasn't freshly made for us. But it was the best that we could get. A piece of erzatz margarine and that was everything – day after day. When I think about it, I don't know how we managed to survive. I know I was demented. I couldn't think of anything else. Just bread.'

Not even fear of the electrified fences entered his mind. Just, as he said… just bread. The saying is that man does not live by bread alone. The Buchenwald prisoners did just that. If you could call it bread. If you could call it living. 'No-one will ever understand what starvation is until they have suffered it themselves. I remember what it felt like – when you can have nothing on your mind except thinking about having a piece of bread.'

This was starvation, simply that. But it has had unexpected side effects: the one day observed by most Jews in the world and to most the hardest day of the year is for Ben, the happiest – the 25-hour Day of Atonement fast, Yom Kippur. 'It is my favourite day – because I had starved for the earliest years of my life, never knowing if I would ever have something nourishing to eat again. On Yom Kippur, I know that that evening, I will be able to eat again – anything I want. And with my family.' Probably only another Holocaust survivor would understand that.

The lack of food was everything, permeating every thought. But it was just part of the inhman regimen. 'Once you were inside,' Ben recalls, 'there were people who were in control of you. All kinds of people. The Germans had it very carefully organised, just as they did in all the camps.' And, as in all the other camps, there were collaborators, some of them Jews. 'They were inmates like all of us.' But unlike the other inmates, these stole food 'and did other terrible things. Everybody talked about them when they got to the camp.'

The treacherous inmates inspired almost as much fear as did the doctor who decided who would be fit and who would be left, unfed, virtually unclothed, to simply waste away and die. 'They seemed to be able to do anything they wanted – because if you complained, things would be much worse. They could tell any story to a German and no-one would think anything about it. Very few would dare go and say, "Look what X did to me" because you knew what the result would be.' That result was often summary execution with a guard's gun (either from a bullet or from a crack on the head from his rifle butt). 'There was a better chance of surviving if you said nothing. The most important way of surviving was to lie, not to be in front, just pretend you know nothing and then to look busy. Some children survived because they did say nothing.' That was the rule outside the camps, too, in places like Piotrkow. 'It was a question of luck. Some Jews survived simply because they lived in small towns and villages and were perhaps taken off to work in factories. Children and families who didn't have nearby factories were not able to survive. Sheer luck, that's all.' And that was the rule for survival in Buchenwald and all the camps. The best wish you could give anyone would be to offer the blessing, 'Be lucky'.

'It was not such a strange atmosphere in this camp as might have been expected. Some people from my home town were there. They had gone to Buchenwald some six or seven months before we had got there. When we looked at them, it was clear that there was almost nothing of them left. They were just a set of bones. They didn't have a change of clothes, so everything they wore was in tatters and falling off them.'

As he said, it was no wonder – either about the cause of their current position or the fact that so many of them didn't survive. They were literally being worked to death.

By then, Ben knew that his father – the man who had, mainly because of his determination to survive and his inspiration to find ways of doing so – was one of those who had been killed after leaving Buchenwald. 'It was terrible for me. I couldn't stop crying for a very long time.'

Moishe had been told that he would be leaving the camp and going to work in a tank-weapon factory. A list of numbers was read out by a guard. Ben's camp number – 94790 – was read out. All the numbers were read. They stopped before it came to number 94813. Moishe's. 'His number was not called out.' It took some time before Ben realised he would not see his father again.

Actually, the number *had* been called out just a short while before. And this might have led to Moishe's downfall. 'He wasn't there, so I said he had gone to the toilet and then the guards went out [of the barrack room]. I waited to see what happened and watched him coming back in. I remember I said, "What happened to you?" He took out a big piece of bread and he said, "Take it". I said, "Where did you get it?" I told him that I had said they were looking for him and that he had gone to the toilet.'

That was how it all started – or rather how it ended. The next stage was after the number was not answered. 'He was going to be somewhere else. He was equipped for a journey because they gave him a jacket to put on. That was the last time I saw my father.'

Ben discovered that the man who had been his guardian and guide all his young life was gone. No-one told him. He just wasn't there. 'One day after we had been given our prison clothes, my father disappeared. When I looked up, he was not there. He was 38 years old.'

Actually, Moishe didn't 'just' disappear. Ben did see him being taken away. 'I started running back to him, but I was stopped by the men in charge of the block [where we lived]. One of them put his hands around me and said, "Don't worry – the war will soon be over. You will be fine." I was then taken away and I said, "Thank you. I hope I will see him again soon".

'There were four boys of my age who were in the same spot, with their fathers. One of the boys and I usually slept in the same bunk. The other four stayed with their fathers whose numbers actually *were* called out and answered. I was not that lucky.' I suggested to Ben that he must, inevitably, have been terribly jealous of the other boys. 'No, not at all. I was broken-hearted but I was pleased for them. I remember saying, "Good luck to you".' Luck was not a usual commodity in Buchenwald.

He later found out what had happened to the man who had meant everything to him after they were separated. 'He was at the concentration camp until the end of February. The 28th to be precise.' February is a funny sort of month and when people have birthdays then or when other things happen, the date stays in mind even when others that feature more significant occasions are forgotten. Ben will never forget February 1945, a month when things held so much promise for troops shortly to storm Berlin, for families who could look forward to the return of loved ones in uniform and perhaps, in rare moments of optimism, even the inmates of death camps.

Surprisingly maybe, the prisoners, banned from listening to clandestine radio sets which really did not exist, had an inkling, too. The guards talked of the Russians coming and it was clear that there were changes afoot. Buildings were being destroyed – and then there was the wholesale removal of the inmates. Ben didn't go. But Moishe did. When the Russians were coming closer and closer, he was put on one of the death marches.

The marches had become a Nazi speciality, a last chance of the feeling of power, leading to wholesale murder. Once they realised that not only was the war lost, but the enemy was, quite literally, at the gates, this was all they had at their disposal. Moishe didn't survive it. As Ben says today: 'If he had been put on the train as I was, he would have survived, finished up like I managed to do.'

The terrible details of that last death march were relayed back. 'They were walking – in rags and many without shoes – and kept walking to different places where they could rest (the guards needed to rest, too). At one place, a few of them decided to try to run away. My father was one of those who ran and didn't make it.'

To most people, one would suppose, the details of that march, specifically focusing on one particular person, would be lost in a cloud of mixed memories. But Ben, soon after his liberation, heard what had happened to his father. 'Somebody came to see me and said, "There is someone here who was with your father." He took me to see this man. Straight away, he said: "Now sit down." I thought there was something else wrong and he told me, "I was with your father when we got to a certain place and some of them decided to run away. He was among them. Most were caught and shot, but I am not sure if he got away". Plainly, he did not.

'You cannot imagine what a shock it was for me to be taken away from my father, because it was understood we would always be together.' As he said, he didn't stop crying for days, possibly weeks and months afterwards.

In Buchenwald itself, the organised almost statutory killing (by guards who needed no excuse to use their rifles) stopped. 'They weren't killing us any more but they let us die of starvation, much to the satisfaction of the guards still there. They killed people by starving them.'

There were actual fights – because one of the people deputed to look after 'serving' the so-called meals was distributed by, among others, a man called Yanik – who kept some of the food back for himself and for others whom he favoured. He knew they would do things he asked them to do. Ben swore he would fight him when they were liberated, just as he had the boys who were in punch-ups when he was a boy.

It was a regimen that lasted for the time that Ben was in the hell of this camp. He could, however, always think of the alternative, that there was perhaps just a chance that he might actually leave the place – alive.

But things were to get worse. He was moved from Buchenwald to a place not exactly on the international map. It was called Schlieben. He thought that at Schlieben, since it was not one of those places where, with a notably terrible reputation, the food would surely be better, the place a whole lot cleaner and the work almost pleasant. The train journey took a day and a half to a place which Ben said was the worst he had ever been to. His hopes for it were ditched immediately. He thought he was about to be released. Released from all those feelings of desperation, that is, which he still felt when a bowl of the usually inadequate soup was poured all over his thin clothes.

'It was to be four weeks of hell – the worst time in the worst place I have ever been in.' He had said that about Buchenwald, but now he was ready to abandon his own previous judgment.

The interesting thing is that the 'kapos', prisoners ordered to do the SS's dirty work (like preparing people for the gas chambers at Auschwitz and Treblinka) had virtually taken over the camp. 'They were the ones who kicked and shouted', Ben recalls. 'There was one kapo who was a gypsy. He was very handsome and strong and wore beautiful clothes and shiny high boots. He was homosexual. There were two boys among the prisoners who fared better than most because he fed them.' Probably with more than just food. As for Ben himself: 'I used to wrestle with him. I felt I was being reborn, being able to do that. He laughed at me, because I was much smaller than he. He stopped laughing when he realised I was winning. He didn't say another word.'

Some were being killed by overwork in other parts of the camp, others by over-zealous guards for whom it was their favourite sport. Ben doesn't think that his own work there was particularly onerous. 'I was a servant. I had to carry cinders.' Cinders? 'They called them cinders. Actually, they were explosives. Explosives for anti-tank weapons. It very often took just two minutes to finish the job. Then, I'd start again 24 hours later. A German checked that I did this properly; very lucky because I got a job with a few other boys to work inside. This was winter and I was working with a group of German women. Surprisingly, they were quite nice – and never shouted at us. But they watched us losing weight day after day. It may seem amazing to other people, but to me it was a very good job indeed.'

Ben and the others bore the sometimes invisible scars of their previous incarceration. 'It felt as if my chest was stone dead.' He had at 15 already seen so much. As he told the writer David Epstein in *Sports Illustrated* magazine: 'I go almost crazy when I think about it. [My father] was killed like a dog and buried like a dog. Somewhere in a hole and I'll never know in what place he was killed. I just imagine they threw him in a dustbin or buried him in a place where there is no sign of anything. I didn't expect to feel this way now. And I find it difficult to digest.'

He was put into a group consisting mainly of German women – not, on the face of it, an ideal arrangement. Women guards at the camps had a reputation for being even crueller than the men.

'There were 12 of us boys working with the women – who didn't give us anything to eat, but mostly ignored us, pretended we didn't exist.' Which was a near perfect arrangement.

Two of the women were teenage sisters, one 18, the other 16. 'They were lovely girls.' It was altogether a peculiar arrangement. Here was Ben, riddled with insect bites, just freed, unexpectedly, from the torment of Buchenwald and talking – and being spoken to – by young girls who didn't want to cheat or ill-treat him.

Then there was a girl called Rosemary, forever after known as the girl on a bicycle. Every day she came to the camp by bike. 'One day when we had our break, I asked her if I could have a ride on the cycle. She said I could – after I told her that I wanted to see how strong I still was. After all, she and all the other women could see how we had been deteriorating. "Of course," she said, "come on". Just a week earlier such a request to a German by a young Jew could have resulted in a bullet from an SS man's pistol. But these were changing times.

'I got on the bike and I was in heaven. I could see immediately that I was still able to ride a bike. I was so excited that I didn't notice a German, about my own age, coming towards me. He shouted "Halt. How dare you?" We went to see Rosemary and he demanded, "Did you let him ride your bike?" She said yes – and then added the magic words, "Mind your own business". Ben had never before heard an argument between two Germans – with one of them strongly coming out on his side.

But there was a result of the 'conversation.' The young man was another of those who were in charge of the food distribution, an envied position. Ben describes him as 'Hitlerian. He had a horrible fat face.' The following day, he was serving the watery soup, slightly better than the kind at Buchenwald, but not exactly quality eating. 'I came to him with my bowl, the only thing I possessed, and he said, "Do you want soup?" I said yes – and he poured it all over me. He said, "That's all you are going to get today." The bastard!'

He knew he wasn't going to forget either people in a hurry – the kindness of the girl cyclist and the 'bastard'. 'I said to myself, "If I survive all this, I'll find him and give him a fight". But then I thought about the kindness of Rosemary and decided I was never going to look for vengeance. But he did still think he would look for his father, if and when the war ended while he was still alive. 'All the time I thought about my father. I thought that maybe he was still alive. Maybe, he had gone to Piotrkow.'

It was a hopeless dream.

Rosemary, however, was no dream. She was one of the people who treated him well – incredibly well, he recognised, when he contemplated his situation. Another was a German Communist who had previously spent years in Buchenwald. He gave him an encouraging piece of advice: 'Keep saying, "Not well. Not well". It was something done in the bigger camps – another survivor, the much loved Rabbi Hugo Gryn used to tell me how older inmates would instruct the then 14 year-old Hugo to say he was 18. That way, he could possibly avoid the gas chamber by having a job. In Ben's case, it was more to avoid a job – which in his state could have killed him. All that prompts a question – what sort of Nazis were the people in charge, both starving their slaves and yet not planning to kill them off by working them to death if they were not well? Strange, indeed.

It was easy for the Nazis to change concentration camp factories that made 'panzerfausten', anti-tank weapons, from where there had been gas chambers. Gassing them was totally unnecessary. Jews were dying simply by being ignored. That was why the request to ride on the bike was so unusual. And so was his relationship with others in the camp – like Rosemary, although there were none really like her. As Ben told me: 'They had only started making the weapons at the start of 1944. Had they started at the beginning of 1943, the war might have lasted a longer time.' And the women might have been harder to get on with. 'Now I worked with women who were so frightened because of what was happening to the Jews there and they feared they would be punished.'

He was working in a part of the factory called the Zinderparkraum. The story of Rosemary and the cycle was not the only happier memory of the hated Schlieben. One was of a lad called Jakub of whom he would write, 'his image never faded from my mind, but whose whereabouts I [had] never been able to establish. I felt that, although I did not remember Jakub's last name, he was one of those who I last saw in May 1945.'

They did get together again several years later. Jakub had gone back to Poland after liberation.

'I arranged to meet him at [an] hotel in 1993. It was the 50th anniversary of the uprising of the Jews in Warsaw. When I came out of the lift, I recognised him instantly, although he first ran up to [another former inmate] named Krulik, mistaking him for me. He had hardly grown taller and his face, although aged, appeared to me just as I remembered him so many years ago. Any doubts about whether I would recognise him were immediately dispelled the moment I cast eyes upon him and asked whether he still had a limp. How surprised and overwhelmed he was at what was a most moving encounter between the two of us! It was very encouraging to reaffirm that the passing years had not dimmed our memories.'

The people who arrived there may not have been in the infamous lice-ridden striped 'pyjamas'. But, for four months, Ben and his fellow survivors of Buchenwald, had had no underwear. 'I hadn't had a change of shirt. Can you imagine the cold working for hours a day in winter?' He had been bitten by insects on the marches from the big camp to the new one.

But it was not quite the end of the camp journey, although things began to get better. He was among the former inmates of Buchenwald and other murderous places taken to Theresienstadt, the camp in Czechoslovakia which had been acting as a kind of way-station to Auschwitz and other institutions from which people were not expected to return. Ben arrived there on 7 April 1945.

They were sent there for reasons that were to be kept totally secret. As a last throw of the dice, the Nazis were planning to install new gas chambers. They were not going to lose a last chance to kill more Jews.

For a time, that was the main object of this camp. But there was another reason for the Nazis' interest: they were also making anti-tank weapons there far away, it was thought, from the bloody battle zones which were increasingly becoming less and less satisfactory to the Germans, an understatement in itself. They were still making the 'Panzerfausten' there. It was another Nazi last-ditch hope. This was the brainchild of the misguided Berlin officials who kidded themselves that they could turn the tide. The old phrase, 'never kid a kidder' was part of the game – Nazi officers who wanted to bring a sense of reality to the situation were shouted down.

It was into this atmosphere of a false dawn that one of the last transports into Theresienstadt came. Among them, one Ben Helfgott. His job was to pack the weapons with explosives.

Ben contemplated the women with whom again he was working. 'For the first time, these women were talking about the work they were doing and how much they hated it. They were nice enough to me, but I thought, "I am not going to cry for them". Even so, he recognises to this day that these female workers could have been cruel to him. They could have beaten him for the sheer fun of it, an underweight, poor Jewish boy who really had no idea what was in store for him. But they didn't, even though they would never have been punished for doing what most Nazis in the camps did.

'I was very lucky to work there,' he says now. 'There were just two boys there, me and another one and two men who were given the job of repairing watches. But no-one gave us any food.' Which was a reason why crying for the women, in particular, was not on his agenda. 'They never thought of giving us even a little piece of bread. They saw how we were going down and down. Our bodies showed all our bones. It was terrible, but none of the women thought of feeding us even a crust. There was one woman, who was saying that the Russian soldiers were violating German women every day, who was always very kind to me. But she wouldn't offer me a piece of bread, either.'

The Germans, he maintains, 'didn't hurt us physically. They didn't even shout at us.' It was a case of being grateful for the traditional small mercies. Another mercy was that there were no mirrors around. 'We couldn't see how bad we actually looked. I imagine we were like the people who survived the death marches, like the one that was to result in my father's death.'

Hitherto, this had been no death camp. There were no gas chambers. They had an orchestra and children acted in plays and drew pictures. That was exaggerated a thousand fold by the Nazis who gave the place a look of happy homeliness – when the Red Cross came calling. The visit in 1944 and the 'lucky' residents were filmed in one of the Nazis' classiest public relations exercises. It was a visit not repeated in any other camp. The international organisation was banned – had they come it might have exposed what was really going on there. They could have seen the starvations, the deaths, the thefts of valuables as well as lives. Not a single letter was ever delivered to a prisoner. But Theresienstadt was different. Just how different was discovered by the same Red Cross organisation when they discovered the plans for the camp such as the building of the gas chambers – just a few weeks before the end of the war.

The Red Cross in Geneva had been keeping an eye on Theresienstadt once the first whispers were heard that all things were not as pretty as they had been led to believe on the visit and film. 'People who were working [on what would be the execution site] there had managed to pass on news of what they were doing to the Red Cross.' The head of the operation was persuaded to stop work. It was an open secret that the Germans were finally being ravaged and the men working on the site were warned – perhaps with more hope than fact – that they would be among the first to be hanged by the Allies. In fact, they didn't wait for that to happen. The officers involved all committed suicide.

'Now we had those fresh clothes, even though, pretty obviously, they were not of the best. We hadn't had different clothes from 2 December to 20 April. I had no shoes. My trousers were even more ragged than they had been before. But, best of all...best of all, we had proper bunks to sleep in, but I was so afraid of bed bugs that I always slept on the top of the blanket.'

As Ben recalls: 'We didn't have to work any more. They gave us fresh food. Our clothes were replaced.' They had to be.

The condition in which they arrived in a place which was to seem like some strange kind of paradise. And sleep he did. 'In fact, I slept for the whole of the first day – bitten by lice and bugs.'

Those omens, which had seemed so dominant in the inmates' thoughts, for once, looked right. After seven days in a cattle truck with virtually nothing to eat, anything would have looked right. 'When we arrived, a Jewish man who was one of those dishing out the food, told us: "Be patient, dear people. There will be enough for everyone".' He hadn't heard such kind words from a person 'in authority' since the days before the Nazis moved into Piotrkow. He even had the courage to ask if there were a ping-pong table there. There wasn't. Why he thought of such a thing can't now be explained. It indicated a mind set.

But there was the food and there were the clothes, provided by the Red Cross, who had by now realised the 'pup' they had been sold by the Nazis. The strange thing was that they were taken in by the Germans at all. They probably knew that things in 1944 when the film had been made were very different in every other concentration camp in every other place where they were located. But they wanted to be able to show that they were making inquiries – and put up with the little fact that they had been banned by the Nazis from every single death factory. The fact that they accepted this is one of the big indictments of the organisation that all other people lauded and continues to laud. The fact that they doubtless knew that no food parcels or other communications reached those for whom they were intended – at least since the 'Final Solution' in its full horror had been instituted.

The trains continued to run from Buchenwald. Heinrich Himmler still had plans to gas the men, women and children in the cattle cars somehow. Instead, the trains went to Theresienstadt. The last batch arrived on 8 May, exactly a month after Ben was crammed into the train. It was VE Day, the day the war ended. They had been travelling exactly a month – ironically since the camp was liberated. 'You cannot believe how many dead people there were and the others were taken to hospital.'

Among those in that hospital was his cousin Gershon, the son of Sara's brother, Marcus Klein. His condition was much worse than Ben's. He was seven years old and almost dead.

It wasn't the kind of hospital that the world's cities like to boast about. It was crowded – mainly with typhoid sufferers. But it was more than had existed for Jews in Occupied Europe before and the medical care was exemplary. The doctors were all Jewish. They were previously treated as prisoners but for a little while now they had been part of a strange regime in what had become a very strange concentration camp – since, in fact, the Nazis who had been in charge there realised there was no future for them.

Ben didn't make much use of his new much more comfortable bed. For three nights, he went without sleep. It wasn't that he was kept awake by ill treatment. It was the thought that liberation was about to come. The Red Army was just a very few miles away and everyone in the camp, guards and prisoners alike, knew that the Russians were about to change their lives for ever.

Ben heard the final, best possible, news early in the morning. 'By that time, I couldn't keep my eyes open, even though I knew it was all about to happen. A boy came and shook me. Two words told him it was all over. "Wake up!" He had waited almost six years to hear those words, shouted excitedly but not with the menace he had come to expect in the ghettos of Piotrkow, in the glass and wood factories, in Buchenwald, in the two places which had begun to slowly restore the faith he instinctively had in mankind.

'Wake up,' shouted a boy again, 'We're free!' Free! It was unbelievable. Ben wasn't sure whether to believe it or not. He was now barely conscious. But he ran out – and there was no-one to stop him. 'I saw people walking into the street. I knew there was a town nearby, a place we, of course, had never been allowed to visit.' Now people were going there, to Leitmeritz, about two kilometres away, as if they were on a shopping spree. They had no money, but what they 'bought' was the air of freedom. Before long, Ben joined them. Who was going to complain if he did? It wasn't easy to be free.

Not for any of them. They hadn't seen shop windows for years. Now they soaked up every item on display. Everything, of course, was in short supply. But none of them had seen so much food for years. They could see fruit. They could watch children playing – just as they had in places like Piotrkow.

And some of them tasted a fruit that Ben had taught himself to despise – the fruit of victory and retribution. The 82-pound bag of bones had to adjust to a thing he thought would never enter his life again. It was really, incredibly, undeniably called freedom.

'The best thing that happened,' says Ben, 'was that we were clean. My chest was still sore from always having blood coming from scratching myself all the time. When I got there, from that moment on we didn't go to work. We could sleep all the time we wanted and we got rations which, in comparison with what we got in Buchenwald, was marvellous. A big piece of bread and some butter – not a lot but it was something. And the soup was much better, still made from potatoes. But not just from the skins.'

He had to thank the Red Army for that and he has never forgotten it.

The other Allies were suspicious of the Russians, but the inmates in this camp regarded them, literally, as liberators. 'The Russians were very good', Ben remembers. 'They treated us like kings. The first day when we were liberated, they said, "Today is your day. Go out – and do whatever you want to do today".' But, they emphasised, it was only for that one day.

Ben said his needs were few. The only thing he wanted was a decent pair of shoes. He got them – and a sliver of revenge at the same time. 'A Hungarian soldier was running around. I stopped him and said, "I don't want anything. Just give me your shoes". And he did.' Actually, it wasn't quite as simple as that. As Ben explains: 'He said, "I want to keep my shoes." A Russian soldier was nearby and heard what was going on. He told the Hungarian; "You had better take them off and give them to him".'

Shoes are not easily swapped. What if they weren't the right size? 'I made sure that they did fit', he says now with a smile.

The wheel had begun to turn. He was giving orders to one of his captors – who a few days before could have shot him merely for daring to talk about shoes or anything else. The need was simple – to go out into Leitmeritz and try it out. 'As I was walking, I saw two young women, perhaps just 18 years old – and they were beating up a German woman who had with her a little boy, perhaps about eight years old. The girls were hungry as we all were and all I could hear were her screams. She was crying, the little boy was crying, the baby in the pram she had been wheeling was crying. The woman was pleading with them, "What do you want?" It was a question he himself asked of the probably crazed tormentors. 'What are you doing?' Ben asked them. 'What do you mean?' one of them asked him, 'What do you mean, "what do you want?" They have taken everything from us. We want it back. And they killed my mother and father.' That was taking things too far for him. It could be the root of his feelings for post-Holocaust generations of one-time enemy countries. He got hold of the woman with whom he had been arguing and pulled her away from the young mother. It was not enough. He pushed her down a dell alongside the pavement where she had been walking. It was a moment for deep thought. The most natural thing probably – only probably, however – could have been to, at the very least, walk away. The hatred in the hearts of most of the camp inmates was palpable.

A moment of supreme irony then occurred. 'The woman thanked me,' Ben recalls. 'I pushed her away. I said, "Don't thank me, just go".' Remember, this was a 15 year-old boy talking. 'I was so upset and you can imagine, I am still sensitive about it. When I walked back to the camp that day, I could hear Jewish voices crying "Kill him! Kill him".

'I saw a Nazi on the floor, his uniform torn. There was a mob of former prisoners kicking him. People brought water to pour over him. I was upset. I had seen mobs before and they can be terrible. They get so beefed up that they forget what they are doing.'

Liberation was a whole mixture of reactions and decisions. Ben says that most of those who were well enough to make the trip into town were to go to the nearest bank to get money. How that was managed is another one of the mysteries of what happened at this time. Where were the bank documents stored? How could they, at this earliest of stages, get over the fact that one of the first of the Nuremberg laws, which applied in the Occupied countries as much as in Germany itself, stipulated that Jews were not allowed to have bank accounts any more than they could have money to bank.

None of that affected the young Helfgott. 'All I wanted was to get food, bread. While the others wanted a bank, I wanted a shop that sold food.' The question of money didn't arise either. 'Everything was free for us. The Germans had been kicked out of the town. I came across a place where there was sugar and rice. I took a bag of rice and one of sugar and put it on my back and left.' Of course, this wasn't shopping. It was looting. 'Certainly, it was,' he agrees. The sugar and rice were turned into a rice pudding – which he shared among his previously starving friends.

It was wrong. Ben, as he forcibly argued, understood why it happened; why it occurred in this town as it happened in every place where there were inmates who had suddenly found a freedom that they didn't know how to deal with. There were stories of death camp guards being, not just assaulted, but killed by men still wearing their striped pyjamas. You could understand, but not approve. Yet it did happen and there are those who say it is not something for which apologies are due. To argue with them is to put yourself in an impossible situation and one for which everyone who never saw a gas chamber or took part in a roll call should never stop being grateful. Only personal experience could begin to explain, to understand.

They look at the war criminal trials after Nuremberg and think that what they did was only what they are certain for which the judges would have failed to convict. They point to the thousands who were jailed only to be freed before the end of their sentences.

And yet Ben survived – and so did his sister Mala, who puts it all down to the short time both of them spent in concentration camps. 'I think,' she says, 'that because we were only deported into camps at the end of November 1944, and so we were there for less than six months, played a big part in our survival. Some people lived for a year and two years there, but I, for instance, was only in Ravensbruck for about two and a half months – then off.'

It is all part of the Holocaust story. All part of the human condition. All part of the confusion as to what is really justice.

# *12*

# Free…But

*"I tried to conceal my true feelings'*
*– Ben Helfgott*

There were no words to adequately describe the way he felt. Free, of course. But free from memories? Of course not. Free of resentment? Today, he still emphasises that he bears no grudges against either the twenty-first century Germans or the people of Poland. But free to resent the years of starvation, the murder of his parents and the theft of his childhood? Of course.

Something else was involved, too. A change in everything that happened to him in the late spring of 1945. The war was still on. The Nazi generals had yet to assemble on Luneburg Heath and surrender to Field Marshal Montgomery. And yet. Ben and every member of the tiny remnant of European Jewry still in the camps or still in hiding had to come to terms with a situation that until sometimes just days, sometimes hours before, had been the subject of their dreams. Victory, when it came, brought problems.

Ben, as we have seen by now, was always resilient. Yet a phrase was suddenly only too relevant to him. Here he was, all alone. He was a man who looked like a boy. At 15, there were no more concessions for him in this new amazing situation called freedom. Any more than there had been under the Nazis. And the phrase? One coined and used by anti-Semites since the thirteenth century. He was…the Wandering Jew.

He went back to Piotrkow. It was a horrendous journey. He had had plenty of those in the last four years, yet for once in that mini lifetime, he was not scared. The thoughts of the pogroms that followed liberation in several parts of Poland did not enter his mind. He caught a train. Actually, he caught a whole collection of trains, one after the other, justifying in that word 'caught'. It was as though the trains were running away from him. When he did catch a train, he often had to sit, bend, crouch on top of the carriages, like characters half a century or more later in a James Bond film or something from Bollywood, having to make sure that he was one step ahead of the next bridge or tunnel.

He travelled like that for four weeks, packing his pathetic belongings in Theresienstadt for the journey, first to Prague. It was a place with which Ben admits he fell in love. 'After what I had been through and what I had seen, it was such a beautiful city. And people were walking around. Free! I started running. I went to the cinema. There were a lot of Russian films, very communistic. But very interesting. There were also some British films, which I enjoyed. And I started reading Czech papers. Surprisingly, I could talk very nicely in Czech.'

He stayed in a house where a few other boys were living. It was a tiny room about half the size of this room here (he pointed to where we were sitting, in the living room in their comfortable home in Harrow). 'I started the morning at about 9.30 – a luxury in itself – and I walked past the river. I managed to find some money so that I could row on the park lake for about an hour. The fresh air was marvellous. At about 11.30 I would go to a kitchen [set up for former camp inmates] and have some soup. Not like the soup we had in the camps. It tasted wonderful. From there I would go to another kitchen and have some more soup there. And I'd go to the synagogue. It was something to do.' Not at all the thing the newly-liberated Ben would think he would do. His days as a follower of his ancient religion were over (although his sense of Jewishness, its heritage and his loyalty to his fellow former sufferers were certainly not).

There were two weeks spent in Prague and he enjoyed every minute of his stay; his first experience of real freedom. 'I lived such a lovely life for once. It was something so special. I was learning and eating to my heart's content. It was so special. But I decided I had to go back – to Piotrkow.'

From Prague, he went first to Germany, then to the Polish border and finally to Piotrkow.

Ben himself does not tell of one particular incident on his trip back to his home town. Nevertheless, it made a big impression on his fellow former citizen of the town, Harry Spiro. He told me: 'While he was there, he had several books with him. He was walking with another survivor. Two or three Poles came up to them and took away everything that Ben himself was carrying. Because he speaks perfect Polish, he heard one of them say, "Let's kill them – otherwise they'll recognise us". Ben, though, somehow or other, talked his way out of that fate.' Knowing Ben's attitude in later years, Spiro adds: 'Imagine being in a situation like that – and still say that we should have good relations with the Poles!'

The event did nothing to make Ben forget the purpose of his visit 'back home' – which, of course, it no longer was and never would be.

Nevertheless, here he found, among those survivors, two of his aunts. One was Irene, the wife of Fischel. 'The first time I got there, I was able to tell Irene that her daughter Hania was alive and with my sister Mala. She asked, "Why did you leave them?" I said, "You know what I will go back and get them." Quite a statement for a 15 year old.

There was also his mother's sister Gucia (she was the one whose wedding Ben and his father had attended in the ghetto; she was now 29 years old.) There were two other women living with them. One was Bronia, Gershon's cousin. Gershon was still in hospital in Theresienstadt. 'When I told her that Gershon was alive, but very ill, that was the moment that I decided to go back to Theresienstadt to fetch him and take him back home.'

That part of the endeavour was achieved. He collected the newly-recovered Gershon and took him on the trip back to Piotrkow. Another long journey, but it bore fruit – literally. 'The Czechs, on seeing us, showered us with food.'

It really was an incredible situation, a moment for reflection, an occasion for thanksgiving – to the Czech people who were the first human beings he came across in six years with no connection to any of his experiences, in the ghetto, in the camps, in the factories. 'We were greatly encouraged by this spontaneous reaction of brotherhood and friendship.'

When that sort of thing happens, one is inclined to think that the world is made up of only the good and the kind. Not a feeling that would last.

It was when they crossed that border into Poland that the true relationship between Jews and Poles struck home. We have seen how Ben thinks so well of many of his former fellow countrymen today, but if the question of forgiving on behalf of others (those who perished during the Occupation, who would have been the only ones who could possibly offer their own forgiveness; he was not prepared to act as the proxy for the dead) isn't really part of his psyche, forgetting certainly is not. He arrived with his cousin in Czechochowa to find himself in the middle of their own personal pogrom.

Instead of being treated as they were by the Czechs, as human beings worthy of being 'showered' with the necessities of life ('food, warmth and sympathy' he put it), the newly liberated Polish police, with whom he had the terror of meeting, were up to their eyes in the joys of trying to finish what the Nazis still had left over. The venom of anti-Semitism had found an outlet with the arrival of the two youngsters.

Whereas those Czechs had restored his faith in humanity (he said he had never really lost that faith but now it was 'bruised') he could not possibly think the same of the Poles. His former countrymen, not so much restored a faith in humanity, but changed so many feelings of sympathy for the Poles into a hatred of certain citizens of the country. Perhaps what the Poles really restored for him was the cliché of this being a nation of Jew haters, even if he had not previously experienced it himself and has always refused to believe it of the whole nation (as we proved when we went together to Piotrkow).

In the late Sir Martin Gilbert's book *The Boys*, Ben tells of his horrific experiences at the hands of people whom he had wanted to regard as friendly, even if not actually as friends. As Ben wrote years later: 'When I recall the nightmares of the Holocaust years, there is none that fills me with a greater dread and horror than the one I experienced after my return to Poland soon after my liberation.'

It was to totally distort that word 'liberation'. Certainly, it was not what it felt that day. As he wrote: 'Liberation found us in a stupor, in a state of utter exhaustion and emaciation. It took a while to awaken from our five and a half year nightmare. As long as we had been struggling for survival and had lived from hour to hour, we had not entertained any thoughts about the enormity of our loss or about our future. Now, it gradually began to dawn upon us that we were, at last, free and that freedom necessitated a complete readjustment.'

That would have been enough of a culture shock, without anything terrible happening again.

The war had stolen their childhood. Now the 'peace' was threatening to take away the hope that the two boys had during all their previous suffering. It was a factor that kept Holocaust victims going. It was not for nothing that the national song of the Jewish people was called 'Hatikvah' ('The Hope') and is now the national anthem of the State of Israel.

But that day, it seemed – literally – hope*less*. Indeed, when the boys arrived at Czechochowa, hope was the last emotion either felt. As Ben wrote, he was, 'like so many of the flotsam and jetsam that was traversing Europe in overcrowded trains, returning to their respective homelands. Both of us looked emaciated and our hair was still conspicuously short.'

Two starving, dirty boys about to suffer the ultimate example of profound disappointment – to say nothing of unspeakable horror. As Ben wrote, remembering a time that would have been beyond the human capacity to forget. 'We crossed the Polish-Czech border with bated breath, full of excitement and expectation for a brave new world. The train stopped in Czechochowa, well known for its pilgrims to Jasna Gora, the most sacred of [Catholic] shrines in Poland. At the station, we were waiting for the train that would take us to our home town. Hundreds of people were milling around, talking and gesticulating excitedly, when suddenly two Polish officers accosted us.'

They may have anticipated that someone would want to know more about these apparent strangers who, nevertheless, spoke faultless Polish, but not, as was happening, to have that conversation turn into a hostile interrogation. 'Who are you?' they asked. 'What are you doing here?'

Of course, it wasn't difficult to see who they were. Jews. Jews who were still skeletons, Jews who were unkempt. Jews who were dishevelled. Jews who were just children, but old – very old – for their years. Ben told the men their story. They said they had just left a concentration camp (they may have thought that would evoke sympathy, but soon were to change their minds about that).

The policemen wanted proof – of the fact and their experiences. Undoubtedly their appearances made their identities obvious. But it suited the men in uniform not to reveal that it did. The boys showed their identity cards, issued at Theresienstadt. 'They were still not satisfied and ordered us to come with them to the police station for a routine check. It seemed rather strange to us, but we had nothing to fear. Fortified by our experience and believing in a better world, now that the monster that had tried to destroy the people of Europe was vanquished, we walked along with the two officers, chatting animatedly about the great future that was in store for the people of Poland.

'The streets were deserted in the prevailing darkness, as there was still a curfew after midnight.' That was particularly a problem because the street lights had yet to be restored. It made what happened next more frightening than they could have imagined. 'My cousin and I were getting tired as we carried our cases which contained clothing we had received from the Red Cross. Casually, I asked: "Where is the police station? It seems so far." The reply was devastating and shattering: "Shut your fucking mouth, you fucking Jew." They shouted, as loud as any Nazi screaming at prisoners leaving their cattle cars for the journey to the gas chambers.'

'I was stunned, hardly believing what I had just heard. How could I have been so naïve, so gullible? The Nazi cancer was removed but its tentacles were widespread and deeply rooted. How had I lulled myself into a false sense of security? I believed what I wanted to believe. I had experienced and witnessed so much cruelty and bestiality, yet I refused to accept that a man could be wicked. I was grown up in so many ways, yet I was still a child believing in a beautiful world.

'I was suddenly brought back to reality and began to fear the worst. Here I was in the middle of nowhere with no one to turn to for help. My thoughts were racing. My heart was throbbing faster and faster. On the one hand, I was castigating myself for allowing myself to be lured into this seemingly hopeless situation.'

But could one as resourceful and determined as Ben Helfgott had shown himself to be just lie down and accept what seemed now to be the inevitable end of it all? 'I was scheming about how to extricate ourselves from a clearly dangerous situation. The Russian were still well in control [of Poland's government, such as it was, and its administration] and I was hoping against hope that if I were to see a Russian sentry, I would shout for help.' That was indeed wishful thinking. As he said, 'There was no Russian to be seen.'

Things only seemed to get worse. They were taken to a dimly-lit house. One of the policemen had knocked on the door, which had been opened by a young Polish woman – who, along with the man in uniform, ordered the children to open their suitcases and then took a pile of their Red Cross clothes for themselves. 'They took most of the clothing and announced that they would now take us to the police station. It seemed inconceivable to me that this was their real intention, but we had no choice and we had to follow events as they unfolded. As we walked in the dark, deserted streets, I tried desperately to renew conversation so as to restore the personal and human touch.' That was even more wishful thinking.

'It was to no avail. I tried hard to conceal and ignore my true feelings and innermost thoughts, pretending to believe that they were acting in the name of the law, but they became strangely uncommunicative. After what seemed an eternity, we arrived at a place which looked frightening and full of foreboding. The buildings were derelict and abandoned; there was no sign of human habitation, all one could hear was the howling of the wind, the barking of the dogs and the mating calls of the cats.'

It all got worse when talk was replaced by guns.

'The two officers menacingly extracted pistols from their holsters and ordered us to walk to the nearest wall. Both my cousin and I felt rooted to the ground, unable to move. When at last I recovered my composure, I emitted a torrent of desperate appeals and entreaties.' Never could appeals have been more from the heart. Here was, after all, a young boy who had seen so much, involving an enemy everyone knew to be an enemy. Now, he was facing what was almost a firing squad from people who could easily have been his Piotrkow neighbours.

'Haven't we suffered enough?' he begged. 'Haven't the Nazis caused enough destruction and devastation to all of us? Our common enemy is destroyed and the future is ours.' Reading it now, it sounds more like a speech to the United Nations. But Ben says he recalls the exact words he used. 'We have survived against all odd and why are you intent on promoting the heinous crimes that the Nazis have unleashed? Don't we speak the same language as you?'

And then, things began to change. Ben recalls that his pleas were accepted by at least one of the policemen (they seem to have been genuine cops). This one said: 'Let's leave them. They are, after all, still young boys.'

The guns were put back in their holsters, but the torment (verbal now) continued. 'They made a remark that still rings loud in my ears. 'You can consider yourselves very lucky. We have killed many of your kind. You are the first we have left alive.'

That may or may not have been true. But it sounded as if it could have been and that was enough. 'My cousin and I looked at each other, unable to comprehend what had transpired. We were trembling and completely shattered by this experience. Racing through our minds was the realisation that we had been nearer death in a free and liberated Poland than at any time during the ordeals of more than five years under Nazi tyranny.'

The man boasted that they were left alive – as though he was doing them an undeserved favour. Left alive? Alive to tell the story and to begin a new kind of life. But he recalls: 'I cannot help thinking of the many survivors who returned to Poland after the war and were killed by the Poles.' It is not what he says now when he is once more decorated at the Polish Embassy in London. On the other hand, the Poles he meets today are different people of a new generation.

The fact that they were able to get back to Piotrkow at all was a miracle in itself. He made up his mind that this could no longer be regarded as home.

The few Jews who had also gone back there talked only of two things – how did they survive? Who else was still alive? That was when the news he dreaded but knew already inside was confirmed. Thoughts about his own father were primary in his mind How was it that he wasn't selected to go with Ben? 'This is something I have been thinking about again and again.' His father was dead. But his younger sister Mala had survived. So had Irene's daughter, Hania.

One thing is certainly clear about this reunion and this family. Every Holocaust story is in some ways different. Mala's story represents another chapter in the history of what is now called the Shoah. On 28 November 1944, she was deported. At first, as she told me, she thought this meant the liberation had come. 'There were just 1,000 people left in the woodwork factory and 650 in the glass factory.'

She describes the scene: 'We were lined up in the labour camp, all of us standing together. We knew that the Russians were already close, but for five months they had not moved.' (The theory was – and has never been disproved – that they wanted the influence of the Polish Government in Exile in London, and which had supported the Warsaw uprising run by what was now called the Free Polish Army – to be discredited. America's President Franklin D. Roosevelt had secretly accepted that the country would be in Russia's 'sphere of influence' and the last thing Stalin wanted was to have the 'Free Poles' win this last desperate battle; when he thought his aim had been achieved, the Russians moved in to Warsaw.)

Mala had been one of the women who were taken off the train at Czechochowa and sent to work in one of the four major munitions factories there. With the Russians just a few kilometres away, they were moved again – to the women-only camp at Ravensbruck – one of those hideous places that has become as well known in Holocaust histories as the death factories of Auschwitz. (Her cousin Gershon's mother, Frania, had died at Ravensbruck just a few weeks before.) There were the same deprivations, the same starvation, the same humiliations from the same breed of women guards and the same hopes against hopes that they might soon be freed. And yet, comparatively speaking, it was better for Mala and her cousin than it was for others. Judging by some people's experiences, things were not so bad.

'I was personally never badly treated', she told me. 'Nobody beat me up or anything like that. But I did what I was told.' Which was not always easy, even if no work was expected of the two girls. 'We had to stand out there from six in the morning in the freezing cold. I mean we went there in November and then in December and January. It was really terribly cold.'

But they were moved after a couple of months.

From Ravensbruck, she was sent to a place that, particularly in British eyes, summed up the horrors of the concentration camps which had no gas chambers, but like Buchenwald was in the business of killing Jews by starvation and beatings. Bergen-Belsen was the first big camp to be liberated by the British troops who took newsreel cameramen with them – men whose cameras were recording the piles of bodies, both of the hundreds of thousands of corpses and of the living dead, emaciated skeletons with hearts still beating beneath the bones. That was where Mala was when the soldiers stumbled on the camp and reported with horror what they had seen. With her was Hania. As she told me: 'I remember on arrival, we went up to the barbed wire and told people who we were and asked if they had seen …So and So, all names we could think of. We didn't know where the men had gone. I don't suppose Ben knew where the women were either.'

Bergen-Belsen was a factory of starvation. The piles of corpses shown in those newsreel scenes are testament to that.

And yet life *had* been worse. Mala said: 'Actually, I was very lucky in Bergen-Belsen. I had a bit of luck because there was a children's home there. I pleaded with them to take me in.' She was told that there was no room, it was so crowded.

'The Germans were sending people from other camps to Bergen-Belsen. There was just no end. When the kitchen was broken up, there was no food.' The children's home offered some hope when they found room for the two girls. 'We had been interviewed by two women, nursing sisters and a doctor – who was called 'doctor' but was actually a dentist. At first they wouldn't take me, so I asked them 'would you take my cousin? She is only seven.'" But the assessors (Poles or Ukranians, she can't be sure which) took sympathy when they realised Hania wouldn't go anywhere without her. They were to stay together – at least for a time, as we shall see.

It was indeed a good move. 'There was actually a little more food because some people would go into the kitchens and beg for something extra for the children. It wasn't that we were being looked after, but we were with other children of our own age It was different from being in the main camp. Even so, I was one of those who caught typhoid there.'

Like her brother, Mala heard that liberators were at the gate and that perhaps those hopes might be coming true. 'I was in my upper bunk by the window and I saw people running about. I realised it meant that the liberation had begun.'

The logic of the situation is that people who suddenly found themselves free after all those years in which their childhood had been stolen from them, would be ecstatically happy. But if this was a silver lining to the story, a big, very black cloud was there, too. It was just a few days before her liberation that Mala heard that her father had been shot on the death march. So any emotion she felt would be mooted. Actually, it was more than that. There was no emotion. 'No emotion, believe me. First of all, I was pretty ill. I think I was recovering, but I was still ill. There was no dancing in the streets for any of us. It wasn't like what I have since seen on television.' At that time, the camp was known simply as 'Belsen'. History has recorded the correct double name version of the horrific place.

Not for her, either, the relief expressed in kisses to a liberating army, as one particularly evocative movie scene recaptured. 'Probably older people were more aware of what was going on than I was. I don't remember. I remember being transferred to a hospital and I remember that when they came to me with a stretcher, I said, "I'll walk to the ambulance". But, of course, I got on to my feet, took one step – and collapsed.'

She now thinks it remarkable that she recovered at all. 'It was amazing what a quick recovery it was for a lot of people who caught typhoid. I was, after I left the hospital, in a pretty good shape.'

The camp didn't close immediately after liberation. For five years it was used as a displaced persons' (DP) camp. 'A few people got busy. They set up a sort of theatre, I think in a tent. They had, I recall, a Polish pianist. I remember him, a very handsome man, a Christian. There was a choreographer, a redhead, a very lovely looking woman. She was a dancer and she organised a few children in the children's home to do a routine. She taught us a little bit of ballet and a little bit of cabaret dancing. It is amazing. I remember performing there.'

In time, Mala, like most of the other Bergen-Belsen survivors, had to travel yet again. With Hania, she was taken to Sweden.

When he heard that his sister was alive, the man-child called Ben Helfgott was on a rescue mission. With Bronia, one of Gershon's cousins, he set out for Bergen-Belsen – but couldn't get there. 'Communication and transport was chaotic,' he now remembers. He was not the only one who was disappointed. Bronia had gone with him when she heard that her cousin was also there and had survived.

Somehow he was going to try to find the girls no matter what. He knew that they were now in Sweden.

First, though, there was a new development in his life. He was now sure that the two girls were alive, but that new development could clash with this – if for only a short time. 'I decided to go to Bergen-Belsen to bring the girls away from the country. There was only one way I knew to get there from Poland and that was via Czechoslovakia. But somehow I decided to stop on the way and when I got closer I could see people running around, looking very happy. I said, "What's happening?" And I was told, "We're going to England". I said, "Well, I'm not going to miss that, but I will go first to get my sister." I got as far as Pilsen. The Americans were there at the time – this was June 1945 – and when I got there I met Bronia. When we said we would go to find them, we were told it would take a very long time – so I thought there was no point. Together with Bronia I tried to go to Bergen-Belsen but we were told that transport through was impossible. Then we heard the girls were in Sweden.' From Bergen-Belsen and now...to Sweden.

Meanwhile, his aunts would have been happy had he stayed in Poland – although it wouldn't be long before they also left the country. 'One of my aunts said, "I'll look after you when you come back." But I didn't want to go back. I thought it might make me miss going to England.' The aunt went to Germany – just another of the ironies of this story. 'In Germany, she met a man who she had known from her childhood. He had been married, but his wife and their child did not survive. He was a very close friend of my father, a cousin and an uncle. So she married him. He was a very nice man and they stayed in Germany for a while, before going eventually to Australia. He was quite a good businessman and in Australia he had a factory making sweaters. He said, "I love this life." He proved to be very good on textiles and things like that. Actually, he did very well. Hania (now known as Ann) had two children, boys, one became a lawyer, the other an accountant.' Another post Holocaust tale.

His trips 'home' were not without their own distinctive terrors. Early on, he and a friend – shades of Czechochowa – were attacked by a group of Polish youths, shouting at them, with every other word being 'Jew'. It is not certain if they knew whether Ben spoke or understood Polish. He heard one of them say 'Kill him'. Ben knocked him to the ground and they went away.

Ben is convinced that the experience of the Holocaust years went to making survivors work that much harder – so they became successes. Not everyone, I suggested. There were survivors who did not do so well. 'Yes, there were some.' And it was those in mind for whom a generation later, Ben was himself instrumental in setting up the '45 Aid Society. As we shall see, it was to become one of his proudest achievements. And one of the reasons why joining in the trek to England was such a good idea.

Ben heard about the offer for youngsters from Theresienstadt on his third trip back there on his way, he thought, to Bergen-Belsen. 'England, I heard. I knew I had to be one of those to go there.' That was when this15-year-old man became one of The Boys.

# 13

## The Boys

*'I started loving England before I even came to live here'*
*– Ben Helfgott*

The United Kingdom had a good reputation as far as the Holocaust was concerned. Maybe the word 'comparatively' should be included in that sentence. There had been severe limits on the number of Jews admitted to Britain at just the time when a home in the country was most needed. After the war, the big concern was that they would come to the United Kingdom as a way-station to going to Palestine, ruled by Britain under a League of Nations mandate – already the cause of Arab-Jewish disturbances that looked very much like a strange kind of civil war; both populations living in the same country that they didn't recognise as being governed by a nation that they believed was not entitled to be there.

Also, despite appeals from international Jewish organisations, Britain had, like its American allies, refused to bomb the rail links to Auschwitz.

That was one side of the coin. On the other side was the famous Kindertransport which allowed 10,000 Jewish children to settle in Britain before the war. Now, the war in Europe over, one of the last decisions of the government headed by Winston Churchill was to say that 1,000 youngsters under the age of 16 without parents could come to live in Britain. As it turned out, they couldn't find 1,000 to fill the quota. Seven hundred and thirty-two of The Boys came – as a group who would soon consider themselves more The Brothers and Sisters. Few people would find themselves part of a more loving family. And those who still survive still consider themselves that way.

They hadn't, of course, come from one concentration camp. The problem was finding them – not even rounding up 732 was going to be easy. Says Ben: 'They [the organisers of what was hoped would be a mass exodus from Europe] rang through to every concentration camp. In Theresienstadt, there happened to be 300 of us. The point was that out of the 300, only 150 to 200, maximum, were under 16, the age requirement to get to England. Belgium had become liberated and the Swedes decided to take some of the ones who wanted to go to their country. There were some from my home town who went there because their boy and girl friends were already in Sweden and decided they wanted to go there. France said they would take the youngsters who were liberated in Buchenwald. About 200 to 300 went to France.'

Ben loved the idea of going to Britain. Arza, the woman later to become his wife, recalls: 'Ben had always been an Anglophile. He remembers the pride with which his father wore a suit of fabric made in England, the cutlery at home made in Sheffield and the world maps with most of it coloured in pink marking the British Empire. Anyway, how could anyone resist being an Anglophile: Britain had just won the war.'

If he had been given the choice of countries that could offer him refuge – which he manifestly was not – he would have chosen the United Kingdom. As he told me: 'I had learned so much. I knew a lot about it. I knew the politics and about Churchill because I was so interested in everything about the country.' He also was ready to learn the language.

Studying English after 1945 was to be an act of devotion, almost the beginning of a love affair between him and what was to become his adopted country. In fact, he puts it like this: 'I love England. I started loving England before I even came to live here – and in the early years when I was studying history'.

The Boys (and the Girls) were housed in a hostel close to Lake Windermere, one of the great English beauty spots. It was set up by a group called the Committee for the Care of Children from the Concentration Camps. The committee was like the other organisation specialising in helping people who were suffering the effects of persecution, the Central British Fund (today known as World Jewish Relief – whenever a country suffers an earthquake or other natural disaster, WJF is there to help survivors, 99.9 per cent of whom have no Jewish connection whatsoever).

There was one particular heroine of this story. Joan Steibel, who worked with Otto Schiff and the people who had run the Kindertransport and now worked with Leonard Montefiore, Elaine Blond and Lola Hahn Warburg, who was a non-Jewish woman who took The Boys under her wing. 'A very nice woman, a spinster'. Later, they would have lessons on Britain, its language, its traditions and before long its own London youth club. At the same time, they were given advice on finding places in schools and universities – among them Rabbi Hugo Gryn who, just six months after arriving in Britain, remarkably following years in Auschwitz, won a scholarship to Cambridge, taking the exams in English, a language he didn't know before, along with other Boys, being taught it in his new country.

Ben Helfgott arrived in Britain on 15 August 1945, the day that the Japanese surrendered, thus ending the Second World War. There was no selection process – a phrase that haunts all survivors. Ben says: 'No selection

whatsoever. Whoever had survived and was under 16, they came to England.'
It could have seemed a very touch and go situation, but there are no records
of any of The Boys regretting coming. Certainly, none (orphans all) wanted
to go back to Poland or Lithuania or anywhere else.

About three weeks after his arrival, Ben was introduced to a man from
Argentina who told him the most important news he had received since
leaving Theresienstadt. He was going to Sweden to meet a group of young
Jews there who had been liberated from Bergen-Belsen.

He had had no news of Mala since the first indication that she had been
in the camp. By then, he couldn't be sure that she was, in fact, there. 'I asked
him to look to see if Mala was among the Sweden children.' Two weeks
later, he discovered that, yes, she was. 'I received a letter from the man,
writing on one side, and on the reverse, Mala herself writing to me.' It was
a message he could have prayed for. But, if it was almost accidental that
they made contact, it was also proof that he had made the right decision.
'If we had made it to Bergen-Belsen', says Ben now, 'we would never have
found her. She had already gone to Sweden.' For Mala it was a passport to
a new life.

It was one of the miracles of the end of the war in general, to say nothing
of the Holocaust that Ben and Mala's Aunt Irene had been in a camp called
Skarzysko-Kamienna. The fact that she survived had another aspect. The
camp was another of those places to which Jews, ironically, had been forced
to help the Nazi war effort – manufacturing ammunition. The skin of a
number of the slave labourers turned yellow after a time – a sign that before
long they would be dead. Irene escaped both fates.

How the two Helfgott siblings had first got to know about each other was
a product of the bush telegraph that had been so active during the Holocaust
years. Ben had gone to Piotrkow and heard about a notice plastered on to
the walls of what had been the ghetto there. It listed the names of survivors
– a place for tears from people whose family was not included on the poster.
But those of Mala and Hania (Ann) were there. They were in Sweden. Ben
immediately made arrangements to get there – by the proverbial hook or by
crook.

The Swedes had taken a number of survivors from the camps and offered
them homes. Mala enjoyed being there. She remembers: 'They organised a
kind of school, like a boarding school. They gave us lessons and we got down
to learning.'

The schools and the homes that went with them were distributed
through the country and Mala and her cousin were in one of them. The
trouble was the age differential between them. 'We went through a [settling
in] process. At first, we were children of all different ages. My cousin Hania

was with me, for instance, and you wouldn't have a seven year-old and one of 14 like me in the same class.'

Peace in Sweden had a remarkable effect on Hania and her relationship with Mala, who told me: 'Hania had been with me from 1943 to 1945 and was so attached to me and wouldn't let me out of her sight. But once the war was over, she shed the fear and didn't mind being with other children. It was like turning it all upside down.'

I wondered whether this was a cause for friction between the cousins. Did it betray a sense of ingratitude – after all, a 14 year-old could be quite sensitive and a child of seven could more likely carry on in her own way, unthinking of another's feelings. Neither seemed to sense this. As Mala says: 'I think I was relieved. It had been a terrible responsibility. It was not something I would have told her, mind you.'

Things, however, were not so straightforward – at least for aunt Irene, who also decided she should go to Sweden. But she was so confused, knowing that finally she and her little daughter would get together again. The trouble was she was so flustered that she had no idea where she was going to go. She read the destination not as Sweden, but as Switzerland. In Polish, the spelling of the two countries is remarkably similar – Szwajcaria for Switzerland and Szwecja for Sweden. So Irene caught a train that would take her to Switzerland. She discovered the truth of the matter before it was too late.

By the time that Ben caught up with the girls Hania had not only found a new sense of confidence, she had gone a stage further and already left –and had been able to embrace her mother, although that took some time.

The truth of the matter was that she didn't want to meet her mother at all. It was a shock to everyone in the children's home and it was a shock, in particular, to Mala. This is one of the untold stories of the Holocaust. Understandably, the legend is that children who had lived on their own for years couldn't wait when they heard that a parent had returned on to the scene. At the same time, parents would look forward to be able to be reunited with their children. The second is, in a majority of cases, undoubtedly true. The idea of children being equally pleased at the prospect is by no means universal. Mala saw that, too.

'Everything was chaotic after the war,' she says. 'The trains hardly ran at all and when they did, they stopped for days. Irene set off on this journey and she was meeting people on the way and she told them, "My daughter has survived and I'm going to Switzerland to get her." And they said, "Not Switzerland. Sweden". She said, "Oh, well then I have to go to Sweden". Just like that. 'My aunt told me the story. She got as far as Hamburg and then she started visiting the Swedish Embassy to get permission [to go looking for her daughter].'

It wasn't as easy as that. 'In the port of Hamburg, she could see all the ships, wishing she could take one because it was very difficult to get the permission she needed. She kept going to the embassy day after day and then she met someone who told her what was happening in Hania's life. "Your daughter is no longer in Sweden", said the woman. "She is on her way to Palestine – and she is on a ship from Germany to Marseilles". Irene was getting desperate. As she later told Mala, 'I said I must get to Marseilles, but I don't know if her ship is still there.'

Mala recalled the second part of the conversation with her aunt. 'She made her way to Marseilles and the ship was still there'. Youth Alyah, the organisation which to this day looks after young people who want to go to where at the time was not yet Israel, had chartered ships to take 'DP' youngsters to what they believed would be the promised land. Irene managed to get aboard and was able to talk to an official. She said: 'My daughter is here and I have come to collect her and her name is Hania [Hannah] Helfgott.' 'They looked down the list', says Mala today, 'and they said we have got a Hannah Helfgott here, but we can't let her go because she is in our care. We are responsible for her. We can't let any children go – and, anyway, how do we know you are her mother?'

It was the kind of bureaucracy that gets in the way of what Irene thought would be, at last, her happy reunion. It was understandable on both sides of this equation. Among the terrors of the Holocaust's end was that of child trafficking. Not a lot, but it was known that it happened. Irene asked the only reasonable question she could think of: 'Why don't you call her and ask her? Let her come and see me and ask if I am her mother.'

Then came the outcome that this mother, who had not seen her child in more than two years, could never have contemplated. Hania was, shall we say, slightly less than delighted about the prospect of reunion than her mother. She came up, looked at Irene and announced it was all over between parent and daughter. 'Yes', she told the incredulous, uncomprehending official, 'this is my mother, but I don't want to go with her'.

Mala looked for explanations for her cousin's behaviour in destroying her mother's dreams. 'She had been without a mother for a long time. She had spent over two years in Sweden with a lot of other children and wanted to stay with her mates.' But Irene was having none of it. 'Of course my aunt was very upset, but she was a very strong woman and, of course, eventually Hania did agree to go with her.'

There are no records to show how many children did spurn their newly-survived parents, but as Mala says, the case was not unique – and not just with Jewish children who didn't want to leave their friends for their mothers and fathers. As Mala herself recalls, there were any number of children sent by anxious parents away from German bombing in London and other major cities – not as evacuees to the British countryside, but to America and Canada – who didn't want to return to the fog and austerity of their home country.

'There was one family', she told me, 'who said that the girl was at school and she was graduating, going from one class to another. She was told [by someone in authority in the camp]: "We have a real surprise for you. We are bringing your mother over for the graduation". This girl was disappointed. She wasn't interested in her mother coming.' Of course, it could simply be a case of nerves. We don't know if girl and mother were, in fact, ever reunited.

As for Hania, it was probably a case of it having been so long since they were last together that the experience seemed just too much. That was not the only problem. When they finally did meet, Hania was about to go with other surviving children to Palestine. She made her way to Marseilles from where the ship to Haifa was about to leave. It was a battle to be won by her mother – and, instead of making the trip to the not yet established state of Israel, she and her mother went to Germany – and then to Australia.

As we have noted, Irene was to marry another survivor, Abraham Korn, and it was a family of three who made the treks. Mala remembers Korn as being 'a wonderful man – what a great father he was to my cousin! He died quite unexpectedly. It was after them doing well in Australia and they had a very nice lifestyle.'

Meanwhile, Ben, the dutiful brother, was spared this kind of trauma when Mala re-entered his life.

'I find it very difficult to describe emotions,' Mala says now. 'What can one say apart from it was wonderful to be together again. When I did meet him ultimately, it wasn't a surprise because we had been corresponding for quite a long time by then.' But she adds about that reunion: 'I never believed I would see any of my family again. I thought they had all gone. Of course, there was the possibility of my father and brother being alive still, but I hadn't heard anything about them. It was just a possibility, but I didn't imagine it was probable.'

Now, Ben and Mala had been reunited. He had traced all her steps and when she arrived at Tilbury Docks on 24 March 1947, Ben was there to meet her. Mala recalls. 'Ben had established where I was and he wrote to me. He was the first person who had ever sent me a letter.' Just before their meeting at Tilbury, she recalls Ben 'wrote a lovely long letter [in Polish]. He was a very good writer. I remember when I got that first letter, I couldn't believe my eyes. I picked it up and I started reading it. I read it walking through the grounds of the lovely big house which served as our Swedish school. I recall shouting out, "I've had a letter from my brother."

It was not as though this was the first intimation that Ben was also alive. 'I knew that already. I had heard that, rather. But to have an actual letter was more tangible. After that, we corresponded with each other and kept sending photographs, which showed how much we had both changed. Some awful photographs. His were OK, mine were terrible. We were always swapping pictures with my friends in Sweden. It was a craze.' One of Mala's big regrets is that none of Ben's letters have survived. It was, of course, enough that both human beings *had* survived.

The emotions both felt at their reunion is one to be left for the imagination. All Ben would say to me was, 'Of course it was emotional.' Mala says: 'I find it very difficult putting emotions into words. It was obviously very exciting and I was very happy. The committee had arranged for me to go and live there [in London]. With me was a girl who came with The Boys. She had had an operation and went away for convalescence, which people always did in those days after surgery. The committee people said, "She will be away for two weeks, so you can use her room, then we'll find somewhere else for you, proper accommodation". But I stayed there for quite a long time.' Her brother was ready to go on watch, not always with her complete approval.

As she remembers: 'Ben was acting like a big brother and behaved as if he were my father, even though he was only a year older. He kept telling me what to do, what not to do. He had some very old fashioned ideas. When I started wearing lipstick, I must have been at the very least 16 and a half, but for quite a long time, he was absolutely disgusted. He thought it was terrible and made me seem like a girl from the streets. Of course, he felt he was responsible and now I understand it.' Not that she completely forgives him, naturally. I said that he probably felt the need to be protective. 'Protective, yes. Exactly.' But she points out: 'In fact, it was not that we were a family any longer, or so it seemed. We weren't living in the same premises.'

She was being well looked after in those first days in the city that would thereafter be her home.

'It wasn't a hostel, but a private lodging house. Our landlady was a Mrs Neuberger, who had come from Germany. I was using that single room. Next door were two brothers of the tenant of my room, Rosalind Gross. They were sharing a bigger room and when Rosalind came back, I slept on the couch there for quite a long time. It was fine. We got on well and she was OK. She already knew the language and was working.'

It becomes obvious that Ben and his sister had a lot in common. As she says, 'My first priority was to learn English. It had been in the curriculum in my Swedish school and I thought I could speak the language until I came here. Then I realised I couldn't. So I set about learning English and I did quite quickly. Not because I'm clever, but simply because I had to. Then I went to a secretarial college.'

She was happy with the idea of becoming a secretary. So were the people who had provided her with both a new home and a new life. Indeed, when she was given a number of options. She thought it a perfect way to make the progress in learning English which she craved. The most surprising thing about Ben, this young man who put learning and study above everything else, thought she should become a dressmaker.

She says now over and over again, that her big brother was 'very good and meant well and wanted the best for me. But he didn't realise that I had something to say, too. He was part of an era with old-fashioned views when parents – and he continued to consider himself almost a parent – told their children, "You will do this" or "You won't do that". Psychologically, Ben was still in that era and he just thought that he knew better than I. After all, I have to admit that at that time being a secretary was not a very prestigious thing to do. But that's what girls were doing and it was more acceptable than sitting by a [sewing] machine. Anyway, I was good and have always been good with a needle. But there was no need to spend my days over the machine.'

Almost two years had elapsed since their joint liberation, two and a half years since they were taken away from the woodwork factory, but they were not strangers to each other. There was no question of not recognising brother or sister. They had sent photographs, all taken after the war. Lists, similar to the ones in Piotrkow had been put up in the Swedish centre where survivors were known to be and a British delegation had gone there to assess the situation – armed with the information some of the youngsters wanted to hear – and some they did not.

Ben was not over-emotional, Mala recalls. 'He came with a friend called Nathan Wald, who was to die in America. It was emotional for me, though. We hugged.'

The strange thing is that what Ben's sister remembers most about the occasion was not so much how she felt at meeting her brother, but the surrounding sights and people. 'I remember saying to Ben, "Oh look, a *murzy*". Murzy is Polish for black. I had never seen a black man before. Ben told me, "Be quiet. There are a lot of them here. You don't talk about them".'

She was not one of The Boys – in the terms of arrival in Britain. 'I was under the Central British Fund, which had its headquarters at Bloomsbury House.' This was the headquarters of the same organisation which had found homes for the Kindertransport children less than a decade earlier. 'They took me to a place in Maida Vale [just north of the Edgware Road in Central

London]. They allocated me there because the girl who had occupied that room was a survivor from Hungary who was now convalescing after a not too serious illness in hospital.' It was only temporary accommodation.

As for The Boys, they immediately forged those friendships which might have seemed incredible in any other circumstance. They had come from all over Europe and suddenly total strangers speaking different languages became not just friends for the moment, but many of them vowed to themselves that they would stay friends for ever after. That they have remained so for more than 70 years speaks volumes – in any of those languages (although it has to be said that most of them did have a common tongue, Yiddish).

Most of the organisations searching for homes for the homeless would regard a sudden influx of 732 youngsters a task they might wish they didn't have to worry about. But these were boys and girls with the psychological baggage that doesn't take too much imagination to contemplate. They were as grateful as anyone in their situation could show, but for some there was a sense of anti-climax. For others, the terrible fear of what could lie ahead.

They had had years of deprivation and of that fear. For so many, there was the feeling of being almost sub-human – because no human should ever have been expected to exist, let alone survive, in the conditions they went through. Children should never have been exposed to what they saw, dead bodies all around, often the bodies of parents and other loved ones. What has to be recognised is that this was the beginning of a life that Helfgott was to take into old age. It also established his ideas of brotherly love. The other Boys, to use a convenient cliche, could be said to be a family.

They were met by Leonard Montefiore, scion of an old, almost aristocratic Jewish family known as 'The Cousinhood'. 'I went,' says Ben, 'together with a group led by Mr. Montefiore and we came to Trout Beck Bridge, which was between Windermere and Ambleside. During the war they were making airplane parts there. But they put us up there when the Air Ministry decided they didn't need it any more.'

'The first thing that happened was on the day after we arrived. We were seen by doctors and dentists.' Both the doctors and dentists were amazed at the specimen with which they were presented when young Mr. Helfgott came before them. 'I had the best teeth', he remembers. 'I was in very good shape and already very strong.'

He settled in like a puppy in a new home. 'For years I had not slept on a fresh bed. Normally, I woke up all the time at night, but I slept and slept and had to be woken up by a man who looked after us.'

There was also a German Jewish woman who looked after The Boys. A sort of fairy godmother? I asked. 'No', said Ben who didn't want to elaborate.

But it was a very close family indeed, that first group in Windermere in the picturesque Lake District. They were nothing less than a brotherhood.

Other groups followed – though not to Windermere. A planeload of Boys came from Munich and a hostel was established in Southampton, where Dr. Oscar Friedmann helped with the same sort of regimen as was taking shape in the Lake District.

'We were reborn there,' Ben now remembers. 'For the first time we were doing what we wanted to do.' (He does not include the times spent in Prague and going to and from Piotrkow in that statement.) 'We started the day with breakfast and then we waited for the post'. There were always vague hopes that there could be news on the way of the sudden discovery of family members whom they knew, in their hearts, were already dead. But some were lucky. 'When the post came, we could hear the occasional cries of "Oh my sister has arrived. My father has come".'

The jealousy of the others could not be hidden. 'I remember one boy going up and asking, "Is there no letter for me?" I wouldn't say there was envy but…Yes, there was envy. Particularly when some did realise that a parent or a brother and sister had, after all, survived.'

As far as Ben was concerned, it was a time for fun. 'We played football, volleyball and they took us out in coaches. It was beautiful, so nice. We went to the cinema about three or four times a week. I saw them and I concentrated. I tried to remember words I learnt from the movies.' And he started reading the British newspapers notably the popular broadsheet paper, the *News Chronicle*, a much admired intelligently written paper that folded 15 years later.

But these were not the only language 'lessons'. As he said, 'We started having English lessons and were learning maths. It had been much easier at school.' Of course, time was more pressing now. They had to prepare for further education and a career. No-one was going to give them an easy ride as far as that was concerned.

The organisers expected the children to be excited by the food, their new clothes and the beautiful scenery of the British countryside, particularly at Windermere. What they were not expecting was their thirst for knowledge. They thought that, like the average British 15 and 16 year-olds whom they knew, the idea of education might be something to be suffered. This was not the case with The Boys, who realised that it was yet another thing of which they had been deprived and, therefore, had to be scooped up as if it were a last meal and not, in effect, the first.

They were astounded by British life. It seemed so free, so perfect – to some. To others, it was not what they had hoped for at all. The religious ones were given every opportunity to follow their faith, within the obvious restrictions. The ultra-Orthodox community in Gateshead were there to help – it was one of its rabbis who distributed those first cups of cocoa, along with cakes and *white bread.*

That food might not have been considered 'properly' kosher, but these strictly observant rabbis took the injunction on for *pekuach nefesh – for the sake of the soul.* This clearly stated that in the case of sickness and particularly with the threat of death overhanging them, health and the saving of life took prority over everything else. But even Gateshead, home of the only top *yeshiva* (Talmudical college) left in Europe offered a kind of religious service that wasn't totally familiar to those who had gone to *shul* in Piotrkow. As far as possible, religious children were put together, as were those from secular homes and from Zionist backgrounds. But Windermere was not Piotrkow, a name previously unfamiliar to the people running the hostel, but now well known to them all.

It was not just the refugees who found Britain a strange place. A lot of the country's native citizens did too. Those who remember the country from before the war were bitterly disappointed that peace hadn't meant reasons to just be happy. Food was still rationed – indeed the newcomers had to realise that even their favourite white bread (or that of any other colour) now had to be bought with ration coupons, something that hadn't happened even during the darkest days of the war. The Boys were sampling the first sweets and chocolates they had tasted in at least six years, but these were limited (they were briefly taken off the ration and then promptly put back on ration 'points' because there were not enough of the goodies to go around). An egg, a fantastic treat, had to figure in their diets only as a result of their temporary ration books being passed on to the grocery shops nearby.

Being together without the threat of guards wanting to shunt them off to gas chambers or have roll calls in the middle of a freezing Polish night gave opportunities for The Boys (and The Girls) to compare notes with each other, or even to write down their thoughts. But even the sense of all being in the same shaky boat did not come easy. As Ben was to remember: 'There were many who found it difficult to describe their experiences. They preferred to ignore and even to suppress their recollections.'

Ben, who has always seen it almost as a sense of duty to do just the opposite of that, understands those attitudes. 'It took us a while to awaken from over five years of nightmare. As long as we were struggling for survival and had lived from hour to hour, we had not entertained any thoughts of the enormity of our loss or about our future. Now, it gradually, began to dawn upon us that we were, at last, free and that freedom meant a complete readjustment. But how could we readjust without either a home or family support? We suddenly realised we were alone.'

The logistics of the operation had to include dealing with those deprivations and fears as well as finding the mostly teenagers homes. But it all happened. As usual, members of the Jewish community rallied. The late Sir Martin Gilbert quotes Leonard Montefiore outlining the job he had taken on. He did it seemingly out of a sense of responsibility. His ancestor, Sir Moses Montefiore, travelled thousands of miles in the Victorian era rescuing Jews of his generation from persecution. Lionel Montefiore was to say, 'When we got down to considering what could be done, there were immense difficulties. No money could be sent out of the country and even if money had been sent, there was nothing to buy. But if we could bring the people we wanted to help to this country, then the currency difficulties would be cleared out of the way.'

The Home Secretary in Clement Attlee's new Labour Government, J.Chuter Ede – its 1945 landslide victory had been confirmed less than two months earlier – was the one to give the green light once Churchill had gone into Opposition.

The excitement among the young refugees was without parallel in either their lives or even those of other orphans of their age in other countries. 'When I heard I could get to England, I knew that was going to be the most important thing for me', said Ben.

Others felt the same. They were overjoyed, but they also worried about the future. They couldn't believe there were people out there who wanted to help them. They also knew, when they settled down to consider the future, that before very long, they would have to stand on their still fragile feet, although that would take time. For the moment, there was the sense that they were with family. Some were part of the same actual family, but they were in a tiny minority. Most were in the queue to go to England on their own. However, there was that link between them – the fact that they had all come from the camps; everyone knew what the other knew, had seen what the other had seen, had scrambled for the same crusts of stale bread or been fed the same soup that smelled of excreta. It was immensely strong.

When they talked, food was inevitably at the top of their conversations. Perhaps the wonder is that they were given any food at all in the camps. As it was, Ben admits he had became 'demented'. As he said, 'I saw fathers fight sons for a crust.' There was one man who swapped a diamond for a slice of bread. In Claude Landesmann's epic documentary film, *Shoah*, there is an interview with a Pole who did find a loaf for a starving Jew in exchange for precious stones. He showed no remorse. 'They couldn't eat the diamonds,' he says.

Ask for an explanation for such cruelty, from someone like Ben Helfgott and he says: 'I was always hungry. I went to bed hungry and woke up hungry.

All I could ever think of was bread.' The answer was quite simple: it was all part of the business of dehumanising the Jew before killing him. That was why a new life in England was going to be so vital.

Others might not have been so articulate, but that summed up most of The Boys' experiences. Some were 'landsmen' – as the Yiddish word denotes people from the same towns – who before the Nazis murdered their kinsfolk had played the same games. Some came together for the first time, though they had lived just streets away from each other. Several were from Piotrkow, like Harry Spiro, who had been in the same ghetto and worked in the same glass factory as Ben Helfgott, but who, until that moment had never met each other, even though from that time on they became inseparable and life long friends. Another was Josh Segal. And then there was Pinkus Kurnedz.

Talking of names becomes a roll call of Jewish history. That didn't cross the minds of the young people who assembled in Prague, ready for the flight to London.

In addition to The Boys were 30 much younger children (some as young as three). All were loaded into a fleet of 12 Lancaster bombers, a particularly appropriate choice in an age when there were virtually no civil aircraft (the airlines hadn't existed during the war). The big black Lancasters, crewed by RAF pilots and navigators, had symbolised for Britons the bombing of German cities that contributed to the war's end. If that, in itself, was seen as a gesture of hope by the people in the concentration camps (particularly those in Auschwitz who had hoped without success that rumours were true – that the railway line to Birkenau was going to be attacked by Allied planes) – to The Boys using those aircraft with their trademark double tail to now save lives was that, too.

The planes landed at Crosby-in-Eden – close to the Scottish border, to be greeted by, among others, members of the Women's Voluntary Service – the ladies of the WVS who in their ungainly green tweed uniforms were on the scene whenever they might be needed. In the war years, they helped young British children on to the trains that would take them to new temporary homes in the country, away from the German bombing targets in London and other big British cities. The WVS were on hand to help wounded troops off other trains – with cigarettes and mugs of tea at the ready.

Many of the women were schoolteachers, who wore their uniforms in the classrooms. It was said the rough tweed made good blackboard wipers. Their experience working with children was now invaluable.

This first group of Boys (and Girls, of course) were taken to the hostel at Windermere. Most reports stated that they were all happier than could be imagined. Just being in the country seemed enough. Leonard Montefiore reported the time he took a group of them in an old truck that broke down.

He apologised but one of The Boys told him not to worry. 'It's an honour to break down on a British road', he said. If any of The Boys could imagine a time when those roads would be theirs, as familiar as the streets of Piotrkow and the other places from which they hailed, it was, it seemed, mere fantasy. The idea that they would one day become British citizens, marry and have children here and enter its professions and be in business and represent the Jewish community to which they now proudly belonged, would be too much to contemplate. It was the same with others who would choose not to stay in Britain but to make their new world, *in* the New World, in the United States and Canada, and in other places of which they had hardly ever heard. Not all were like Ben Helfgott, who had spent so much of his early childhood reading and studying the world outside Poland. And not all were so successful. It would be Ben who would find a way of helping those who needed it with his '45 Aid organisation. For the moment, that is another story.

The matter of settling in, particularly its problems, was not something that could be easily ignored. Settling in to ideas of a freedom that for many had still not developed in any sense of normality. Ben recalled the secret hiding of food. The youngsters took time to grasp that they could easily get what they needed (or even just wanted) to eat. Yet to many of The Boys, the idea of being able to – legally – eat *real* food virtually any time they wished was beyond comprehension.

That feeling of becoming 'demented', to which Ben had referred, was, as we have seen, all part of the far-seeing Nazi policy. Now, there would be no more examples of fathers and sons fighting for a slice of bread – most of The Boys had no parents. It was all in the past. 'There was', says Ben, 'no need to hide the best white bread, to say nothing of fruit or cakes.'

He didn't forget those days when he arrived with his fellow Boys. The memories were fresh then and they are as clear now as the day he went to work in the glass factory. What had to be considered was the entry of the world of bureaucracy. Westmorland County Council, then the local authority for Windermere, recorded how The Boys were given a cup of cocoa on arrival, followed by a medical examination – a doctor and nurse were looking for signs of infection – and shown to their beds. Their names were taken – although, amazingly, not all the teenagers knew their names, although most did. The years in concentration camps had taken that knowledge away from them, just as they had taken away their parents.

Their clothes were removed and parcelled up. If that seemed a little too like what happened in Buchenwald and the other foul places, there was the reassuring sign of being given a warm blanket, a comfortable bed in which to sleep and a complete set of *new* clothes. There was nothing about the old shirts and shorts and ragged coats they arrived in that they wanted to keep. Nothing of sentimental value.

The council report was not exactly a happy one: 'Their condition was not as satisfactory as first appeared. Many of them were obviously above the age of 16 (which was supposed to be the upper age limit) and, indeed, they openly confessed that they had understated their age so as to be allowed to come.'

As for their health: 'They appeared on the surface to be stout [a very 1940s word] and well nourished, but this proved to be surplus fat which apparently accumulated since they were properly fed and had been released from heavy work. In many cases septic scars were visible on their limbs and bodies and in some cases these were still discharging.' The report did not mention that many of the scars came from being beaten in captivity. It did say that a number of the youngsters had been suffering from typhus, which was always present in the camps.

Others had TB. The 'Tuberculosis Officer' noted that many who had made it to Britain had shown that they were pretty tough. He said that it gave 'some idea of the numbers who must have succumbed to this disease'. Some of the inmates (not a term to be used at Windermere) were unable to sleep, had bad dreams and were showing signs of extreme nervousness.

There was no getting away from it. Tuberculosis was the biggest – a huge – problem. The British Government basically refused to help – because any sufferers should not have been there in the first place. Having TB was a principal reason for foreigners being excluded from entering the country. The efforts made to both cure the sufferers and make sure they were allowed to stay in Britain indicated how dedicated the organisers and other volunteers were. A remarkable woman named Lola Hahn-Warburg, a member of the Warburg banking family, found a solution: she arranged for an empty ward at a sanatorium in Ashford, Kent to be handed over to her. She was a woman who would never accept the word 'No' as being a final answer. Ben would remember:

'She was a formidable woman with a tremendous sense of purpose, with a devotion to young people who played a tremendous part for those whose health was worst affected.' In that they were helped by a man who as a child had been in a Frankfurt orphanage and recognised all the symptoms. Oscar Friedmann, who helped sort out psychological problems and became not just a kind sympathetic ear, but a sort of father figure to the youngsters.

No-one yet said that arrangements at Windermere were ideal, although they had sports activities and were encouraged to spend as much time as possible in the open air, not least on the banks of the Lake. They began learning English – with astounding results, which Ben himself showed and so did others like Hugo Gryn. However, the council report said: 'From the time of their arrival from Prague, there was a delay before the camp could be adequately organised. Food for a few days was definitely poor in supply and cooking, and although this was recognised by the children, there were no complaints.' That last sentence said it all.

As for Ben, he began to think about sports again – not that he ever had forgotten about them. Next to his virtually wiped out family and the next piece of bread likely to come his way, sports and study were the principal matters on his mind. He wanted to lap them up like a kitten offered a saucer of milk. 'I now wanted to catch up on my lost years – and to do sport. I didn't know anything about weightlifting, but I believed I was a natural gymnast.' He had practised at Theresienstadt. 'By the time I came to England I was ready to do anything. I was back in physical shape very quickly.'

Anything that could be listed under that one word 'sport' fitted the bill perfectly. He quickly became table tennis champion there. No problems with that as these were at Theresienstadt when the first thing he asked was whether they had a table tennis table there. 'Imagine that', he says now. 'Table tennis at Theresienstadt Weird! Weird!' But there *was* one gap in his sporting activities. He was a very weak swimmer. 'I just couldn't take to it.' And he never has.

Over the years – and really until comparatively recently – there have been Holocaust survivors who didn't want to talk about their experiences. Ben has never been one of them. No-one could consider him a totally modest man, but talking about the Nazi years is something of a crusade. It took some effort and quite a bit of persuasion. His friend Harry Spiro recalled for me: 'I have never pushed it, but I have always agreed to talk about it when people asked me.' There were those Boys who wanted to put it all behind them – literally. That annoyed Ben. As Spiro says: 'I said to him, "Leave them alone. The time will come. Or if not, they should not be condemned". I told Ben, "They cannot feel the same way as you and I".'

They all felt differently, like Morris Malenisky, who came from the same town as Ben. He was very different – a man who kept himself very much to himself; had secrets from his family and, although, loving in his own way, somehow maintained a distance from those who should have been close to him – like his daughter Angela Cohen, now the head of The Boys' own 'club' the '45 Aid Society (which is more like a friendly society, specialising in helping survivors like themselves and letting the world know about the Holocaust and their experiences in it).

The idea of having and knowing grandparents was a joy from which Angela Cohen and others like her were denied. 'I knew the name of his mother was Hannah.' Angela is close to an English version of Hannah, which means that she, following the ancient Jewish tradition, was named after her. She also knows that as a Cohen (in that tradition, a member of the priestly sect) her father would be the first called to the reading of the Torah in synagogue – so that was an indication of his own father's name. 'But he would never talk about his parents.'

It was Ben who helped Angela Cohen put her family story in perspective. And part of that story was for a survivor to keep the tale to himself.

'Ben said to me, "Did your father ever tell you anything about himself?" I said, "No". So Ben said, "I'm going to tell you a story." He recalled that they had made the same journey – from Piotrkow through the camps.'

'They knew each other right from the beginning of that journey. My father came from a very frum [religious] family. Ben's was more secular. But they weren't best buddies or anything. Yet my grandparents were bakers and Ben's family made flour or sold flour, so there was a kind of connection there – through cakes and bread.

'Anyway, Ben tells me this story. They had gone from one concentration camp to another. When you got out of the cattle cars, you would look at the state of the inmates to see what kind of camp you were going to. Lots of times, the inmates – those in the camp already – would come to the trains to see what was going on – and would try to find out about where they came from. If it were someone from their own home towns, they would try to find out if they knew the fate of their own parents – if they were alive or dead. Ben told me that he saw three men coming up to him, all dressed in their striped 'pyjama' uniforms. They came up to him and he looked at these emaciated men. Body lice were literally falling out of their wispy hair. They were almost skeletal. Ben told me my father was one of the three.' It wasn't her father, but his near contemporary, just a couple of years older. 'Of course, by the time Ben told me this story, he wasn't that man any more.'

Whether this was a unique story or not, it illustrates another demonstration of the Holocaust syndrome that The Boys at Windermere and Southampton were experiencing. Of course, all the survivors had indelible memories – of the days they were deported, when they went to the camps, how they were mistreated by guards. Yet there are subtle differences in the ways they reacted to liberation and freedom. Ben, for instance, is lucky to have found a loving wife and to have brought up adoring children and grandchildren. Angela Cohen has memories of Morris Malenisky that confirm the love of a man deprived of family life who marries and sires children with nothing else left for chance. 'My father never changed. He was really a clever businessman but he never gave his family the pleasure of turning his business, a milk bar in Stamford Hill, into something bigger than it was.' She recalls her father who, like so many survivors, like Ben himself, was small of stature and strong in physical ability. 'He was five foot four. He never changed. He had the energy of six men. He was so powerful and strong and worked and worked and was very clever, but never became sophisticated.'

But, saying that led to another phenomenon. The effect of being a Holocaust survivor on their children. Books have been written on the subject. A British-born rabbi in Holland devoted his – to use a non-Jewish but appropriate term – ministry to helping this second generation. Psychiatrists have made fortunes dealing with cases over the years.

All this explains, I hope, why the Malenisky story fits into the Helfgott tale at this juncture and why, perhaps, Ben's story is not as typical as one might initially have expected. Cohen explains: 'My father felt that our lives shouldn't be too easy – because I would become too complacent. Dad very much lived to those rules and it was only after he died, really, that we found out what exactly he owned and what he had.'

There were countless incidents that confirmed that fact. As she recalled: 'He filled in all the details [in his tax returns and so on]. But he never let his family know. We had been to Israel as a family umpteen times – and he would go on his own. He was one of The Boys.' How much they would find out about him or let others know about themselves is another of the mysteries of survival.

Plainly, there was nothing that could alter that effect, but The Boys were able to help each other, through the depressions they suffered, through the memories that were locked away inside, and Leonard Montefiore and the others were doing more than anyone else's best could have been. They not only did their best to make life as pleasant as possible, they found ways of making them aware of the good and the simple things going on around them.

Entertainment figured high in the world of The Boys, most of whom seemed to have a happier time than Morris. They played gramophone records (Al Jolson was top of the pops a few months after the arrivals in Windermere and Southampton, as a result of the biggest musical movie of 1946, *The Jolson Story*). They listened to the 'wireless' (no-one in Britain called it 'radio' yet) and were fascinated by the James Bond of the day, *Dick Barton 'Special Agent'*. And they went to the cinema, many of them (although, not, as we have seen, Ben) for the first time to see swashbucklers like Errol Flynn, movie 'greats' like Clark Gable and glamour girls like Betty Grable or Lana Turner. Some had their first experience of Shakespeare through Laurence Olivier's *Henry V.* They knew that Derby County won the FA Cup Final and they had got a better grip on the strange British political system than most natives. Hugh Dalton, the Chancellor of the Exchequer, became the most unpopular man in the country introducing one 'austerity' measure after the other. The Boys couldn't understand why. After all, neither he nor the Prime Minister Clement Attlee was organising any pogroms or stopping the newspapers saying unkind things about the Government.

Of course, they were aware, too, of other happenings going on in the world during their first year in England. In Nuremberg, ten Nazi war criminals, like the former German ambassador and Foreign Minister Joachim Von Ribbentrop, were hanged after the first trial of its kind in history. Most telling of all for The Boys was what was happening in Palestine – war between Arabs and Jews was heating up and both sides were battling with the British who were administering the League of Nations' mandate. It was the year when the King David Hotel, headquarters of the British military, was blown up by Menachem Begin's Irgun Zvai Leumi. In pre-war Germany that sort of thing would have led to a Kristallnacht. True, there were a few anti-Semitic demonstrations in parts of Britain and the press was not kind (nor were the newsreels shown in cinemas which concentrated on the bodies of dead British officials with hands visible beneath the wreckage). But it was but nothing compared with what the Nazis would have done.

Ben knew about all these things. Seemingly this was another vital chapter in his 15 year-long life.

# 14

## A New Life

*'You can't imagine what a prop we were for each other'*
*– Ben Helfgott*

Ben was at Windermere for four months. Ask him for an instant thought about the place and he is in no doubt. 'It was wonderful.' But why? The answer took no thinking time. 'Because we were all together. You can't imagine what a prop we were for each other. It helped us so much. We were happy because we were all in the same boat – in other words, all of us were alive. We were, as I say, learning. Not just from the cinema and the newspapers. We were going to museums, anywhere we wanted to go. We had nothing to lose, just to enjoy everything we were doing.' The Windermere organisers provided the wherewithal for that enjoyment to happen.

There were always some things that could not be swept away with a few kind words. 'I'll never forget the nights. I knew that my mother and father had been killed and the memories – and the dreams – kept recurring. During the first three months, I kept thinking in particular about my father because I didn't want to accept that he had been murdered. I thought that it was unbelievable. When we were living together he had taken such risks and always had come through. He would always get out. I liked to think that he had escaped with a few other people – and with a few children who would have finished up where I finished up.' He said that he couldn't believe that Hitler's order that any Jew his troops found should be shot could have included his father among them.

Ben had been told there would be a home for him. He had lived in Birmingham, Britain's second city, with a group who had decided and had permits to go to Palestine (it was three years before the establishment of the State of Israel).

From Birmingham he and the other boys moved to London. He was one of 30 boys transferred to a hostel at Loughton, one of those parts of the county of Essex always thought of as being in East London.

The Boys were given a week's work. They were each paid £1. 'We said "It was nice of you to give us work. But £1? You didn't do us any favours. You took advantage". So we walked out.' It was perhaps the first time that Ben

Helfgott exercised his talents as a leader – and an amateur trade unionist, to boot.

'It was the most wonderful hostel – probably due to the man who looked after us, called Heiny Goldberg – a man whose family left Germany before the war. He was very good.' The hostel was actually a converted large period house that he remembers affectionately. 'It was a beautiful building surrounded by a lot of land, where we could play football.' Another sport for Ben to chalk up. 'We were all very friendly, but we had groups. A few people in each – this group, that group. It was also close to a Jewish community who were nice to us. They had a club where we were welcomed. They had a rabbi who came from Czechoslovakia. A group of survivors came up to us as soon as we went there for the first time. They said, "We would like to help you". Every Friday they came to us with extra food.'

'The rabbi asked me what I wanted to do. I said that I wanted to catch up with what I lost. I want to study. There were other boys who said the same thing and he said, "I will try to see what I can do" and he was as good as his word. He told us, "I have spoken to the council and they would like to help you." They organised a bus to take us to West Ham Town Hall. Two MPs were there, including the future Lord Elwyn-Jones, who was the Member of Parliament for Plaistow and later became Lord Chancellor. I later became very friendly with him and his son.'

One of The Boys, Jerry Herszberg, won a place at West Ham Education College, where he studied mathematics – and was so good that he began teaching the subject there. They became very close, Ben and Jerry, which may today sound like an ice cream company, but in 1946, theirs was a serious friendship and one of those bondings which seemed as though nothing and no-one could drive them apart. 'You cannot imagine how close we were. We went everywhere together. We never did anything that we were upset about. It was a wonderful friendship that meant a lot to me because he was one of those people to whom I could speak and know it would never go any further. It was very special.' After graduating with a first class degree in mathematics, Jerry went on to Kings College, London where he completed a Masters and a Ph.D.

But there would be problems. 'He wanted to marry a woman who was 15 years older than he, with a child of about 12. She had come here, to London, after spending the war years in Russia. I remember saying to him, "Jerry, what are you doing? You have so many girls you could take out." He had always had girls; he was very good with girls. He was a nice boy. Nothing special to look at, but very intelligent. When I got married he was my best man. We would invite him for breakfast every Sunday, sometimes lunch. He didn't marry, but he always had a woman. Then, quite suddenly, he didn't come for two or three weeks. I asked him why and he said it was because of our children – they were very small. "I don't want them to run around", he said. It was the first time I had had that reaction.' So the big friendship turned into the big drift apart. 'Maybe it was my fault'.

The Council officials thought it was time Ben went to a British school – and an appointment was made with Dr Harold Priestly, Headmaster of the county grammar school at Plaistow, then in the heart of London's Docklands. 'I and one other boy were given an exam. We talked and the head said he would take us. We would start on 1 September 1946 – and in the fifth form, the lower fifth. After three months, the head said he would put us up a year – so that we would be ready to take the 1947 examinations.'

It was 'further education' in its truest sense. For Ben and for the others before long, it meant more sport, more time for study – thinking about going to school for the first time since he and everyone else round and about were herded into the ghetto. And there was also a club for them called Primrose. And a hero of an athlete called Yogi Mayer.

# 15

## Primrose

*'He is solely responsible to his own conscience'*
*– Yogi Mayer*

Primroses are beautiful flowers of assorted colours. The word has political associations. It was, by repute, the favourite bloom of Benjamin Disraeli, in whose honour the favourite redoubt of British Tory politicians adopted the name Primrose for their 'League'. The Primrose Club had no political associations, apart from the fact that a few of its members would share an intense desire to see every surviving Nazi strung up from every lamp post in Germany.

They all had good reasons for this. Every one of them had been in a concentration camp. The average age was about 16 and none of them had any parents. For them, Primrose was a life saver. And if it wasn't for the building itself it was because of its leader that they settled down to their new existence in *their* new country.

Paul Mayer (Yogi was a nickname, which became the only way anyone knew him by and was plainly adapted from the famous American sports personality, Yogi Berra, to say nothing of the cartoon character Yogi Bear) was a brilliant German athlete who had found, with his wife Ilse, asylum in Britain in 1939, only three years after being rejected by the Olympic selectors in Berlin. He attended those 1936 Berlin games as a sports reporter, while he 'moonlighted' as a physical education instructor for Jewish children (he would not have been allowed to teach non-Jewish pupils). His prowess as an athlete – he was also an outstanding swimmer – made him the idol and mentor of the youngsters he taught.

All that made him the ideal man to take over the two houses in Belsize Park, the North West London suburb which, appropriately, had drawn other recent emigres from Nazi Germany. The Primrose Jewish Youth Club was set up with the help of private donations from within the Anglo-Jewish community in 1946. He immediately knew what it was going to be for – to help The Boys and the few Girls among them to see value in life again.

Yogi was to write about his Primrose members and the teenager they had voted for in their first election of officers: 'After a very short time, it became evident to me that within this very active and volatile group of young people, there was this rather quiet boy Ben Helfgott who, because of his popularity, became the obvious choice as chairman for the newly formed committee of the youth club. Soon, this representative body of members became very much involved in self-programming and so, among other more cultural activities, an extensive sports programme was started. Ben proposed that weightlifting would be of special value to those boys of whom many were emaciated after years in concentration camps, slave labour camps and death marches.

'Within a short time, I, as a former PE teacher, noticed that Ben had not only regained his physical abilities, but also had the inborn strength of character required to reach the top level in sport. I have never met a person of the integrity, determination and unselfish involvement as Ben Helfgott. He is solely responsible to his own conscience.'

Undoubtedly, he saw sport as the fulcrum of his aims, which put the young Ben Helfgott and himself immediately on the same course. He might even have had the young chairman in mind when he said that his hope was to 'harness the survival skills' of his new members.

The idea for the club came from Oscar Friedmann, the same doctor who had done so much for The Boys when they arrived in Britain. Says Ben: 'When he died we discovered he had been an orphan, a German refugee who came to this country before the war, and lived in an orphanage, which explains why he wanted to help us.'

Yogi – everyone called him that – played football with the boys and taught them cricket on nearby Hampstead Heath. That had two purposes: both games were intended not only to build up the youngsters, but to instil in them what he considered British ideas of fair play. The idea of kids who could barely speak English, whose background included both the *shtetl* and the camp, complaining about being out LBW and maybe even clapping a player with a 'well done, Sir', sounds ridiculous. But there was great method in his apparent madness. He wanted them to, as soon as possible, be immersed in the culture of their new community.

He wasn't entirely successful in that – although a few of The Boys (and Girls) did make the journey to what they did consider the Promised Land. If he did not completely get his way in that, he not only continued the work that Friedmann had begun. He was a restless individual who took it upon himself to act as a kind of PR man (a species that had not yet arisen). 'He was in touch with several leaders of the Jewish community in Britain and persuaded them to come to our hostel.' That hostel was now where Ben lived – so that Primrose represented both his home and his leisure – and where he did his school homework.

Belsize Park to Loughton was quite a trip – but nothing to someone like Ben who had, by then, made many more journeys. 'From the club it took me an hour to get to the school and we would invariably be late. It was very embarrassing because when we arrived, it was already in the midst of assembly and they had started singing.' Depending on public transport in the 1940s was a hazardous undertaking. Ben Helfgott, master of languages and chairman of Primrose, had to let his case be told. 'I asked to see the headmaster, Dr Priestley, and said we are Jewish and would he mind if we didn't take part in the assembly. Actually, I was sorry not to do so, because I liked joining in and singing the songs. But he excused us. He was very nice.'

The head was another of the inspirations of those years, a man who, long afterwards, signed a copy of his autobiography for Ben as a gesture of his appreciation of the boy's talents. 'We had some very fine people come in to see us. Not all were Jewish. But there was also a future Israeli Prime Minister, Moshe Sharett, who I remember spoke eight languages who visited us.' That was enough to impress the newly-elected Chairman of Primrose.

The club was affiliated to the AJY, the Association for Jewish Youth, so they had plenty of opportunities to mix with other kids of their faith, but who had lived in a different world. In a way, these newcomers to the Jewish youth scene became sort of mentors to youngsters from the indigenous clubs. Sports of all kinds were on their agendas – football, table tennis, cricket, athletics, swimming. All for Ben, except the swimming. 'We became partners of the AJY.'

This was always going to be more than just a boys' club. If it were only that The Boys needed partners to dance with, it was important that it was not what today would be called gender based. In those days, it was a simple matter of mixing the sexes – for this was a place where youngsters had to be taught how to relate to young women.

Girls did come. After all, for them it was a chance to meet boys – boys whom they hadn't known before and ones whom they before long got very used to being with. 'Several of our members married these girls', Ben remembers.

But it was not just a case of just mixing with (here comes that word again) the opposite sex. Strictly speaking, that is. Hardly a single Jewish family in Britain hadn't lost relatives, close or distant, because of Nazi oppression. But it was important that The Boys got to know others from outside of their 'family'.

Primrose, by then, had grown from an initial 35 members to several hundred. Young British-born people from the West Hampstead/Belsize Park area were invited to join and many did. Primrose offered activities and leadership like few other clubs outside the East End, the bastion of institutions that had become household names, like Brady and Oxford and St. Georges, both of which were also affiliated to the AJY.

Ben was not the only one who lived at the club. So did Harry Spiro. 'It set me up to open a shop and become a tailor. We did everything together and, when I had my shop, I would think, Yes, we lived there in one room and it was breakfast there and dinner. You weren't pushed into anything. It was a place to meet other people, who had the same problems and had gone through the same terrible things. Ben was completely different from the rest of us. He met a lot of people outside the club. He was involved with them almost right from the beginning.'

Life was changing for the refugees in all sorts of way. Some were, like Ben, beginning to go to school and some of them to start their first jobs. In that, he was also their counsellor. He put it like this: 'Primrose is a substitute for your lost families.' A substitute named not after a human being, but the local telephone exchange – PRImrose. Phone exchanges and human beings at the other end offered a lot more opportunities than the cold numbers of contemporary communications.

Harry Spiro says that the club was a 'life saver'. So, there was an all-out effort to support and help settle in. But it wasn't confined to sport or even counselling, although if you were a little bit clever you could work out the associations that were in Yogi's mind. He believed in the youngsters, while still spilling out their hearts, learning how to socialise. He did it in a way boys and girls, who 24 months earlier had been starving, had to discover, just as they had to learn to play on a sports field. He established what became known as the perfect coffee bar – serving only kosher food (there were religious youngsters among his flock).

The bar was legendary – thanks to the Viennese cook Mrs Mahrer, who Yogi discovered and was brought in to make the best pastries in London, and the kind of apple strudel you couldn't yet read about in English language cook books.

Harry Spiro describes Yogi – as if he needed to do so; the facts about him spoke for themselves – as a 'great influence'. As he says today: 'His priorities were to keep us fit, not just by us playing football, but by insisting on the observing of rules and regulations.' Surprisingly, Spiro says that, for all that, Mayer was no confidante or counsellor. 'He never did anything like that. But he was worried about how few girls there were in the club – to say nothing of how few there were, altogether, among the young survivors. So, in addition to the sports instructions, there were dancing lessons. Just to give The Boys a chance to meet local girls (mainly brought in from other, more conventional, youth clubs) and learn how to behave with them.

Ben was now sharing a room with another Polish-born survivor, Roman Halter, who was to become a world-famous artist. He would talk about 'going home' there. It was at the club that he met his friends, where he did his homework until about 10 o'clock every evening. It was where he had his supper between playing table tennis and doing homework, which not surprisingly he thoroughly enjoyed. 'It was a very nice supper. I also had breakfast there before going to school and took sandwiches made in the club for lunch.'

He doesn't forget easily, our Mr Helfgott. Table tennis is a particular memory – as we had already seen, but now it was no longer a 'weird' fantasy. I wondered if he had worked at the game as he was about to work at his other sports, in all probability he could have become a champion of the table. He doesn't think so. In fact, there are all sorts of reasons he advances for that not being 'on'. 'I didn't have the height', he explains. 'Well, the point is I always wanted to win, always tried to win. If I had carried on with table tennis, I would have got better and better, but I could not have taken it up seriously. However, what I lost in height, I made up in my jump. I jumped faster and faster.'

The fact is he has never allowed his five-foot, four-inch height be a barrier to anything, never allowed it to worry him. But a question arises. A great many survivors are short (by no means all, but a fair sprinkling of them). Could all those years of deprivation and incarceration have something to do with that, with living on a diet of foul-smelling soup and a crust of bread? 'No. I don't think so', he maintains. But his answer almost repeated and confirmed the question. 'There were some boys who were taller than I, the same age. When they came to Britain, they grew.'

Primrose only lasted for three years, although its presence in the Anglo-Jewish youth movement scene was immense and, in many ways, its influence lives on, certainly in the lives of its old members. But when the lease on the houses ran out, there was not enough money to buy anywhere else. Yogi went on to do a similar job in London's East End with the legendary Brady Boys Club – working with English Jewish youngsters, some of whom had other problems of their own. He did that job in the evenings, while during the day he was art and PE teacher at the Orthodox (which he was not) Hasmonean Boys School in north-west London. He then became Youth Officer for the London borough of Islington. Eight years before his death at the age of 98 in 2011, he wrote a book on Jews in the Olympics, in which he listed 400 Jewish medal winners. Among them, of course, Ben Helfgott, who would never forget his mentor, a man with an idea that took suffering stateless young Jews on the way to becoming productive British citizens.

Primrose was Mayer's legacy. Helfgott remains one of the legatees. 'I owe him a very great deal,' says Ben today. But while Mayer did so much to provide the new life that he and his fellow Boys would come to enjoy, had he wanted his members to forget their past (and there is no evidence that he did) he would have failed. 'It is always there,' Ben says.

Primrose was his life but so was his school. Economics and history were the subjects Ben liked best, alongside British Constitution. It was another reason for Ben to study British newspapers and now it was *The Times* on which he focused. This was not *The Times* of today, an attractive tabloid-shaped paper still regarded as the journal of record, but with brighter writing than 70 years ago – which was difficult for native Britons to penetrate, let alone people who were settling in to an entirely new country and culture. 'We had a teacher who told us about *The Times*. I started reading it and I have read it ever since.'

He also remembers reading the *New Statesman*, which today calls itself a magazine but then was an intellectual journal, offering current affairs with a distinctly leftward slant. He also read *The Economist*. Boasting? As I said, he just tells it as it is – and was.

Ben was brilliant at Plaistow and, no doubt about it, he knows he was. But to him, it's just one of those things, to quote a song probably sung and danced to around the record player at Primrose. On the other hand, he is not afraid to analyse what went into those achievements, successes that amazed envious other Boys. As one former member told me: 'We thought he was getting a little big-headed about it all, but before long, we accepted it was just him. He didn't think he was doing anything extraordinary – and neither do I believe he was boasting. We always talked about how we spent our days and that was what he was reporting.'

His 'reports' to the school were echoed by the ones from the school to him – had he had parents they would have spotted how clever their boy was; although they would have known that anyway.

He puts it down to memory. But memories can take you just so far. It was what was behind those memories that counted. The analysis of facts, again. But also there was the point, that despite getting facts down on paper, sometimes it took time to assemble those memories. He will actually say that his memory was not that good. So he had to find ways to compensate. It was a gift he has kept ever since. He knows certain facts. Events, dates and names are at the tip of his tongue. But sometimes that seems it's where they are going to stay. His method has been not to panic. Ten minutes later, they will come back. At least, it's just one of his methods.

Let him explain: 'I had five different subjects in the sixth form – economics, economic history, British constitution, German and geography. When it came to the final exam, it was geography that presented the problem.' Not that Ben didn't know what the examiners expected of him, but getting it down on paper in the limited time allowed to deal with the question in the final test was a different matter – a problem faced by most clever youngsters who know all the answers and want to put them down in the fullest detail if only the clock said they could do it. So he had to come up with a ready answer.

'I was very good at geography,' he remembers. 'I started writing the answer to the first question – which was about the effect on the economy of New Zealand after the introduction of the railway. Because I have a visual memory, I made a map and started putting down the names. I knew Auckland was the biggest city in the northern island. I knew the names of the rest, but I couldn't think of them. The map was blank in that vital regard. I was sitting there and I realised it had been 15 minutes and I hadn't even started writing. I thought I had better leave it. I'll write about it, but I won't use any of the names. While I was writing, I was all the time thinking about the names. I had to put the names down. And I couldn't recall them. I had finished three questions, but I had only half an hour to answer two more. I did that and stuck at it and just as the exam was about over, I remembered the names. I went out with a friend for a bowl of soup. I thought him extremely rude and insensitive when he laughed at my tale of woe. On questioning him he explained that I was so distraught that I was eating my soup with a fork and hadn't noticed!'

And that was it. The exam was passed. Higher Schools Certificate was his.

The schooling was – on paper, at least – the most important factor in establishing his future. It would open the doors to university and to all that would follow. Plaistow, in reality, formed the bedrock of Ben's own introduction to British society (of course, Margaret Thatcher was to say there was no such thing, but Ben would consider himself testament to the opposite argument). The idea of a grammar school summed up exactly what it was – an education denied to many others, boys and girls who might not have appreciated how lucky they were. He was now doubly lucky – a word he would never have used about himself and about his life up to that point. The incredible thing was that he was having an advanced schooling that normally would have required a selective test (the unloved '11 plus') to get in. He not only did well there. He did exceptionally well.

The hunch of the rabbi paid off and so did the faith the headmaster had in putting him up from the lower fifth to the next form. In that time English became, if not his mother tongue, then that of his adopted mother, Britain. He was a prefect at the school. All chalked up in the school records. It led to his being admitted to Southampton's University College (it would be some two years before the college became a university). To read economics.

He doesn't think it any great achievement, but one of the results of years as a prisoner is, paradoxically, a failure to accept any day as different from the one before. In a way, success one day followed by another – 24 hours later – is taken for granted.

So, bearing in mind his history, we now imagine what followed – that he was a brilliant success at Southampton, stood in his gown and mortarboard at the graduation ceremony as he collected his first class degree, amid the cheers of his friends who had made the journey to the south coast to view his amazing achievement.

Not quite. After a year at Southampton, he packed his bags and left. It wasn't that he wasn't doing well there in academic prowess or that his sporting talents were being ignored. He enjoyed his time at the college, made lots of friends and fitted in perfectly. But, he thought he could do better for himself. He was impatient – and had got a job as a clerk in a City firm. 'Of course, I now regret it', he says about the one blip in his life since arriving in Britain. The college regretted it immediately. A letter from Professor P. Ford (they didn't go for using first names in 1950) was kind and encouraging. The professor wrote: 'I quite understand the way you feel you should now be as independent as you can. You may rely upon us to help you by advice in any way we can. I am glad to know that you enjoyed your time at college and I hope it will remain one of your pleasant memories.'

It fitted in with his attitude to study and social life. Dr Priestley recognised that. When he left Southampton, Ben told him he wanted to be a teacher. Could he send him a reference? In 1951, Priestley did it – glowingly. Ben didn't take up teaching, but according to his old headmaster, he could easily have done so. He wrote then: 'I first came into contact with him shortly after the war in 1946 where, as a refugee, he entered the Plaistow County Grammar School, of which I was then headmaster. In spite of enormous difficulties including the necessity of learning English, he succeeded in a comparatively short time in obtaining not only his London University matriculation, but also in passing the High School Certificate examination. He was subsequently admitted to University College, Southampton, where he obtained exemption from inter B.Sc. Mr Helfgott is an earnest and keen student. When he was admitted to my school, I was struck by the rapidity with which he identified himself with it and his popularity with the other pupils. He made an excellent prefect, exercising his authority with understanding and very effectively. I have every confidence in his becoming a first rate teacher as he has always been interested in social work of every kind.'

All this would bear dividends when Ben applied – and obtained – British citizenship, which at the time was called being a British 'subject'. Dr Priestley was again a referee. But not the only one. 'A man from the Home Office came to see me and we talked British history.' Ben, who believes in telling a story as it is (or as it was), says: 'I overwhelmed him. Somehow, it came out in conversation. He just said, "I wish everybody knew what you know." We talked politics. I had picked up a lot from the *New Statesman*, but then I realised I couldn't read everything, so I switched to *The Economist*. The man came to me and I was teaching *him* British history.'

The pattern had really been set at Plaistow. Before long, he was actually *feeling* British – if parts of him could never be that. 'I have never felt a foreigner here apart from my first time as one of the Boys. People ask me how long have I been here – because I have an accent. I say I have been here for more than 70 years. And, remember, by the early 1950s, I had eight or nine languages at my disposal.'

Ask him what he gained from Southampton, he will say that it helped him develop into a man – not just a Holocaust victim. 'I'm not really very clever,' he insists unusually modestly. 'I have always been a serious student and I was there, too.' If it helped him to study, it also helped him to mature. It made him think seriously – that word again – about his future. A future, he decided, that would be in business. He yearned now to become a normal British youth. He was in the midst of the training that will never stop.

It was 1952 when Ben left the club life and the hostels in which he had spent all his time since arriving in Britain. He says that he didn't fend for himself with feelings of deprivation. 'We had everything. We didn't have a lot of clothing. We just lived from hand to mouth. When I later went to work, I went to lunch. I bought two rolls for a few pence and that was that. I never felt, though, that I was missing anything.'

He had girl friends. 'Of course, I liked girls,' he recalled. I was very normal in that respect.' So normal that he had been 'going steady' with one girl for five years. But it should have been clear that it wasn't going anywhere. In 1960, he started living with 'Sylvia'. Sylvia was a pretty redhead. She was an intelligent young woman – how could someone like Ben tolerate one who was not? – and it seemed they had a great deal in common. 'We were interested in a lot of the same things. She was knowledgeable about music and we went to concerts together. I liked all this – and the theatre. She was a very good cook. She spoke perfect French and Italian and was very good telling jokes. She was quite a character.'

But after a year he says he realised he was making a mistake. 'I realised we had problems.' It was a matter of what used to be called incomparability. But at first all was very good for them both. 'One of The Boys was giving a party to which we went. But after about 20 minutes she came up to me and said, "I'm so bored. Let's go." I said, "I have come here to be with my friends" and she said, "Who is more important?" So I said to her "come on. I'll take you home".

Then she said "I am so sorry." So I carried on with her but I decided that the longer I was going out with her, the more I wanted no more of it.'

One of the problems was Sylvia's parents. They didn't like the idea of their daughter getting involved with a Holocaust survivor. It was a problem apparently faced by other Boys. Somehow, for parents looking for nice Jewish sons for their daughter, being a survivor was not a recommendation for a marriage. 'Her mother said, "You don't know where he comes from. He's got nobody". Her mother wanted her to marry a doctor. Actually, she was quite a girl. 'She had been to university.' Her father was more enthusiastic about him. 'And they both decided they wanted to make a wedding. Her father said I had been invited so often to my friends' weddings that I should replicate one of them for myself.' But Sylvia said that was precisely what she did not want.

Ben had little or no enthusiasm for the idea, but agreed to take a step which, in many middle-class Jewish households, was considered to be the first move towards the marriage canopy, the 'chuppah'. 'She said her parents wanted to see me and that is what happened. I didn't want to get involved. But she had a lot in her favour.'

Later, when Ben did get married, she wrote him an angry letter. 'Why did you do it?' she asked. 'I loved you so much.'

There had been another girl in his life before he met Sylvia. That was in 1959 and he had not yet thought in terms of what for a time would be his philosophy – keeping away from Jewish women. The mother of 'Joan' was a doctor. 'I liked going out with her but one day she didn't turn up for a date – I had been invited somewhere and she was coming with me, but she wasn't at the place where we were to meet. I didn't want to see her again and she married someone else. She had been born in Canada and went there to live again. Suddenly, I had a letter from her, saying she wanted to see me again. We met again and I asked her why she hadn't turned up that day. She didn't have anything to say.

'Of course, I still used to go out with girls, but I was very careful with Jewish girls because I didn't want them to start thinking of marriage – I just wasn't ready to do that yet. But I went out with a lot of girls. Usually, we went to the cinema, but again not with the Jewish girls. I didn't want to get hooked.' What the girls thought was a different matter.

These days, Ben will admit that he was afraid that being tied to a woman would cramp his athletic style. There were also a couple of other things on his mind. For one thing, he had started his first job after deciding that the idea of being a city gent was not for him. He was now training for a job with one of the grand British companies, Great Universal Stores, headed by the Anglo-Jewish businessman and philanthropist Sir Isaac Wolfson. Ben soon became a branch manager in Watford.

# 16

## Weights

*'I can do that'*
*– Ben Helfgott*

The other thing on his mind was rather less exciting, one might think. He had taken up weightlifting. Taken up? He was entering into one of the outstanding chapters of his life.

Thinking about it, weightlifting is the last sporting activity you'd expect of a nice Jewish boy. Even less could you imagine such a physically draining activity as lifting outrageously heavy weights, the subject of a thousand cartoon films, with the plate-like discs either end of the sturdy metal bar on which the lifter depends before he can begin the job.

Actually, Ben Helfgott was not the first Jew to think he could be good at lifting weights – and doing pretty well at it. Until Ben came around, the most famous of them was the Polish (again) Siegmund Breitbart. If that fact surprises, so might the thought of this Jewish weightlifter also being a Jewish blacksmith. He probably realised that if he could lift a horse's leg, the irons that were the tools of a weightlifter's trade were easy meat.

In the 1920s Breitbart was regarded as a big star – not least among the Jews of America in general and New York in particular – after emigrating to what was not yet known as the Big Apple. What was already the biggest Jewish community in the world, having snatched that title from Poland with the big immigration of the late nineteenth century, took each show business personality – and for him, this was undoubtedly showbiz – to their hearts once they heard that they had the same genes as they did themselves. Al Jolson, Sophie Tucker and Irving Berlin had arrived on immigrant ships just a couple of decades earlier. The Gershwins were New Yorkers by birth, but that didn't matter.

Breitbart was an immediate hit. In 1923, 85,000 people helped him earn $7,000 in one week to see what the fuss was all about. Here was a fellow who billed himself, not as a weightlifter per se, but as a strong man. (Could anything appeal to Jews more? A strong man! So different from the legends.) He was certainly that. He had a number of specialties such as rolling half-inch thick metal bars into scrolls or hammering with one blow three-inch thick planks of wood or biting through chains. Houdini, another immigrant and son of a Hungarian rabbi, regarded him as competition, even though escapology wasn't Breitbart's game. Aged 35, he was six-foot, two inches tall, weighed 225 pounds with a 50-inch chest, 18-inch waist and a whole lot more statistics that were strictly for the enthusiast. He died in 1925 after an accident he, of all people, should have been able to avoid. A rusty nail pierced a thigh during a performance. Plainly, his eyes were not the strong man's strong point. Another theory was that he invited people to punch him in the stomach. One did and it killed him.

Ben, at five-foot, four-inches tall, weighing 154 pounds (11 stone) couldn't compete with Breitbart's achievements, which could be called, in effect, kinds of freak shows. What Ben Helfgott had set his sights on was purely sport, and one that he took so seriously it was a kind of science.

Not as impressive perhaps as the great illusionist or the Polish-American star, but even those figures were too much for the organisers of the sporting events he would enter. He was a lightweight (in athletic terms, that is). He had to lose six pounds in three days. 'I didn't eat as much.' On the Friday before the big event, he drank three glasses of water, two glasses on the Saturday and drank or ate nothing on the day of an event until he weighed in. Of course, doing without food was no novelty for him. But this was different. Just how different he never needed to explain.

But why was weightlifting his cup of tea (yes, he became very English)? It was during his long summer holidays from school that he decided to take up the sport. He would walk to a swimming pool in Hampstead Heath just a mile from Primrose in an effort to cancel the only sport in which he did not excel. But it was still no good. It was after finally getting out of the water that inspiration struck. He saw three young men and their coach lifting weights.

The truth was that, as in all the good stories, he said to himself, 'I can do that.' He had already wrestled there, but weight lifting?

Truth to be told, he didn't like wrestling – he thought it was brutalising and demeaning. As his son Maurice told me: 'Dad said, "I didn't like what it did to me. When someone plays unfairly, you know, they kick when you are not supposed to be kicked or pulls you away when you are not supposed to be pulled." His instinct was to fight back and to do stuff to the other person as well and he really didn't like it. Whereas what he liked about weightlifting was absolutely him. With the bar he could do what he wanted with no risk of hurting anyone. There was no competition. You lift the heaviest bar you can to win. If you don't lift the heaviest bar, you lose.'

But when he did first pick up a weight, it was all new to him. Ben Helfgott a weightlifter? Up to that moment it was something he hadn't thought of. 'I said to the coach, "Can I try to lift weights?" He looked at me and asked, "Have you ever lifted weights before?" I said, "No". He said, "Do you know how much these weigh?" I said, "Yes. 140 pounds."

That was quite a weight and the coach said no. He didn't know just how difficult it was to say no to this young man. But it would have been quite an effort to even pick up one of the set of weights, as if it were a bag of potatoes, let alone do it properly. Ben insisted. The man said, 'I'm not taking any responsibility.' So, as Ben put it, 'I went to one of the weights – and lifted it.'

It was a matter of instinct. Without a single lesson, he knew how to do the lifting and put that instinct into practice. 'No effort was required. To me 140 pounds required no effort at all. From then on, it was what I wanted to do. Before long, the 140 pounds had become 180. Then I added another five. After that, it was not quite so easy. I struggled and that was it. The record for lifting weights like this was 209 pounds, which was not all that far off.'

The coach was suitably impressed and decided to start a weightlifting class. Meanwhile, Ben had told Yogi Mayer about it. He suggested that his protégé should go to the next Olympic Games or, at least, the 'Jewish Olympics', the Maccabiah. But he couldn't go. No matter how important that was to him, his school studies had to come first and there was no way of his having the time .

He went in for trials, however. There were four other boys in his class. He told the judge that he would start with an attempted weight of 190 pounds. 'Who is this boy?' he heard one of the other competitors ask. He was already trying to break the British record by half a pound – 210 of them altogether. 'Your had to have your head straight. I lifted quite easily and came first. And that was how it first started.' His training – although like a musician, he would never stop practising – lasted a year and a half.

Weightlifting is something of a mystery to people who have never picked up barbells in their lives and have no ambition to do so. It seemed to lack the excitement of athletics, the glamour of Wimbledon tennis, the gentlemanly clapping at a Lord's test match and certainly the cliff-edge tension when Spurs and Arsenal are drawing minutes before the end. Ben, however, has never doubted he made the right choice.

'It was a sport that depended entirely on me. It was the weight and I. I liked playing tennis but I always had to find someone to play with me and was always concerned whether he or she would be available when I wanted to play. I had no trouble with weightlifting. All I needed was the body and the weights – and when I started to play, I had both. I improved very quickly as much as anything because I was writing everything down and learned. It also gave me stamina and determination – but I would never overdo it. I trained three times a week after school and then work.' Which I suppose would be a question of objectivity. To anyone watching the Helfgott progress, it could appear that he was obsessed with his choice of sport.

And that was the crucial point when it came to being 'hooked', as he called it, to a woman. 'I wanted to become a British champion and I became a British champion. And the Olympics were not far away. I thought I would train more seriously than ever. The following year, the championships were going to be in a series of different countries and I thought it would be a good opportunity to travel – none of my friends were travelling in those days.'

He was making serious – you could call them 'weighty' – plans for the not so far future. 'I thought that after 1956, I will finish, and then I heard that there were going to be championship games in Moscow and before that in Warsaw.' The Communist countries had realised that their all-encompassing devotion to most sports – including weightlifting – was marvellous publicity for their countries and their culture. As the world found out, they were not wrong as far as sports were concerned, but exporting their way of life and their culture to the West was going to be another thing altogether. It was indeed a strange paradox. The Cold War was close to freezing point, but sport was opening a few doors, even though the doors that both President Eisenhower and First Secretary Malenkov, who had succeeded Stalin, had most in mind were on the bomb bays that could at any moment open for a hydrogen bomb to be dropped.

Ben was now entering more and more championships and before long, he was British lightweight weightlifting champion, breaking records all the way – from 210 to 248 pounds. Now here comes the strange thing. 'Does that record still stand, 60 years later?' I asked. 'I don't know if it still stands', he says. There was a reason for that slight but significant doubt, apparently. The Helfgott category has been abolished. And, he says, he was responsible for that happening. It was a question of the judges who decided these things. 'There were usually three judges, which meant that the winner was chosen two to one, if not three-all. I, for instance, by the time of the championships, had developed a style of my own and it was difficult to see the way the body was moving. Sometimes they saw and sometimes they didn't.'

So what *was* the right way? 'The weights should be lifted straight up without the lifter moving – although it looked as if he was, because in a second the lifters would shoot up. I was very good at this, but sometimes I passed and sometimes I didn't. I said, We can't keep going on like this, because there were complaints all the time. But we did away with it.'

From that point on, it gets a little technical and a matter of learning a new vocabulary. 'We did away with the two-hand press – and the snatch and the clean and the jerk remained in. So everything changed.' I tried to get to understand the words, which I was assured were *all* clean. The 'snatch', for instance. 'It means lifting the weight in one movement. You use your body as you lift.'

For Ben, the important thing was that he was engaged in the sport he loved (no other term will suffice here). The love brought appreciation from other experts in the field. Then there was an official from the British Amateur Weightlifting Association. One of their officers ruled that Ben could become a coach when he was 19 (this was now 1948). There was never any money due for his weightlifting. He was going to the Olympics in London that year. When he attended the world championships in Stockholm, he paid his own fare.

All the time, he was training four to six hours a week, either at the nearby Maccabi building or at a local school. Weightlifters today would regard his regimen as too easy. To achieve the status that came to Ben, they are expected to train every day.

The Weightlifting Association appoints judges. Ben explained the procedure to me. The judges go to a club or other centre for where a championship is being competed. 'You have to go to the person dealing with the events and tell him what sort of lift you are intending. Then others follow. You can't go down, you can only go up.' In other words, previous achievements continue to count – until they are followed by a higher score. The best competitors like to see what others have achieved before going to the judges themselves. If those judges know that a competitor is up to breaking a British record, they pay special attention.

Ben had already become British champion, before he started breaking records. The British championship was achieved in 1954 in a competition in Stockport. It was the eleven stone championship – in other words, the contest for men weighing 11 stone, which Ben did.

All the time he was doing this, he had to think about his health. Anyone without his training would have risked getting a hernia. But Ben got one just the same. It wasn't caused by lifting weights, he maintained, it came from 'stretching', obviously part of his own weightlifting manner.

In 1952, he entered London's Royal Free Hospital, just a hop and a jump from Belsize Park, for surgery on his appendix. He was not a good patient. The day after the operation, he got out of bed and made a handstand. But a nurse was not impressed. She shouted, 'You mustn't do that yet.' But Ben was having none of that and, even now, when he makes up his mind, nothing, but nothing, was going to get him to change his mind. 'I could control my movements completely.' He was sent home early because he was considered by the surgeon to be well enough. One cannot help thinking there could be other reasons, like his determination to get out. Or the hospital couldn't wait to get rid of him.

And the training went on. But training didn't mean lifting weights. It is a system that he continues to this day. 'It is far from weightlifting. It is using every part of my body. I exercise to keep my muscles in shape. Also standing exercises. I work every part by bending, stretching, everything. Competition is training for fitness. For fitness you don't have to lift heavy weights to make progress. You can't avoid some illnesses. The fact I did what I did was partly due to luck.'

It was also a paean to the Holocaust victims. There were those who doubted that there could be a connection and even if there was, no refugee from the camps could have the health or stamina to see it through – apart from the obvious one, of a survivor being an athlete of Olympic standard. But he knew all along that it was important that a link be made for others to know about. 'I felt', he said at the time, 'as if I was representing all the Holocaust victims whose talent had not been allowed to come to fruition'.

But even he knows the limitations. 'The body needs a rest.' As in Israel where the rule is that Jewish farmers should give the soil a 'holiday' every seven years. It is there where religious kibbutzim make a formal sale of land, so that the biblical law can be averted. 'I compare it to maintaining a car. A car needs oil as we need food. If you look after your car, the car lasts longer. If something goes wrong, you have it repaired. If the body goes wrong, you try to treat it.'

He was travelling a great deal now – taking part in competitions and seeing other athletes at work. He competed in the 4th Maccabiah in 1953, the World Championship in Vienna in 1954 and again in 1955 in Munich. An important competition overseas was the one in Warsaw in 1955. Ben decided he wanted to go. It would be his first visit to Poland since that second trip back to Piotrkow. 'I knew I wanted to go very badly but people were saying "You're crazy. They won't let you out." Some said I was only a child [he was]. I wrote a letter to the secretary [of the weightlifters Association] and said that if I were held up in Poland, it would be against my will. I thought I would be all right. The organisers here in Britain were mainly Communists and the chief organiser was a Jew.' So Ben went.

Ben's trip caught the wider public's attention. For the first time, the media became aware of the name Helfgott. A BBC producer interviewed him about an early trip back to Poland. The war was now a memory. Poland was on the other side of what Winston Churchill told the world to call the Iron Curtain. 'I told him exactly what I thought. It was summer and there were no children running around without shoes. I knew there were 1,000 excellent schools I had heard about. But, of course, there was another side. When I met a Polish man for the first time since I had lived there, he turned around before he would answer my questions. When we finished the BBC interview, the presenter gave me an envelope. He said it was my fee for doing the interview – about £15. A lot of money at the time. I protested that I was just an amateur and, therefore, didn't need to be paid.'

The following year, it was in Germany – Munich, to be precise – the city that sparks terror in Jewish minds for the rise of Hitler which began there; and then, a few years later, for the murder of Israeli athletes in the 1972 Olympic Games.

He believes he was the last person to see the Israelis before their killing by the Black September terrorist group. 'I was with them until about 1.30pm, speaking and drinking coffee. Then, at 7.30am I was woken by a phone call, telling me they had been taken hostage. I've never forgotten them.' Even with that experience, coupled with his own suffering, nothing will allow him to hate all Germans. 'If I started hating every German, I'd start to hate other people and I refuse to fall into that trap.'

He had wanted to go to the Olympics in 1957, but he had an injury that put paid to the idea.

'I was manager of a Wolfson store. We had 40 salesmen who were in cars. They were earning about £7 a week. From time to time I went out myself to see how well the salesmen were doing. There was one customer who hadn't paid his bill for a month. I knocked on her door. She came out and accidentally closed the door behind her. She couldn't get back in. I saw there was a window open on the floor above. I told her, "I'll get you in straight away. Don't you worry." Quickly, I managed to shin up to the open window. I tried to put my hand down to the window, but I slipped.' For once, the athlete had made a mistake. 'I fell and my hand was bleeding heavily. I was rushed to hospital, where they said I had to have an immediate operation. I was in hospital for two weeks.' It was 1957. Soon after returning home, he was invited to compete in a meeting in Moscow. 'I was there for three weeks. I had the time of my life.'

Going to the Soviet Union and meeting people was rare in those comparatively early Cold War days. But Ben did both. 'I met a lot of young people and when they discovered that I was Jewish, they came running to me. They told me what was going on.' Jewish life was difficult under Stalin. Synagogue services were attended only by the elderly. Jewish organisations were banned. They were not allowed to emigrate. 'They came round to meet me at the choral synagogue. I asked them how Jews were getting on. They were all silent and I told them, "Your silence tells me exactly what is happening here". One of them tapped me on the back.' There were thousands of people gathering where Golda Meir, Israel's first ambassador to the Russians, attracted 100,000 Jews, more than had gathered in any Soviet location since the 1917 Revolution.

One of the many events he was to go to were those 'Jewish Olympics', the Maccabiah. The Maccabiah was an act of faith. An act to which Ben Helfgott subscribed. Others went to Israel out of pure Zionism. Some went because their religion called them. Ben Helfgott, Jewish to his core, went for sport. To him, a man who, since 'recovering' from the Holocaust had restricted his formal Jewish observance to three days a year in the synagogue and family gatherings on Friday nights and Passover, it was a combination of all three. But his pure faith was in sport. The Maccabiah gave him all the opportunities he could possibly imagine.

He was still at school when the 1948 War of Independence broke out as armies and air forces of five Arab countries invaded the new country just after it had been declared by David Ben Gurion, head of the Jewish Agency (the unofficial Jewish 'government' set up under the British Mandate for Palestine, and now the first Israeli Prime Minister).

He told an English teacher that he was leaving school to emigrate to Israel. The teacher begged him not to go. 'They're fighting out there', she said. 'I intend to go and fight', he answered. 'I liked her very much, but I said it was something I had to do.' 'I would like to talk to you more about that', she said. And then she admitted defeat. 'I can see that I can't persuade you.' But she told him he had exams in three months and should wait until they were over. By then, the war was over. So he thought about it again.

At 18, he hadn't quite 'made aliyah', as the phrase for moving to Israel now goes. He had to content himself with going to the country as an athlete. The 1950 Maccabiah games were his first international competition. It was just six weeks after the first time he had ever competed – at a session at London's Maccabi club, a stone's throw from Primrose in Compayne Gardens in West Hampstead. He was lifting more than his own body weight. He weighed 154 pounds and was lifting 260. To train and to lose some of that body weight – he was five pounds heavier than he should have been – he tried all he could to sweat it off. He would go to the famous Parliament Hill Fields, very popular then and now with upper middle class families walking their immaculately kept dogs, run around and practiced the shot put and discus. 'It was very hot at the time and I used to wrap towels around me to make me sweat even more.' Small he might be, but he was all muscle, in perfect tone. He had to keep his measurements but lose weight at the same time. Israel awaited him. 'When we British athletes arrived, the stadium was not yet ready. They finished it an hour before we were due to be there and start.'

The little money that he had went on travelling – to sports events. Such as going to the 1956 Olympic Games in Melbourne. And going to Israel for the first time in 1950. That anyone was able to go there was virtually due to one man, Pierre Gildesgame (real name Hildesheim) who was a cousin of one of Ben's uncles. He was known as Mr Maccabiah and without him the Games would never have happened, certainly for a British team. Collections were made within the Anglo-Jewish community to raise the money to send the Maccabiah athletes to Tel Aviv. Ben contributed £15 himself.

Inevitably, it was a country that, as exemplified by the world-famous Yad Vashem memorial – now a combination of museum and shrine – relives the Holocaust every day of the year. Ben went to Tel Aviv and its nearby Ramat Gan stadium – then a poor area hardly a shadow of the place today. It was an opportunity, not just to practice his sport and win medals, but also to meet people, some related, all part of his family. Just like The Boys, every survivor was indeed his family.

'I came across survivors, mostly a little older than I, and in most cases these were people who had got married and many of them were doing very well. They were people who came from families of shoemakers and tailors and some of them were now doctors and lawyers. It convinced me of how the world would have been so much better had not six million Jews been murdered. What they achieved for Israel could have been done for countries all over the world. It is not a point made often enough.'

There had been two Maccabiahs (Maccabiot, in Hebrew) before the Second World War. Ben went to what was the third, the one held in Israel in 1950. It seemed like the challenge of a lifetime when Ben competed in the games on behalf of Great Britain, the country of which he now felt completely a part . The country, then two years old, bore all the signs of an infant, born in poor circumstances, which was just learning to walk. 'They were so poor and when we went there, we lived poor, too. There was no sugar for our Wisotski tea [the local brew, now much improved and much liked]; no coffee. And there was no meat.' As for other necessities of life, such as toilet paper, forget it. We had to use newspapers.' Of them, there was no shortage. Already, Israel had a reputation for having more of its population reading papers than any other country in the world.

If those conditions were bad, try the difficulties of the athletes who were there to make the Maccabiah what they hoped it would be. Not exactly the Olympics, but still the organisers hoped and expected them to be very much the 'Jewish Olympics', with Jewish athletes from all over the world, even from behind the Iron Curtain. 'It was worse for us. They actually didn't have the equipment, the weightlifting equipment. Can you believe that? We had to borrow weights from the Americans. I was very disappointed because I hadn't taken into account what was going on in that country.'

A land building itself up by the proverbial boot straps and sports were not at the top of the nation's priority lists. Music, yes. The Israel

Philharmonic, which had been founded as the Palestine Symphony Orchestra, already had an international reputation, with people like the young Leonard Bernstein adding his talents in the 1948 War of Independence and on numerous later occasions. Athletes were not yet the respected species that was perhaps expected by a violinist or piano virtuoso. 'The people were absorbed with themselves because they were looking for homes and jobs. You asked them questions and they answered "What do you want?"'.

They didn't care about the morés of the sort of society to which Ben had already come to expect and respect. Such as good manners. 'I remember there were some cars on the roads, but not many. I was used to queueing for buses in England, so when I waited for a bus, I assumed I was first in the queue. I was 20 years old then. Two young men, who must have been two or three years older than I, pushed in front of me. They jumped in and I went for them. I had been waiting for a long time and now I was going to be late for something or other. So I pulled them out and one of them came at me with a knife. I was very lucky because some other people came and separated us.'

Nevertheless, Israel was exciting for Ben. An international sporting occasion at last. Another British competitor, the fencing champion Alan Jay, was luckier, as far as the sidebars of the Maccabiah were concerned. Things, as Ben recalls, were so bad that there was no accommodation 'in hall' as university students might have called it. 'Our team were housed in private homes, looked after people we knew as 'Auntie and Uncle'. These 'relatives' all lived in Haifa, where the fencing bouts were taking place. 'Food was in short supply and we brought them baskets of food.' Of course, that was not part of Ben's experience. The two men, Helfgott and Jay, did not meet at that time but both were involved in the Big Event of the 1950 Maccabiah. Says Jay: 'We went into the stadium, looked around at the flags of the participating nations, but couldn't find the Union Jack. They didn't have one at Ramat Gan, but we found one available at Tel Aviv.'

Knowing one in the big city was one thing. Getting to the stadium was another. There was also the problem of the traffic between the two areas. 'There was one solution to making the stadium in time. We put the flag in an ambulance – and it was allowed to race through the traffic to the stadium.'

The results were not outstanding. But, then, the motto of the organisation's Big Brother, the Olympics, does say that the spirit of the Games is not the winning but the taking part and this was an unquenchable spirit.

Things would be easier in the Maccabiot in which Ben took part in the following years. They now had a chance to see how the country was maturing and how much better were the conditions under which they operated in 1950 – when the hot weather almost got the better of them. The food was better – even though Ben was overweight, even while existing on what were hardly luxurious diets. He weighed 154 pounds, six pounds more than he should have been in his class. In the end, he got to the right weight. He says it was easily done. Nevertheless, it was something of a battle.

He won. Six weeks after his very first competition in London.

He was to compete in two more Maccabiah Games in 1953 and 1957. And he won each of those too. That was three gold medals. After that first win at the beginning of a new decade, he could have thought there was only one other place to go. And he went. To compete in the Olympic Games.

# 17

## Olympics

*'When you have done something which you love, you don't stop'*
*– Ben Helfgott*

The Olympic Games would be the pinnacle of Ben's sporting activities.

November 22 1956 was a dreary very late autumn day in London. At the Melbourne cricket ground, scene of the first ever Games to be held in the Southern Hemisphere, it was gloriously sunny. Spring was about to give way to summer – ideal weather for sporting events; not too hot and not too cold – although Melbourne had a reputation for having a somewhat fickle climate, cold rain and equatorial heat all on the summer day. The storytellers would abandon fears of being accused of using cliches, but would have described it as a 'red letter day'. It was also Ben's 27th birthday.

The Olympics moved to Melbourne – still in the Commonwealth, but a different place altogether. It was not like London at all – no sign of the food rationing that was to remain in Britain until 1954; no bomb sites that had still not been filled in. By universal agreement, Melbourne was fairly provincial, but the sun shone a *lot* of the time while Europe shivered and new immigrants still benefiting from assisted passages were increasing the population with considerable effect (the '£10 Poms' scheme was intended to encourage Britons to travel to 'Down Under' 80,000 of them in one year alone).

Previously, Australia's place in world sport had come from the 'Ashes' Test cricket series. Now, the decision of the World Olympic Committee to award the Games to Melbourne put the city and the country firmly on the map. Ben wanted to be a dot on that map and because of the championship that was already his, he got his wish. The Maccabiah gold medal the year before couldn't have hurt.

There was achievement enough in being selected – astonishingly for anyone who didn't know the Helfgott philosophy or the way he interpreted it – nine years after the horrors of the Holocaust. To Ben himself, it was almost a natural thing. He knew he could do it, so he did.

The ambition had, when he thought about it, been with him since he was eight years old. He was shown a pamphlet about the Olympics in Los Angeles and the idea took root. 'I read that a Pole had won the 10,000 metre race. He was a champion.' The Polish press was beyond excitement. For this eight year-old, it was like reading about men reaching the moon decades later.

It was all he could think of. 'When I read about it, I said to the boys I played with, "Let's see who can run longest". There was a square and we ran around it. They all fell about and I could hardly breathe. I wasn't going to give in. I had determination.' It was that which has carried him through his life.

He may not have seriously thought it or talked about it, but perhaps that was when he began to wonder...Could it? Would it? How? And then went back to his studies, going to the cinema, reading the newspapers and, above all, leading the kids of Piotrkow and proving he could run faster, play better football and jump higher than they could. Children have dreams and if this were one, it was as unlikely to happen as the German were about to invade Poland.

It might also have been the start of his training for higher things, although he would not have known it then. As he told me, 'I was not just fanatical about sport, I was fanatical about learning about sport.'

Melbourne was the third Games since the Nazi Olympics of 20 years earlier. But it was also the year of the failed Hungarian revolution and the Suez disaster both at virtually the same time, and was undoubtedly the opportunity of all time for him. The athletes were looked after better than they were in Israel for the Maccabiah. No luxuries, but the accommodation was better and the food quality didn't compare.

'Actually, the Australians built houses for all the athletes. We were sharing a building, the British teams – the weightlifters, the runners and jumpers and two gymnasts.' They all had rooms to themselves – luxuries that had been unknown in Tel Aviv. And the food they were served? 'Terrific', says Ben. 'We had all kinds of food, whatever we liked. It was really amazing.'

They had two weeks to enjoy their single rooms and the 'terrific' food before the opening ceremony with the Duke of Edinburgh performing the necessities of the traditions.

Those ten days before the Queen's husband went on duty were perhaps the most enjoyable part of the trip, for Ben at least. 'It was the first time I could relax and I could eat all the food I wanted.' For someone of Ben's experience it was more than merely memorable. It also gave time for training without any pressure.

When it came to the competitions themselves, he did well enough. 'My first lift was the 235 press and I already had the record of 236 pounds.' The record on the press was at this time 236 pounds and Ben broke the record for five minutes with 248 pounds but was beaten by other lifters.

Prince Philip had come from what was still called the 'Mother country' to open the Games and the ceremonial oil container was lit to signify business had begun. The athletes, every one of them, in those days strictly amateurs, marched past. Ben was among the smart British contingent, blue blazer, white trousers and straw Panama hats. He was captain of his country's six-strong weightlifting team.

It was an almost unbelievable moment. Now the former starving Buchenwald inmate was seeing life which to him seemed to be at its best. At the head of a group of men who, arguably, had to be among the fittest, and certainly the strongest, athletes of them all. It was truly an incredible situation. As he told David Epstein for that *Sports Illustrated* interview: 'Eleven years ago, I was at the point of death.' Now he had the strength to lift a total of 748 pounds. In three lifts.

The winner was, inevitably, competing for the Soviet Union, Ihor Rybak. 'A lovely man', Ben remembers.

It was the first Games in which he competed, but the third he attended. As a spectator, he had been at both the London and Helsinki Olympics – and wouldn't miss another until 1976.

By the 1952 Olympics in Helsinki, the world was finally recovering from the effects of the war. For Ben Helfgott the scars were still there and would never go away, even if he had wanted them to – which he did not; the memories were as fresh as ever and there were so many who did not have the shelter of all-encompassing passions as he did for sports. Not just to be active in the ones that attracted him. No, just being active would never be enough. He had to excel in them. He had to be the best. He had ambition. And he had to see the best. He would have dreamed of being in the British team, but he had just before those Games had his appendix operation and lifting weights would have been impossible.

I would have thought that lifting weights to an Olympic standard would have been a no-go area for anyone who had been in a concentration camp, but he was adamant that that was not so. 'To be a weightlifter', he explained, 'you have to have three things that are imperatives. You have to have a lock. I was very strong, the strongest for my age, but I didn't have that lock. I had to jack it – to keep straight – to keep straight while bending. I didn't have the ability to lock my arm in a certain position. The other thing is you need to have is the position – be in a position, to be in a situation to hold the weight, the centre of gravity of which has to be in the middle of your body. If not, it will bring you down. I need to have hip and shoulder mobility, which I haven't got.'

The question then arises, how could he possibly succeed in his chosen sport? 'To be able to lift heavy weights you have to have lift.' Not as simple as you might think. 'You won't see anyone doing that these days because it is much more difficult. But it is lighter to do, just the same. When you lift it, you then come down with the weight. If I could have done it the other way, I would have been world champion.'

So without competing he had to content himself with being a mere spectator – not an easy thought.

As always, he was being influenced by the athletes, in whose place he now yearned to be. One was the Ukranian-born Jewish weightlifter Novak who, after an amazingly successful career, was, in Ben's words 'going down', although he finished up second. Ben discovered he spoke Yiddish and immediately felt close to him – perhaps too close for Mr Novak. 'I used to go up to him and stand by him. It could have been difficult for a Russian athlete to be seen with one from Britain.' He asked the older man (actually, only about five years older) if he felt endangered. 'He looked at me and said, "I am not afraid of anyone." He was a tough guy.' But not so tough not to die in 1980 in his mid 50s.

'He liked to drink and went to the local pubs. He ordered one drink after the other and somebody said to him: "You are a Jew. I will not drink with Jews." Novak said, "I have not heard you. Say it again." The man did say it again and he got hold of him[the other man] and threw him out. The man broke his hand. The Russians were getting better by then and didn't need him as badly as before. So after the pub incident, it was the end. They didn't want him.'

Helsinki had seen a roller coaster of a war. Fighting one with Russia, invaded by the Germans, and then occupied by the Nazis who had become allies of a sort. Then in 1944, they signed an armistice with the Allies. For a second time, the country became part of the Soviet 'sphere of influence'. After taking a huge indemnity from their Russians neighbours, who also demanded ten per cent of Finnish territory. For years afterwards, the Soviet economy dominated the country.

Russia, in either its Tsarist guise or as the Soviet Union, had not competed since 1912. Now the Helsinki Olympics in 1952 gave the Soviets a chance of international respectability.

What Ben remembered was that it was difficult to talk to any Russian or citizen of one of its allies or satellites. 'They were under instruction not to meet anyone.'

As we have seen, Ben found a chance to override that ban. There were actually two Russian Jewish weightlifters. But they were not the only athletes from the Soviet Union whom he met. 'I somehow could talk to anyone because at that time I was very good at languages.' There were only two countries where he admits he found their languages difficult, Japan and South Korea. 'I loved going there. I had the chance to go to every Olympic event at that time, because I was a member of the International Weightlifting Association. I made lots of friends.' He has a philosophy about that. 'When you have done something which you like, you don't stop. Because once you stop, you are on the way down.'

Of course, Ben had always had the ambition to one day represent his new country in the most important festival of sport the world had ever known. Now all he wanted was to be in the parade of athletes and show that he was good as any of them – and better than most. He might have dreamed of that. But he couldn't be sure it would happen. That he would be the captain of a section of the British team was beyond dreams.

His activities became the pride of the Jewish community in Britain. The *Jewish Chronicle* recorded his exploits and, first, his preparations for Melbourne, the place where his dreams came true. When the Games ended, Ben had come 13th in the weightlifting events. 13th out of 32.

He was third in the two hand press events. There was a disappointment in that. They didn't award medals in that class then. Now they do. 'If they had had that classification in 1956, I could have got a bronze. But, unfortunately, not then.' It would have been nice if the man who would be British champion for seven years could have got a 'gong'.

Of all his proud fans, the most enthusiastic were The Boys. Harry Spiro says: 'We thought it was a great triumph. He showed his strength, determination and talent.' But there were no parties or other celebrations. 'By then, all The Boys had their own lives to live and their own problems to sort out.'

In 1958, he entered the Commonwealth Games in Cardiff and gained a bronze medal. He said at the time: 'Sport brings people together. There's no place for differences. It's a place where you overcome bigotry and racial prejudice because you learn about each other on the playing field.'

If anyone doubted how successful the trip was, the fact that he was selected – again as captain – for the squad at the 1960 Games in Rome disabused them of those queries. But it didn't have either the thrill or the success of 1956. He was down to 18th in those Olympics, but it was a different ball game, to slightly confuse the metaphors. This was the year when the Iron Curtain was just partly lifted, so there was more East European competition than before.

He plainly didn't have an easy ride. Not easy at all. 'There were 37 or 38 people competing in my class. We started at 8am and didn't finish till 5pm in the afternoon.' All in the almost overpowering heat of a Roman summer. But that wasn't the only problem.

There was the question of his weight – once more. Yet again, he was slightly overweight and yet again he had to diet. 'For three days, I only ate very little, light meals, and only one cup of water for the first two days and nothing at all on the third day.' It was no way for an Olympic athlete to start doing his thing, as they might say more than half a century later. Of course, it could be thought that he had performed super-human tasks in the factories and camps where he worked in the Holocaust years on much less adequate diets than he was observing up to a couple of days before. But, as anyone who has experienced fasting, as he still did on Yom Kippur, knows, even one day without food is extraordinarily debilitating. He was in a no-win situation. 'Dieting like that takes away a lot of your strength.' He was stating the obvious, perhaps. Surely, it was not at all good for anyone.

But he did beat the weight problem and went on for his first lift with a 32-inch waist and a 42 chest measurement. But if he could face up to not eating, suffering the heat was still another matter. 'There was no air conditioning in the hall where we did our lifting. I was sweating like a pig.' Even this wasn't the end of the difficulties. He says: 'The other problem was all the waiting that was involved. My first attempt was 242 pounds. I did that and then, after that, I had to wait more than half an hour before it was my turn to go on again, because other people were still finishing off. Every time, I thought it was my turn, there was more waiting. There was always someone still doing their thing and making mistakes, so they were doing it again and again. By the time I had to go to take my second attempt – it was going to be 253 pounds, which would have been a record – I couldn't do it. I did my first and second lifts. It was something I didn't enjoy because of the conditions.' That was how he came only 18th in Rome.

It was the end of Ben's competitions in the Olympics, but not his interest in the Olympic movement or his participation as a spectator. The run ended when politics entered the Games. In 1980, when the ones in Moscow were boycotted by more than 60 countries – ironically because of the Soviet invasion of Afghanistan – the habit was broken. And he wasn't happy about it. 'I had bought my tickets.' The Americans had requested people not to go but for long Ben seemed determined to take no notice of them and still make the trip to the Soviet capital. 'People asked me, "Are you going to the Olympics?" I told them I was. They said, "You, of all people, should not go". I said, "I don't think it right to prevent sportsmen from going to the Olympic Games. They had worked so hard to enter. This is their lives and if they train and are lucky to go". But in the end he submitted to the pressures that were being brought on him by British Olympic officials and stayed at home.

He decided to go to the next Games in Los Angeles in 1984. But then it was family – and a surprising reason for Ben – and religion that stepped in to stop his visit. 'It was my son Nathan's barmitzvah. I was really torn about that. My wife said I should go and she would look after things, but in the end I decided my duty was to be at home and support my son. Not that there could be any competition. Of course I wanted to be at my son's barmitzvah.'

There had been other things that were occupying his mind since he first competed. Other issues that would take preference over the things that not long before had seemed paramount to him, as essential as eating and drinking (when he was not on a diet, that is). He was becoming successful in business, running a clothing factory. Business was good. 'I was thoroughly enjoying it.' Which maybe would seem surprising. Here was a man who was considered – and doubtless considered it himself – an intellectual who lifted heavy books as often as he worked with heavy barbells, bothering with the fashion styles of women. 'It wasn't that', he said. 'I enjoyed travelling and meeting people and then the idea of running a business and using my mathematics to work with figures was fascinating to me.' Also, he wanted to spend much more spare time working with The Boys. And, most significantly of all, he was modifying his objections to dating Jewish girls. Or, rather, one particular Jewish girl – and, what's more, the idea of marrying. Marrying Arza, that is.

22. With Sir 'Ziggy' Sternberg, 2005.

23. Together with Avner Sharlev at the inauguration of the Teachers' Garden at Yad Vashem, given by the '45 Aid Society.

24. Dedication of the ambulance in Israel donated by the '45 Aid Society.

25. Chatting with Prince Charles.

26. 2012: Receiving his Honorary Doctorate from the Institute of Education, University of London.

27. Ben with Holocaust survivor and historian Elie Wiesel. Also with Simon Reis and Jeffrey Pinnick. All three served as Chairmen of the Board of Deputies Yad Vashem Committee.

28. Ben with Prime Minister David Cameron at 10 Downing Street, London.

29. General Petrenko in London to commemorate the 50th anniversary of the liberation of Auschwitz.

30. In discussion with Professor Yehuda Bauer.

31. Ben with the President of Latvia.

32. Reunion time: Halina Heu (left), one year above Ben at school and Ruta Horowitz (right) the only one other than Ben to survive from Ben's school class of 1939 in Piotrkow. Arza is in the centre.

33. With the England football team on the eve of their departure to play in Poland.

arry Spiro and Nathan Helfgott.

35. With the first cousins Katriel Klein and Gershon Klein.

t the 50<sup>th</sup> anniversary of the Melbourne pic Games, 2006.

37. Enjoying the London Olympic Games, 2012.

38. Having received an honorary doctorate from the University of Cumbria.

39. The Helfgott family, 2006.

# 18

## Arza

*'He doesn't like being part of jokes. He is a serious man.'*
*– Arza Helfgott*

Ben used to meet other Holocaust survivors to talk about their histories. Later, their children would come with them. They had to understand how those new Englishmen – now justly to be called 'The *Men*', though they never would be – were adapting to the country of their new citizenship. They never held back in their talks. 'If one of them said "Shut up, you don't know what you're talking about", they took it in good part.'

It was at one of these sessions that he came to meet Arza from Bulawayo. It was she who remembered: 'My mother and I went to see my sister in Israel. I went to England in 1965. After a few months my mother visited me on her journey home to Bulawayo. My qualifications [as a pharmacist] were accepted here so I could practice straight away. Certainly there would be no funds for me without working. I worked very hard before leaving Rhodesia to get the fare and to have enough to support myself.' Arza had come to work and use the opportunity to travel in Europe before returning home. 'Sometimes I wonder how I did it. I knew no-one here but as luck would have it a chance meeting with close friend Becky in South Africa eighteen months earlier, and hospitality from Moishe and Jessie her cousin in London, turned my life on to a new path.'

'Moishe, one of The Boys, married a girl from South Africa,' Ben recalls. 'One Saturday, I was passing where they lived and I thought I would knock on the door and go in and see them. It was around 12 o'clock. Moishe was at home alone. He excitedly asked if I would like an introduction to a nice young girl. Moishe immediately put a call through to Arza and an invitation to tea followed. Soon Arza and I began dating.'

It wasn't a simple invite to tea. Ben had to think of his present girlfriend. 'I said, "How could I? I've been going out with this girl for five years?"' He found a way.

There had been a phone call with Arza first. 'He comes to the phone and says, "Hello" and I said "Hello". I couldn't stop laughing because it seemed ridiculous, because there was no other conversation. What do you say next?

I said, "Would you like to come to tea?" He said, "Yes, thank you". He came. 'He made all the right moves. And the rest is history.' The history of her family, that is. But, in one thing, to his surprise, history was repeating itself. 'He met my mother', she says without hearing what Ben told me about the parents who wanted to get their daughters on the marriage road.

So the big question was: Did mother approve? 'Well, she met a nice gentleman'. But, surprise, surprise, that was not the end of the story. She asked a woman 'much older than I but younger than my parents' to check him out. Not that that would have made any difference. I followed my own instincts. Of course, I had never heard of him.' The Olympics and news of his athletic achievements were all in the past. She had never heard of Primrose, either.

She doesn't remember the first date. 'But I would be surprised if it wasn't something to do with The Boys'. She does recall when the meeting happened because it coincided with the Boat Show that year. 'Becky and I went there in the morning and we were then going to the theatre. I then phoned Becky to tell her there were no tickets.' Depending on which way you look at it, that was either romantic – or not.

She does say that she was not considered a 'female Boy'. 'The Boys are always boys and the girls who came with them are Boys too. I don't know if you knew that.' As far as Ben was concerned, 'When I first introduced Arza to The Boys there was an immediate empathy on her part and an appreciation of my friendship with them all. I liked a lot of things about her and thought we could have a good life together.'

When he met this attractive brunette, Ben was 36. She was 27. He should have known by then what was right about her. He soon found out that he had made a pretty good decision, one for which he has always been grateful. There would be good omens, had he believed in such things. 'By then, I already had my own house, for which I had almost completely paid up within a year.' So there was no reason not to go ahead? As things turned out, that was true. But Ben Helfgott has never been the kind to make impetuous decisions. 'I was already in business.' He was referring to his clothing factory. But he was already involved in another kind of business – giving up his long-running girlfriend and courting the woman from Africa.

'Once we met, we started going out,' Ben remembers. There was something about her that made him give up his reluctance to get tied down to a Jewish girl principally. 'I didn't want, as always seemed to happen, to go with girls who would run to their parents.'

Whether he realised it or not, this was a woman who would provide the backbone to so much of what would turn out to be some of his most significant achievements. In 1966, Ben and Arza were married at the

Orthodox Woodside Park Synagogue in North London. It was March 1966, just five months after they had first met.

It was the synagogue where Mala and her husband Maurice were members. Ben had bought a house in the suburb of Southgate – too far away for him to walk to on Shabbat, which was the Orthodox way of getting to and from a synagogue. That wouldn't have worried him. He wasn't intending to be a regular worshipper. And if he was, he wouldn't have walked. That would have been asking too much of this athlete. But since Mala belonged to that *shul* too, Ben became a member, irrespective of his personal religious beliefs.

So what was there about Arza that struck home to Ben, making her the obvious candidate for the 'job' he never admitted was available? 'I liked a lot of things about her. I could make good conversations with her. She was intelligent and I felt we would be able to have a nice life together. People do talk about falling in love. The real falling in love takes time and our friendship grew as time went on and the more I felt how dedicated she was. She had never cooked, but the minute we married would make the best food you could imagine. What was very significant for me was the fact that she immediately understood my friendship with The Boys and soon developed her own with them and their wives. Last year we celebrated our diamond wedding in the company of our children and grandchildren. It was a time for reflection and I realised how proud I was of my family and how my love for Arza has grown deeper over the years and our bond of friendship deeper.'

The Holocaust was more than 20 years in the past. The Olympics were a decade later. She helped him to settle in, not to suburbia, but to what most people would think of as a normal life. A normal life that was surrounded by Boys she didn't know, but who soon adopted her as an 'honorary Boy'. An honorary Boy who before long would become a mother.

But what about that 'mission' of his? He himself has always refuted any suggestion that that was what his post-Holocaust work was. He says that, if he could help people, that was no more than what he intended to do. Pious words. Perhaps. But the Helfgott story has proved them to be fairly accurate. 'I only think in terms of human beings. Jewish, non-Jewish, black, white, brown. It's a quest that comes from where I was born and my own experiences. There are those in this world who are lucky and other people understand them. Some are not so lucky and life doesn't get better easily.' So Arza had to realise she was not just marrying a man, but also a philosophy. And a cause.

She was supportive and never complained about his work, whether it was in the dress factory or with the Claims Conference which took him, even in his late 80s, to New York. He has been involved with the conference since it was established in Luxembourg in 1951. Nothing was going to stop him going to meetings and advising his colleagues.

Those visits were wonderful nostalgic experiences. 'Back in 1970, I met a few people there from my old home town. We were talking about one particular person, whose name my friends had mentioned. I remember saying, "What, he's still alive?" "Of course", one of them said. "He lives here in New York." He was about two or three years older than I and I had worked with him in the glass factory. His father, I remembered, was a tailor. The father didn't survive. But when he himself went to New York, he decided to do the only work he knew, as a tailor like his father. He expanded his business to the extent that he opened factories in Hong Kong. I phoned him and he said I should come along to his office the next day. He said he had four children – three doctors and a lawyer. He was a millionaire several times over.'

Ben himself has never been in that bracket. But when, in his early 50s, he decided to make another change to his life, Arza backed him all the way. She knew that the Holocaust survivors needed a leader and that Ben would be happier being that than in anything else he could have done.

Arza appreciated that this was going to be no holiday. He had work to do. To him, it was no different from the attitude of the New York tailoring mogul with the doctors and lawyer children. 'When you take the survivors, so many of them were working so hard – and did so much for the countries to which they went, Israel, the United States, South Africa – you name them. They helped turn those places into powerhouses.'

Arza was the one who helped Ben make his own contributions to his beloved causes, to struggle, to find, as we journalists say, a new angle. 'That is his charm. He's very inspirational.' And she gave an example of that inspiration: 'He was involved with the Imperial War Museum and, independently, two members rang him to say they were resigning – and he talked them out of it. He said you don't just resign, you try to influence [the situation]. They stayed on – and to good purpose.'

It was proof that – and not everyone appreciates this – that Ben's work goes beyond the Holocaust and Jewish affairs, to say nothing of his sporting activities. As Arza says: 'He has got a lot of courage, moral courage. He is very flexible. Not black and white.' Perhaps that is why his life would have made a great film – in Technicolor, of course.

Now, to that name Arza. Very unusual. I didn't think I had ever heard it before. 'It's Hebrew,' she says. 'It means cedar tree. It features in the weekly Shabbat service.'

Arza admits that there were times when her husband's wide friendships would involve him breaking off conversations with her to talk to other people. 'Well, I got immune to it after a while, but it was painful along the way.' Memory is becoming a problem with him, she says. 'He has always claimed not to remember names. [He admits it and when one of these forgotten names crops up, he will achieve a way of finding it by remembering a particular book; no problem remembering there about which volume he wants. He has no difficulty remembering dates, as has probably become apparent by now. But he shies away from introducing people. He is embarrassed about not remembering names, even of people he knows well.] Also, he has a hearing problem on one side. So he would never really introduce me because he doesn't always know the other name, and that is a major disadvantage.'

What could also have been a disadvantage were the things that had made her 36 year-old husband tick when they were thinking of getting married. If she could survive those, the forecasts were going to be good. It undoubtedly was a question of priorities. 'He wanted to be with his friends. I knew he would want to do that. He was a gregarious lad and had a commitment to the communal causes about which he was passionate.'

But it was a commitment that she was to enjoy herself – particularly the opportunity to travel; to work for survivors and just for holidays. 'We have travelled to lovely places, made lovely trips. Our holidays have almost always been involved with friends. We are very fortunate. We have friends all over the world. I made contacts, too, from South Africa and North and South America – that was my medina [area of importance to her; Israel is known in Hebrew as 'Medinat Yisrael' the 'State of Israel']. Ben had friends in America, too. Also in Europe and Israel. It has been lovely. It wasn't the traditional sightseeing, touring or relaxing on beach holidays – not at all.'

So who were those 'friends', with whom they spent so much time on holidays? 'A lot of them were relatives. And there are pockets of Boys in New York, in Canada. There are people who Ben has befriended, weightlifting friends.'

Getting to know what might in some circles be called 'Ben's little ways' took more time and understanding than his social affairs did. 'I remember once telling him that I felt cold. I have a back condition and one night we went to bed and at about 12 o'clock, I told him, "My back is killing me. I have to go down and get a water bottle". And what does my husband say? "Well, darling, don't forget to put your slippers on". Needless to say, that was like a red rag to a bull. I could not laugh about it for a long time. Then in the morning, I tackled him. I did go down and get my water bottle. He claimed not to have heard the first part – that my back was sore. He thought I was just cold and why shouldn't I go down and get my water bottle? You have to learn to live with such things. Ben doesn't like being part of jokes. He is a very serious man. I thought that was funny, on consideration. He won't like that.' The good part of their relationship was that she was able to tell the story. But the fact of his seriousness lingers on. 'He doesn't laugh regularly, which is a shame. But there is something about him that is very attractive. A lot of people see that as not being romantic, but platonic.'

I took that a stage further. For some reason or other, I was thinking of the time the Prince of Wales was asked if he were in love with his beautiful new young fiancée, Princess Diana, and he replied that it depended on what you called love. So I asked Arza what made her fall in love with Ben. Her answer was not unlike that of Prince Charles – even though she plainly loves him greatly. 'Oh, come on! It's rather hard to identify. I don't know. Ben has marvellous qualities. Resilience, pragmatism, his abilty to inspire without knowing it, modesty and confidence, courage, generosity of spirit, being non-judgemental and always rising above the trivial.'

I asked her to talk about his greatest asset as far as she was concerned. 'It is the combination of all these qualities that makes him the man that he is and combine to enrich my life and that of others and always able to pick me up by my boot strings.' I didn't ask for an explanation for that. It covered so many situations.

But what about shared interests? Sport? There was a time when that would have resulted in a no-no on that subject. 'I have lived in a house where sport has been a very significant part of our lives. have never been involved in sports for myself, always used to give up on the tennis court or the swimming pool at school. It wasn't my scene at all, but I think as a result, I now go to the gym and do these things.'

'Our children are naturally talented, I think. They were lucky in that they went to a school where the gym master was very good. He was an Olympian in 1948, so he developed a gymnastics team at the prep school and they fell on fertile land. All three of them were captains in their time. They went on to do well in fencing at their school, St.Paul's. What I wasn't prepared to do when I took them to the gym club was to go all the time. I know they could have gone quite far. Then I realised I was going there once a week while other mothers were taking their children five times a week. I wasn't prepared to do that. Perhaps I feel guilty about that.'

What she never feels guilty about is her relationship with The Boys. Now, Arza recalls, 'The Boys were a group of people who had a zest for life that was vibrant, exciting and an influence to enjoy and hold up to my own children. I have always admired and respected them. I have known them for over 50 years and it is wonderful to look back and see how they have matured into the role of patriarch within their own families which have grown to include the next two and sometimes three generations. I know my children and I feel richer for having known them.'

They had settled down happily to married life. One thing she was not going to do was to help him with his business in the dress factory. 'I don't think I could ever work with Ben. I suppose it's because I am quite methodical and organised.' And he isn't? 'Not at all.' She thinks he has 'a librarian's eye for books. Also, he can achieve more in five minutes than I would in a week. But, he didn't go to school as a young child and I think the consequence of education is disciplining, you know getting your thoughts in order. Ben was open about his past and spoke about it – not excessively, but never morbid about it. He has become much more emotional with age.' I told her I had noticed that.

Among those thoughts are organising his diary and accepting speaking and other engagements concerning his Holocaust experiences. 'You know, people ring up and he can never refuse an invitation. I think this may be a part of his story. Mala is like that, too. They always accept invitations and be very charming and very nice about it.'

Sometimes, he is not so charming or nice to her. I asked if he discussed everything he did with her. 'I'd like to think so, but no, I never get messages that he should pass to me from telephone callers. I have had some very unhappy and uncomfortable experiences. I have got over it now and I have come to terms with it because that is how it is. But it has been painful along the way. One time, we went out with friends. I went to have a sit next to her. "Hello", I said. And she cold-shouldered me. I thought, "Okay. I don't know. How is your dad?" She said, "What do you mean, how's my dad? He has been in hospital for six weeks. I said I didn't know and she said, "Well, Ben knew"'.

What Ben always knew was the importance of the brotherhood of The Boys. 'He talks about the friends whom he has lost', Arza says. 'Some were intellectually stimulating and very important to him. He loved them dearly and others had different interests.'

'Different interests' certainly summed up the Helfgott personality. 'Some would say that he doesn't suffer fools gladly. But very few of the people he meets and knows could not be described as friends. Nevertheless, there is no side with him, not a trace of snobbery.' What there is, is not a trace of, to quote his wife, a certain standard. 'He never admits to it. I don't know if you know, but I have a theory about The Boys. I don't know if I am right and I don't know the others intimately enough to know if I am talking out of my head, but they cannot admit to any imperfection.' Ben may not accept that for the others, but it would be difficult for him to deny it for himself.

It is perhaps why a conversation with Ben will practically never include small talk. 'He's very bad at small talk', Arza says. 'I don't think he can do it.' Small talk, anyway, would not generally be something that formed part of the big decisions of Ben's life – such as when he decided to sell up and retire while still in his 50s. Arza backed him all the way. 'Absolutely, I encouraged it. I thought his working life started much earlier than everybody else's and so he was entitled to have leisure time and we could tighten our belts. And that was fine, too. No question about it.'

Even so he seemed to be happy in business. He told me he was – and of that Arza says: 'I think he was happy. He enjoyed the creative side of it.' That still makes her smile. He was, as she says, 'in the shmutter business' [the colloquial Yiddish term for the clothing industry]. It was not the best quality clothing. But, then, it didn't pretend to be – and it sold. Ben never got used to the physical, production side of it. 'He can't hold a needle. Even now I don't think he knows one side of the needle from the other. But he was in the business for a long time – successfully. I mean how does one measure success? But when he closed his business, the expectation was that we would adapt our lifestyle. It's a whole different ballgame, but I think it did excite him to go into the business side of it and create orders.'

'And that was the job he took for himself. He was always good at doing well at whatever it was he did. He never cut the fabric or whatever. I think he was good at buying and negotiating costs – and also they really did make shmutters.'

'When crimplene came in, it was in two seams and there was no belt and that was it. I mean, really no designing there, but he could work out that he could make a certain garment at a certain price. In two minutes, he could do the negotiating and the selling with the buyers. He could do that very well and he enjoyed it. He found it very creative and rewarding.'

But there is always the thought that a man with his brain could easily have been a lawyer, a doctor, perhaps a professor – and be a part-time athletics coach on the side. Wasn't he just a little bit frustrated? She says: 'No. I think there was always frustration. I mean, of course, every business has frustrations. The shmutter business more than most. There was a lot of frustration and aggravation with it; the order didn't come in on time, a lot of things. However, I don't think he was unhappy with it all.'

Retirement for some men means helping (if not actually doing it) with the housework, doing the heavy lifting – to use a phrase much liked by people in the furniture trade. Did that, I wondered, mean that Ben was great at 'shlepping'? He himself stressed to me that they were two different things, the skill and capacity to be a champion weightlifter was not the same as carrying a bag of groceries from the supermarket or moving a couch.

Arza agreed. 'That was a test of my love for him. In all honesty I knew he was a weightlifter, a champion, a record holder, double Olympian. One day very early on, before we were married, he was carrying shopping bags, and said, "I can't carry them." I said, "What do you mean, you can't carry them?" He said, "They hurt my arms". Now you ask me, how are you supposed to react to that? Funny, isn't it? I could have run a mile then. He will go with me to a supermarket, however, and he will take three baskets in each hand, rather than go back again twice.'

Actually, it was part of a continuing story. 'We went skiing subsequently and he couldn't sustain the activity. He can do quick things like weightlifting with an explosive movement. He couldn't sustain anything that involved anything that took longer.'

And yet, and yet... Try to catch Ben Helfgott showing he is tired. 'They [the survivors] have a zest for life and I think they want to make the most of their time – but there are different stages of one's life. When Ben was 50 to 60, there was a real *ruach* for life.[another Hebrew word from a woman who claims she doesn't know the language; it literally means 'wind', but it has also come to mean 'atmosphere' or perhaps a good 'feeling']. He is now 88 and the pace is slowing a little. And yet he has just gone to Israel for a few days. He is going to New York on Monday and coming back Wednesday morning. He is an 88 year-old man.' Not that she was happy about it. 'I think going to Israel, coming back and then going to New York is silly. I think it is a man in his 80s thinking he is in his 30s. He doesn't recognise it for himself and obviously he doesn't feel it physically. So good for him.'

It could be that it sustains him. Arza undoubtedly is part of that story, too.

# 19

## The Sons

*'We recognise the passion'*
*– Nathan Helfgott*

If, as they do, The Boys remain part of his life, then think of another group of boys – whom we'll call The Sons.

There are three of them – Maurice, born in 1967, Michael, born two years later and Nathan, born in 1971. We met, the four of us, at Maurice's house in North London and they talked about their Dad. Life with Father, it might have been called in the days half a century or more earlier when that was the title of a famous film.

There were few holds barred – at least not the sort that Ben used at the time when he did his weightlifting to Olympic standard. Plainly to them, the 5ft-4inch tall man at the head of the Helfgott clan – his sons, his daughters-in-law and his grandchildren – remains a towering figure in their lives.

They never experienced the Holocaust, but they have always been conscious of it and the effect it had both on the man they call Dad and indeed on themselves. Ben has never been one of those fathers who have shielded his children from the facts of his life. Conversely, they have never suffered the traumas of being a 'second generation survivor'. They have, therefore, been spared the psychological effects so many have endured.

So, if they are not personally tainted by problems, how are they influenced by all that happened to their father? Ask them and they are sure to say that it is because he himself has allowed his background from Piotrkow to Buchenwald to form so vital a part of his own life since childhood without it dominating practically everything else.

As the Helfgotts' second son Michael, a lawyer, puts it: 'It doesn't cause him a problem and maybe it allows us to deal with issues ourselves, rather than to see them as difficulties. He was also fortunate to marry our mother, who is a rock. And they are a good team together. He saw the positive in the world and in life. He also saw the dangers, yet to him [the most important thing is] the diversity of the world, which allows people to build bridges and allows people to live together. That is something that he has brought to us, his children.' He took up my own theme: 'It could have been very different.

I know a lot of people who have faced tremendous difficulties in life, including the Holocaust – and it is very hard for them to bring up a family and not bring their pain to their children and grandchildren. Yes, we are still aware of the Holocaust. It isn't something we won't talk about. But it wasn't a burden, wasn't a pain. I know in some ways he has got a hold on it. I have seen and felt the pain that he has suffered.'

Does that mean that there is something particularly special about the men's father? Naturally, all three sons think there is – as most sons would say about a parent. But there will always be another dimension.

The eldest of The Sons, Maurice, a businessman, sees his father's achievements under a series of headings, not least a little thing being regarded as 'a model to the world'. The traditional hope is that Jews should be a 'light unto the nations'. But also there is his work 'teaching tolerance, mixing with people, doing sports, doing and achieving the best, reading, learning. These are the values with which we grew up.'

They are not unaware of the particular and perhaps peculiar lives which second generations have to cope with. Michael believes that a story which concerned his brother Maurice says a lot: 'He was invited to a meeting, to be on a panel on Holocaust Memorial Day. They discussed the second generation and Maurice says he wasn't affected by being one of them. He went a step further and said no-one should regard himself as a victim – simply because of what their parents went through. People in the audience of hundreds of people were upset by that. Several said that yes they did think they were victims. My father didn't say anything. But my daughter found out about [the event] and she felt difficult about it.'

Maurice himself says he is not going to tell people 'how they should feel'. But it is a matter that won't go away. 'In political terms, it is extremely unhelpful to think of second and third generations as being victims.'

Enough about that. Clearly, this is no obsession for The Sons, so I wanted to know about the man himself – seen as they sat around the dining room table on, say, a Friday night. Michael, who in many ways was becoming a sort of spokesman for all the brothers (an impression that didn't last, it has to be said): 'We sat around that dinner table, talking about the Jewish community and world affairs, but he was also telling stories when any question could be asked, no discussion that we couldn't have. He would rather talk about the good things that people did than about the suffering he himself endured. I have heard friends hearing at home that at any time English society could turn on the Jews. But that was not something you heard in our house. We never heard that at all.'

Maurice brought up the question of sport. Of course, that was inevitable when the head of the house was named Ben Helfgott. 'Sport is such a fundamental part of Dad's life, not just because he was an Olympian, but [it dictates] how he feels and how he engages. He loves watching sports and many happy childhood days were going with him to watch athletics. And he had athletics friends. He was always tremendously supportive of our gymnastics. Dad got on very well with the coach to the Olympic gymnastic team, I remember.' That was George Weedon, a close friend.

Retiring from business gave Ben a chance to broaden his sporting activities. 'He was just two years older than I am now', Maurice remembered. 'One of the things he did was to coach weightlifting. People absolutely loved his passion.'

That word 'passion' comes up again and again when The Sons talk about their Dad. Nathan, a businessman, plainly shares his father's sporting enthusiasm, recalls the reaction of people who discover that he and his brothers are part of the Helfgott family. *That* Helfgott family, that is, because there are others with that name, not least the Australian pianist featured in a movie a few years ago.

'They hold out their arms. There is such warmth and enthusiasm. We recognise the passion [that word again] that we recognise in him is recognised by other people, too. There's so much about his personality that infects people in such a positive way. It's hard to say for sure, but there is a connection between a man's personality and sport. It is remarkable that he can commit himself to being a great athlete, lifting heavy weights, while doing so much else.'

And here came something no-one had specifically said before. Ben is extremely competitive. In practically everything he does and he also expected his sons to be, too. Says brother Michael: 'We all used to test ourselves in our family house. We'd ask each other, "What can you do?" And we would test him and see how many times in a minute how many press-ups he could do. He could do 70 or 80 in a minute. Without any problems and wasn't even out of breath. We'd see him get his chest to the ground every time. He has a terrific engine and great strength, no question.'

To them, Ben made clear that he didn't enjoy seeing sports that seemed to him to require less effort and to less purpose. 'He didn't like seeing the tactical runner who just ran a bit – and won the 100 metres.' They talked about the father who before he was a weightlifter was the wrestler as I mentioned before. Michael said, 'You can imagine him tackling the weights. He wouldn't do this unless he was sure he could think of driving in there.' Ben transferred that into his home life, too. 'He saw that we all went to good public schools. Education was so important to him.'

And then came the question, 'What if…' What if Ben had spent the years of suffering in Piotrkow and in the camps in an English school like his three boys instead? 'He would have been at the top of the school. I am talking of high quality. His sense of determination would have ensured it', says Michael. Ben, to him, is both mentally and physically brilliant. 'People have wondered whether this was all due to trying to make up for his Holocaust years. But not every Holocaust survivor became an Olympic athlete. Let's be honest about that.'

Now to a matter that has made me think deeply since I began this book. How much of Ben's determination and his subsequent successes were due to ego? Again, Michael thought, doubted and thought again. 'Yes, I think he has got a big ego,' he said, surprisingly. 'In sport, it's not just how good your competition is. But it's how good is that competition going to be on a certain day? I think it is different from having an ego, however – people who always want to be at the front. Dad wanted to be at the front, but he worked at it. He is going to go all out to compete and wants to be successful. That is his way of meeting challenges.' Ben was always tactical, he told me.

'But that isn't ego. I put myself very firmly on this list. You wonder how should I do a certain thing. Should I go about it? Then the opportunity is lost – and you wonder too much – or if you are not going for it enough. But our Dad...if he has a plan he is totally not going to consider losing. Yes, he does consider, but then he says, "I'm going to do my best" and that's what he did. His record is phenomenal. He was always a winner in Britain. Internationally, it was different. Because he was competing against professionals or semi-professionals.'

Anyone who knows anything about Ben Helfgott can understand that. When he attempts something, he does so only when he knows the odds. In Britain, as we have seen, most of those odds were stacked for him. But that word again. He needed that quality which was all his. Determination. If that was ego, he had that, too. The big problem was making even that work for him. Of course, it nearly always did. But entering the Olympics was always something else. Maybe it was a case of passion versus ego.

Naturally, his pride in his own achievements was transferred to his children. Michael recalls the Friday nights which always included a question directed to one of the sons. Michael, the lawyer, would always be asked: 'What cases have you won today?'

Naturally enough, there are always two views, in the Helfgott family, for the reasons for people's successes or otherwise. When you are talking about close relatives – let alone a parent – the question becomes more difficult to deal with. Ego? Maurice won't put it that way. 'I think it is a matter of self-confidence, combined with his success in sport and life generally. He loves the idea of competition and loves competing. We were brought up with his sense of what it is to be British and to be Jewish. His love of sport [is important because] sport is all about fair play and fair rules.'

One of their early memories, recalls Nathan, is of sitting in front of a television set watching games. 'He shouts at the TV and gets excited. But he doesn't like the hugging of footballers after goals were scored. He gets annoyed.' Michael adds: 'He thinks it is time-wasting, intensely time-wasting.'

And the sport, he believes, always comes first when national sensibilities were concerned. 'The Olympic idea of competing and respecting the individual in a team whether it is a British team or that of another nation is vitally important. If a pole vaulter manages to get the pole higher and breaks the world record, it just does not matter if he is Polish or Russian or from anywhere else. He is a sports fan. But he is not an England-sport fan. He loves Britain and if England does well, that's fabulous. But if the game is good, that's what matters to him.'

If it is by now assumed that Ben is a man of firm opinions, what about disagreeing with him about those opinions? Could his sons argue with him? Maurice seemed doubtful about that. 'If I look doubtful, it is about that word 'argue'. Well, we had our dialogues. I mean when I was 12 or perhaps younger, I decided I wanted to give up Latin at school. Dad thought that Latin was a good subject and it was important. The debate went on for an hour. There was a tremendous effort on my part to establish my right to give up Latin.' Did he win? 'Yes, I did.'

The divisions were not just about their Dad. The brothers are not immune to 'dialogues' among themselves. 'You DID do Latin', Michael says. 'No, I didn't. I did classical civilisation in translation.' Michael: 'Are you sure?' Maurice: 'Absolutely sure.'

Something quite indicative of the authority of Ben Helfgott followed. 'I said I wanted to give up Latin because I really didn't enjoy it and I wanted to give it up.' So I asked, did his father put his hand on the table and concede defeat: 'No', said Maurice, 'I can't imagine he would do that.' Nor can I.

And then Maurice told me how these 'performances' took place. 'I remember that if there were something to debate, then we sat down round the kitchen table and debated it.' 'Yes', said Michael, 'most of the debates concerned Maurice'. The Latin dispute is engraved in all their memory banks. 'I remember', Maurice now says, 'sitting round that table and I remember it [the debate] going on for hours and hours. It was probably no more than half an hour but to me it seemed to be weeks of discussion ending up in nights of discussion. And at the end, Dad said, "OK. You can give up Latin".'

It wasn't the only cause for dispute between father and eldest son. 'I wanted to have a set of drums and I, for three years, played on turned-up ice cream cartons and buckets and didn't even have any sticks. When I had my barmitzvah, I wanted to spend some money on buying a drum kit. I knew it wasn't going to be popular – too noisy.' Not popular? It was an understatement. 'My Dad said, "If you have drums in here, I'm going to leave the house". That's what he said.'

But his mother adopted her role as family peacemaker. 'OK', she said, 'you can have the drums. Go get your drums, but you can't play them when Dad is in the house. If you don't play them when he is here, he won't have to leave the house.' 'So I got the drums. A family debate again, but of course what happened? I did play them when he was in the house – and he didn't leave.'

Michael remembers staying at an Israeli hotel where the country's first Prime Minister David Ben-Gurion used to go to relax from the uproar of the Knesset. Maurice remembers all the brothers were given signed copies of the statesman's memoirs. Nathan: 'I didn't get a copy'. Maurice: 'You DO have a copy'. To which Michael commented: 'Maurice did all the arguing and leading all the discussions'. Nathan: 'I just got on with it'. Meeting them, I could understand it all.

The conversation switched to Ben as a swimmer. Michael says his father is 'a terrible swimmer', emphasising to some degree what his father told me. Maurice: 'He is still very competitive in his swimming. We discussed this one day and he agreed that if I beat him, I could have whatever I liked. I wanted a stopwatch – and I beat him in that race. It was fantastically thrilling for both of us.'

What was also 'fantastic' to all The Sons was the relationship they had with their parents Ben and Arza. Maurice says: 'I always sought and felt tremendous approval from my parents.' Nathan plainly feels the same way. 'When *I* say I sought that approval, I enjoyed it. If I knew I had their approval, I knew I had earned it. They were always very generous with their love and approval.'

What didn't get their instant approval was a matter that also caused dispute around the kitchen table. Nathan decided he didn't want to follow his brothers into a public school. He did go to university, but didn't enjoy it and decided to leave. He says he was 'terrified' of telling Ben about it. 'I was terrified that I had made that decision in the first place, but even more to tell my parents about it. But much to my astonishment when I explained my reasoning why and I explained why I would be wasting more years, actually they both immediately – and particularly, Dad – made it very clear and said, "I think it is a good idea". I was surprised and he said, "Why are you so surprised". He said, "You have done everything I have asked of you. We pushed you to go to school. We pushed you to go to university, you have tried".'

Of course, it would have been hypocritical of Ben, who left college himself before getting a degree all those years before, had he objected – and no-one has ever called him a hypocrite. So Nathan left Leeds University. 'I had a great time there." But he wanted to leave and Ben accepted it. He said, "I never felt that you would necessarily be a graduate. It is so irrelevant to you but I wanted to make sure you had every opportunity. But for you to decide to do something else, that's fine.' 'Yes', said Michael, 'when it comes down to it, Dad is quite pragmatic'. He was speaking as a graduate himself. Both he and his elder brother Maurice went to Manchester.

I suppose what really comes out of a joint discussion like this is the intense pride The Sons take in their father – and pride in each other, too. Maurice cited an example of how, in 2014, he accompanied his father on a more recent trip to Israel where delegates from Britain were accompanied by the then Prime Minister, David Cameron. 'I sat there, holding my father's hand in Israel, in the national parliament of the Jewish state – and the Prime Minister of Great Britain gave the most extraordinary speech in support of Israel and the Jewish people. He cited my father by name and by example. I thought what an extraordinary journey Dad had made – from Piotrkow, coming as an immigrant to Britain, adopted the country [as much as the other way round], proud to be British, proud to be Jewish.'

To see the three younger Helfgotts is to witness a scene that in other circumstances would be a rather long, but loving, private family moment. It was a peep behind the curtains which were suddenly opened. Again, it was dictated by that 'p' word, pride.

The other moment that stands high in the pride stakes is the occasion in April 2007 when Ben was guest of the week on one of the great institutions of British broadcasting, Desert Island Discs. As virtually every citizen of the United Kingdom knows, this is the show when various people of different – but usually staggeringly interesting – backgrounds are asked to choose eight pieces of music they would like to take with them if cast ashore on a mythical desert island. In between, they talk about their lives. Ben's music choices were Elgar's 'Pomp and Circumstance', Gracie Fields singing 'The Isle of Capri', Pablo Casals playing 'Kol Nidre', 'Hava Nagela', 'My Yiddishe Mama' sung, of course, by Sophie Tucker, 'Nessun Dorma' from The Three Tenors and, finally, part of Beethoven's Ninth Symphony. There was one speech choice – the opening ceremony of the Melbourne Olympics.

Kirsty Young, the presenter, was herself later asked to pick the eight people (one for each record all the guests had to choose) who had impressed her most. She selected Ben among the eight (they included Tom Jones, Morrissey and David Walliams and the former MI5 director, Eliza Manningham-Buller) and said she was brought to tears hearing his story of Piotrkow and Buchenwald, through to the Olympics and his home life afterwards.

Young wrote in the *Radio Times*: '[Ben] was one of the most memorable people I ever met in my life, never mind doing my job. He [is] an incredible man. He was really thoughtful, but entirely unsentimental, just inspiring and energetic.'

There were letters from listeners who were moved by the broadcast – like a woman in Brighton who wrote: 'I wept copious tears listening to the programme.'

The repeat of the show was aired on Good Friday, which made one listener John Smith write that it was 'a keystone of the Christian year. I applaud the BBC for broadcasting your programme today and I bless them for the opportunity to hear you talking again.'

A former BBC producer, Thena Heschel wrote: 'I had tears in my eyes which matched those I heard in your voice and wanted to remind you of the old Jewish saying that a Jew dies twice – once when his soul is released from his body, but the second time only when people no longer mention his name.' In Ben's case that is highly unlikely.

Ben and Arza joined The Sons and their families in Nathan's London home to hear the programme, tears falling down their faces. Maurice recalled: 'I am a bit of a sentimentalist, as you can tell by now, and I sat on the couch and I held my Dad's hand in my right hand and my eldest son's in my left hand and we listened to the programme and it was beautiful.'

Michael pulled no punches recalling that day. 'I am totally biased, of course, but I listen to a lot of these shows and this one was really terrific. Dad is particularly good at the personal, one-to-one interview. It is where he is particularly strong.' Was he emotional? It was a rhetorical question and the answer was rhetorical, too. 'Was I emotional? Yes, it was lovely.'

As we shall see, his father's own emotions are a different story. Which, plainly, led to returning to their Dad's Holocaust memories and how it affected them. Michael told me: 'I think this [involves] two things. I remember Mum telling us about what Dad had gone through when we were very young. I don't recall what age I was, but I can remember the occasion very well. The second point is how we learned more and more from the Seder nights when we were children.'

Interesting that. Earlier on, I referred to the significance of the two evenings at the start of the festival of Passover, the occasion when the story is told in most Jewish households about the flight of the so-called Children of Israel from the oppression of the Pharaohs of ancient Egypt. In the Helfgott household, the poignancy of the festival has always been acute. 'On the second night seder, it was always devoted more to my father's experiences, about his freedom and it was about the Jews who managed to come out [from the slavery and oppression of the Nazis]. There was one occasion when it came up and he talked about it in a sort of semi-structured way. Also, there were lots of moments when it came up and we discussed it. It may be different now, but in the 1970s and 80s you couldn't talk about Israel without the Holocaust coming up. You couldn't talk about Soviet Jewry without a discussion on the Holocaust. So, having people around the table, that history of the 1930s up to the 70s was always coming up. Some of the people would throw in little stories of their own. It would inform his attitudes, his way of thinking. I don't recall us saying, "Dad, we really want to know what happened to you" – because it was partly my age and, in any case, it always came up so naturally.'

Maurice was influenced by his father's trips back to Piotrkow 'with Mum'. 'The story I remember about them, when they came back, was about the building in which they were in and my Dad used to jump down the stairs. He was about 60 or whatever and he seemed very old. My Mum was horrified, proud and terrified but Dad just took a huge leap, grabbed the bannisters and swung down 14 stairs in one leap. That was the story of the trip.' When I heard that story, I wondered about the significance of the tale. Was it just Ben showing off, the sportsman demonstrating that he could still do such things? Or was he demonstrating the fact that despite all that had happened, he was able to show that the Germans hadn't taken away either the will or the ability. He was there, fit as the proverbial fiddle, while the Nazi SS men had had to surrender and leave Piotrokow with their green uniformed tails between their jackbooted legs?

Nathan was on that trip. 'I looked at Dad and saw the boy in his eyes and really, I suppose for the first time, I looked at him and saw those moments that meant so much to him.'

At 17, Maurice and Michael (Nathan at 14 didn't go) went with their parents to Poland to place in their minds' eyes the stories their dad had told them so often. It was a pilgrimage to their own past. They went to Holocaust lectures at London's Chatham House and, most memorable of all perhaps, they recalled the many times the late author Sir Martin Gilbert (best known as the official biographer of Winston Churchill, but also one of the most prolific writers on the murder of the six million as well as of the definitive story of The Boys) visited their home. 'We also went to The Dell' – a rock placed in Hyde Park, close to the Knightsbridge end as a memorial to the Holocaust – a new large building will shortly open as Britain's own Holocaust centre. Ben, naturally enough, is one of the main advisers for that project. 'We took an oath and we spoke', Nathan recalled. They took what was known as the Second Generation pledge, to do all they could to ensure they would always remember what had happened during the Second World War and to do all they could to help prevent it ever happening again.

We talked about the publicity Ben has received over the years. Nathan put it into The Sons' perspective: 'When people meet him, they say, "Oh, Ben Helfgott! What a man!" It happened when we were very young and we became aware of how they knew him – in books and magazines, on radio and TV. I would get home earlier from school than Michael or Maurice and I remember Dad watching video cassettes recording a lot of war documentaries. I knew how different our home was from others. While other kids were watching space films or other tapes meant for young people, I'd be watching these war films with my Dad. Or I'd not be watching them – which would often stimulate a conversation with him. I would ask questions about this. He was around for me and we absorbed such things.'

Michael said he saw such matters at that time differently. 'The dinner table where you have a lot of people was open to different opinions. They never imagined this happened [the Holocaust] was never mentioned. There was this silence – until finally, they suddenly opened up. We didn't know there had been people who took that attitude. Our father would throw things into conversation – and he could say difficult things – about what had happened to members of his family. But they didn't ever have to deal with death and destruction [in their own lives].'

Michael then hit on a phenomenon that has struck me myself during my own work on this project. 'When we went with Dad to Piotrkow, I noticed that Dad showed no signs of emotional pain and anguish. Incredibly I sort of wasn't even aware that it actually existed within him. Not that I thought about it before [that visit]. We went to the place where he had last seen his mother and his sister. We went to where he last saw them. He looked into the basement. There is a little window there. I really didn't realise the enormity of what I was witnessing in a way at the time, but that is another story. At that moment, he was stung by a bee and he was a very resilient man and so on. A bee sting can really hurt – and he actually got very upset. And the emotion came out of that. It took quite a bit of calming down actually. Mum was very good and calmed him down. So a bee sting made him emotional, the Holocaust did not. But only openly.' There was probably more in that one story than so many of the tales I myself have heard about Ben Helfgott.

There was one other occasion when emotion broke through. Michael recalled: 'It was when I was 18. I was in America, at college full time, and he was staying nearby. He showed some emotion. And then, in the last five to 10 years, I have seen it when he talks to people and you notice the emotion welling up as he gets older. But we didn't see it when he was talking to us.'

On the other hand, Nathan had seen it when he later also went with his parents to Piotrkow. He saw it on the jump down the stairs. That was a pleasant emotion. On the other hand, when they went to the synagogue, the place where Ben's mother and sister were entombed before being shot: 'I had never seen that with Dad before. He was very moved indeed. It was the first time he had been back there and it was very hard for him.'

As for The Sons, he said: 'One does not know really what his reaction would be and how things we have all had would react on us. How do you think your reaction is going to be after all those stories you have heard for so many years? And I'm not talking about our own family, but about all that happened to so many people, Jews especially, But it's very hard to take in until you go [to places like Piotrkow]. You have to go to those places and see how they processed the deaths and destruction. I remember when we were at Treblinka where there were 850,000 people killed. But all that's left is an extraordinary monument where there is a stone on the ground for every village or town where Jews were killed. They tried to give us some scale to it as you walk among the stones. Dad and I actually walked among the stones, slightly separately. Until then, I hadn't been able to comprehend what had happened and Dad has never tried to make us comprehend what had happened. That has never been his mission.'

He said he 'almost felt happy' that he was, somehow, sharing memories with his Dad. 'In that awful place, I said to him: "Dad, I feel terrible because I also feel slightly elated". He said "Why?" and I explained to him. He just gave me a huge smile and a massive hug and he said, "This is all you need think about. You have got it. That's all that matters".'

Michael's reaction to that: 'When I go to a place like Piotrkow and when I got to some of the extermination camps, the feeling I get so strongly is really that we are so lucky to be alive and what we had contrasted in terms of our family life, the country we live in and the schools we went to, which contrasted so tremendously with what my father had to go through. I think we are so lucky. You know, I didn't feel just about us, but about the Jews in this country. Crikey, we are so fortunate!'

We changed the subject as the last cup of coffee and the last croissant was being served and consumed. What about British politics? What were Ben's? It was a question I had avoided asking directly, myself. 'I think in this country', said Maurice, 'it would be, like most British Jews, conservative. In Israel, he would vote Labour rather than the [leading Government party] Likud.' Did they share those views? All said they did.

After hearing The Sons talk about their Dad, I asked the Dad to talk about them. 'I am so proud of them', that word again, now turned around. 'You know why?' asked the family patriarch, 'they are all *menschen*'. The word I used in the Preface to this book had come full circle, too. 'And that goes for my nine grandchildren. They are not just three sets of three. They are like brothers and sisters. What more could I ask?' What more, indeed.

# 20

## The '45s

*'A practical, very fair, most admirable man'*
*– Aubrey Rose*

People have been saying it for over 70 years. After the Holocaust. After the Olympics. And, particularly, after being in what Arza still calls the 'shmutter' business. What's left? What could be left? What happens when a fellow still in his early 50s decides to change course and – to use a term much derided by others who have made the same choice – retire? The answer is two-fold – the first part is that his wife, as we have seen, thought he'd earned a rest; the second part should be filed under the title 'The '45 Aid Society'.

The '45s, seemingly, could now be translated as The Boys turning into The Men. Whatever you say, they now recognise they are boys no more. The original members included the vast majority of that group who came over in 1945 and found new homes and new lives in Great Britain after the sufferings of barely existing in the death and concentration camps. As the years have gone by, the inevitable has happened – members have gone abroad, to live in Israel, the United States and other countries offering them the freedom and human dignity that the Germans denied. More, sadly, a great number have now died.

But their work continues – helping survivors who have grown old and hit hard times – and every now and again just meeting socially, having an annual dinner, regular get-together occasions, attending each other's children's weddings (and more recently, the nuptials and bar and bat mitzvahs of grandchildren, as well as, occasionally, great-grandchildren). And also within the organisation itself, second generations have joined their parents and, in some cases, taken over from them – such as Angela Cohen, daughter of Morris Malenisky from Piotrkow.

But all the time, they have had the name of their founder Ben Helfgott on their notepaper, originally as chairman and now as honorary president, a man who in 2016 was given a special award for his services, presented at their annual dinner by a British cabinet minister. And, through the years, Ben has made speeches, imploring his colleagues to take part in the '45s work and, by the by, to visit other survivors in Israel.

He shares memories with other members and dreams, all too often nightmares, too – like the recurring nightmare he used to have of hiding under a table in the hope that no Nazi trooper would find him.

The '45s have become yet another cause for, that word again, pride. Pride at the achievements of his fellow Boys. 'When I speak to survivors, most of them didn't have much of an education, but I can see how marvellous they feel that their children have done so well.' In saying that, as we shall see, very much part of the work of the organisation is to help The Boys and others who don't have such a good story to tell. But pride is clearly the emotion that comes hand in hand – a helping hand – with all the organisations and events in which he is involved. Above all, involved with them as individuals.

In addition, Ben helped to establish and continues to work with the Holocaust Education Trust which, besides other activities, acts as a sort of a spokesman organisation to the media whenever – and it happens all too frequently – there are deniers coming out of the proverbial woodwork.

For Ben's sons, the work and story of the '45s in particular became part of their home and their lives. 'It's not about Holocaust,' says Michael Helfgott. 'It's about life. It's a vibrant organisation, doing so many things. I saw it all, when Dad was working for the Claims Commission [see later] or when he was pivotal in establishing the Holocaust exhibition at the Imperial War Museum' – rooms at one of Britain's leading museums in London, devoted to pictures and exhibits of the events that were, for five years and eight months, Ben's life.

What the aid society is really about, says the second Helfgott son, is 'making things happen, making positive things happen within the background of the Holocaust'. His top personal memory of the '45s is, was, as he puts it, 'always in May. My parents dressed up; my Dad puts on a black tie, my mum in a lovely dress, and they went out. Their friends came from abroad. It was always so exciting.'

But in this organisation dedicated to memories of the greatest crime and, for the Jews, the greatest tragedy in history is also a fun occasion. 'Anyone going to the reunion is attending', says Michael Helfgott, 'a happy party. It's a huge celebration of life and their friendships.'

He recalls the meetings held in the family home in Harrow. 'I remember my Dad chairing the meetings. Twenty-five to 30 Boys sitting around the table, we are trying to get to sleep, hearing Dad from up the stairs. I mean they are noisy. In their prime, they were extraordinary, lively, joking, energetic, a fun group of guys. A significant number of them are my parents' friends.'

Angela Cohen says: 'It's because of Ben's energies and Ben's love of The Boys that the '45 Aid Society has flourished. He is responsible for getting the second generation involved. When we celebrated the society's 50th anniversary, we had 450 people there.' The reunion she was planning the following week would have 600 people. 'People coming from the United States and Canada are bringing their families with them.'

Away from social activities what really does the society do? She repeated what I knew already, but went into details. 'We have a fund to help The Boys who fall on hard times', says Angela Cohen. Ben himself says of what was his creation: 'If anyone needed help, we helped. A lot of survivors who went to Israel were helped, too. During the 1950s and 60s we supported hospitals helping survivors.' Angela adds: 'Educationally, The Boys go out to talk to schools. Every year we have a special lecture. When we had a memorial service on the 70th anniversary of the end of the war, Ben sat next to Prince Charles.'

Simultaneously with all his '45s work, Ben has become involved with Britain's Jewish community, the Board of Deputies, which prides itself as being the 'representative body of Anglo Jewry', with synagogues and other organisations sending delegates to its monthly meetings, dealing with matters concerning the community, from the fight against anti-Semitism to taking on the case for the maintenance of the Jewish method of animal slaughter, an issue that constantly raises its head.

'Through that committee, we worked to find speakers [to give talks about the Holocaust]. The most important thing was when the Berlin Wall came down.' That gave many opportunities to involve countries that had been described as behind the Iron Curtain. 'It opened up a lot of new things for us.'

For 20 years, Ben served as chairman of the Board of Deputies Holocaust Yad Vashem (literally the Hand of God; as we have seen, Yad Vashem is the name of the Holocaust memorial in Jerusalem) committee. Then he added to the list of posts he held in Anglo Jewry by becoming president of the National Yad Vashem Charitable Trust in the United Kingdom.

The committee was instrumental in working with the publisher Frank Cass in establishing the Library of Holocaust Testimonies and working closely with Ben's fellow survivors organised a series of talks and lectures in schools and universities. It took upon itself the responsibility of helping to fund the Valley of the 5,000 Communities. Synagogues all over Britain adopted 'Lost Communities'. It also commissioned a survey of Holocaust education in Britain.

One of the Board's leading members, the lawyer Aubrey Rose, who has played bridge with Ben – 'the slowest bridge player I have ever met' – has also assisted him on Holocaust work 'for two years in the 1990s working on Holocaust Memorial Day. People, ambassadors and other important people, always looked up to Ben.' I suppose you could say that is quite an achievement for a man only 5 feet four inches tall. 'He is,' says Rose, 'a practical, very rare and most admirable man. One of the few in communal affairs who have not thought that they have the right to a position or honour.'

Ben was responsible for a memorial 'programme' in honour of his old mentor, Yogi Mayer. Rose was one of the speakers, along with Sir Martin Gilbert.

There are so many people, some well known like the writer Harold Pinter and the actress and writer Ruth Rosen, and some unknown, who can point to the '45s as being responsible for letting 'outsiders' know about the Holocaust. Ruth wrote the script for an evening of thoughts and reminiscences to mark the 70th anniversary of the liberation of the straggling remnant of Auschwitz survivors. They produced a CD of the evening at the Purcell Room on London's South Bank in July 1988, entitled 'Speak the Unspeakable'. Pinter joined Ruth and Harry Ariel to read testimonies from people like Primo Levi and witnesses of the barbarous atrocities of Babi Yar and Chelmo.

The emotions of the speakers as they read the testimonies of victims were high, but the clinical details from SS reports of the machinery used and its success in executions in gas vans, were low key. It was as though they were discussing a new printing press or designs for a car factory. The main problem was filling the vans, because if that happened, it would disturb the balance of the vehicle. Jews were easily disposed of. Vans were expensive to replace.

Another document read was the minutes of the meeting at Wannsee which initiated what became known as 'The Final Solution'. This included a report from Rynard Heydrich, which predicted that 11 million Jews would be involved for appropriate work. Some will fall away for natural reduction. Even people who considered themselves to be Holocaust students quivered as they heard the stories and the statistics.

'It was all through Ben that the evening happened. He raised the money for it.' But that wasn't all. 'I relied on his judgment – which is always spot on. When I talk to him about the things we are doing and need his advice, I can rely completely on what he says. It is fantastic.'

Ben treats the people who have entered his life through the various organisations as his own, not quite family perhaps, but as the twenty-first century version of The Boys, almost as if they were people who because they had done so much he couldn't imagine doing without in his life. Such as another woman called Ruth, Ruth-Anne Lenga, who has spent 25 years or more working for Holocaust education. 'I used to be a teacher,' she told me, 'and Ben has been for me a mentor, both personally and in my professional work. And he has been a critical friend, too.' Which is not difficult to believe. Mr Helfgott has always wanted the good things he does or supervises to be done the way he wants them done.

Another Board of Deputies colleague, Jeffrey Pinnick, noted that. 'The dynamism that he has dictates that he relies on nobody but himself. That can only come from his experiences in the days when it was every man for himself. He is not communicative. He knows what needs to be done and does it. When you are a member of a team you have to find out what Ben is going to do first. You don't ask what he is going to do or how he's going to do it. You just hope he is going to achieve it. Yes, it can be very frustrating at times. The '45 Society are an amazing group of people. Most of the time the others don't know what is going on. He is doing so many things on their behalf and in their interest, but you know he does it in his own way.'

He himself told me: 'I have never, never touched a penny from the money we have raised. Wherever I went, I paid for it.'

He knows a great deal about the raising of money, just as he knows the ins and outs of finance. That is why he has had 25 years involved with the Claims Conference, which is responsible for trying to ensure former enemy countries meet their obligations to Holocaust survivors. Over the years it has arranged for about $100 billion to be paid by Germany. In one year, 2014, it raised around $415 million for survivors. Ben, even in his late 80s, almost never misses a meeting held in the conference's New York headquarters. Once a year, they move to Berlin for their dealings. Sometimes, the meetings are in Jerusalem – where there is always a stop over at Yad Vashem. 'You cannot imagine the effect this has [on newcomers to the conference].'

'There are about ten people around the table at our meetings. I try to speak with the knowledge of my experiences when every day seemed like a year.' There are two representatives on the conference from Britain, one from the Board of Deputies and one other. Ben is there as the delegate from the Board. He is also one of three survivors sitting on the organisation – one from Europe, one from America and the third from Israel.

Plainly, the decisions of the Germans to pay reparations have affected his feelings for Germans. He always denies he has any antipathy to today's generations of its citizens. 'Others don't think like that. Of course, we cannot replace all that we lost but I do believe they try to do their best for us. It's a miracle.'

Of its work, he says: 'The money that the Germans pay is for making good – which they started to do with reparations in the 1950s. The Conference was necessary because there were so many who lost so much but didn't know how to apply for compensation. They started to get paid from the day that this all started. They got an average of £2,000 each – which was a lot of money in 1960.' You can see what a difference the money makes for the Jewish communities of the world, besides the money that survivors are individually getting from Germans, monthly payments in reparations. Then there is 'ghetto money' for those previously forced to work who were not able to do so. 'For the last ten to 15 years, they get almost twice as much as they did before. About three million people in some 43 countries have benefited.'

Education is at the backbone of this work. It was former Prime Minister Tony Blair who said his priorities were 'education, education and education'. Ben could echo those sentiments and so could Ruth-Anne Lenga, who emphasises that her own efforts are not connected with the better known Holocaust Education Trust. She works with the Institute of Education, now part of University College, London. 'What I do include research in the field and teacher education and training. That includes running courses in Holocaust studies, preparing people for masters degrees and Ph.Ds. One of the main problems is with teachers who have, literally, picked up their knowledge of the Holocaust from films and TV broadcasts. Hardly any of them had any training in Holocaust studies – and that includes history teachers.'

Those who had used text books were 'only one step ahead of their students. So then we examined the textbooks and the most common ones were full of problems. One of them was that the only pictures of Jews were photographs of dead bodies or in Nazi cartoons and propaganda.' This is one field in which the names Helfgott and that of the '45 Aid Society frequently occur. The work has to be financed and they – along with the Department for Education and the Pears Foundation – have done a great deal to raise both the money and the awareness, she believes. 'We talked to Ben. I talk to him a lot and he has helped me to understand a few things. He talks about matters that are very close to his heart.'

The people belonging to the '45s because they are survivors or those of the next generation, all have their own memories, their own feelings, their own philosophies. Angela Cohen thinks about her father, Morris or Moishe Malenisky, a man whom I met on my own first visit to Piotrkow in 1983.

He knocked on doors – some of them still bearing the scars of where a mazzuzah had once been. The encased slip of parchment containing the Shema ('Listen, Oh Israel') prayer, established that this was once a Jewish home. Only an indentation in the wooden door frame survived to show that, forgotten by most of its citizens: Piotrkow had once also been a centre of Jewish life. I saw Morris talking in Polish to women whom he had known in the late 1930s or early 1940s and who had known him. An interesting man, for all his problems, speaking perhaps more excitedly and animatedly than his daughter often saw.

'He wasn't a nice man,' says Angela. 'He was not a loving man. He was an angry man. He was a very damaged man. As a result of my father being damaged and not knowing he was damaged, he damaged his children. His ambition [once he had come to Britain] in life was to become financially secure, so that he wouldn't have to ask anyone for anything. He loved his children, but he couldn't give us anything, he couldn't give us love, he couldn't give us financial rewards. And I am being very careful and guarded in what I say because he was my Dad. But I was terrified of him. So in a way, and if I am completely honest, perhaps meeting Ben was very good for me because I understand him. There are a lot of ways in which he is like my Dad and the energy and there is only one way to do things – and that's Ben's way. You can't say no to him. But Ben is a different man from my Dad. And he has Arza.' But what about Angela's mother? 'My mum was very persecuted by my father and life was difficult. Really difficult.'

I have become used to saying 'that was another Holocaust story'. This was one, too, a sad tale few are willing to divulge in the same way. An unfortunate legacy left by a man to his daughter. Just one of the many stories that the '45s, like Ben, hear all the time. We went back to talking about Angela and her father. 'Yeah, Daddy was a tough cookie and I did love him with all my heart. He had a temper. The sentence that followed me around was 'Take no notice'. You know he has been through Hitler.' She said he had parents, 'a brother and three little sisters and Hitler came and took them all and that is why he was like he was. Well, that's true, but when you are a little girl, you don't understand this. And not only do you not understand that, you go into a great guilt. You feel you have to accept that because he is your father. Never mind about my father being difficult, you know violence and whatever he was going to be, he couldn't help it. Hitler came and did that to him. My guilt came about because whatever he did, he couldn't help it.'

And then there was this revealing story – revealing of Morris and of being a survivor. 'Mummy would tell me that my father had his suits and coats hanging in a wardrobe and she would look in the pockets and there would be crackers or packets of biscuits. Dad got taken into hospital years ago, a private hospital. He was placed next to the hospital kitchen and he could have ordered and eaten whatever he wanted. I was with Daddy and I opened the drawer of his bedside cabinet. In it was a knife, a couple of packets of crackers and some butter. That was how he lived his life. He had clocks all over the house, everywhere you went, and they were cheap and nasty plastic things. Because there were no clocks under the Nazis.'

So how was it that Ben Helfgott didn't have these problems? 'He put his energies into his weightlifting, and also into the '45 Aid Society and his other work for the Holocaust.' It was a long, but so revealing demonstration of the effect of those terrible, almost six, years. 'Ben sees the positive. For my father, everything was negative.'

It seemed as if she was on a psychiatrist's couch. Actually, it was the sort of conversation that comes up with The Boys who are now The Men.

# 21

## Finale

*'Having witnessed the Angel of Death, he has become an*
*angel of life'*
*– Lord Sacks, former British Chief Rabbi*

The last competitive weight has long ago been lifted. The last running race has been run. The final jump has been made. But the boy born Beniak Helfgott is still active. Still the focal point not just of the '45s, but also of the whole survivor movement. Still The Boy of Boys. Still consulting his impressive library to fill in any gaps about Jewish history. Still knowing most of those answers himself. And still seeing the link between Jews and Poland – and even between Jews and Germany – as being things to foster.

That was among the things for which recognition was paid in April 2012 at the graduation ceremony marking Ben's award of an honorary degree of Doctor of Literature (Education) at University of London. It was then that the Public Orator, Mary Stirsny, spoke of Ben's 'natural leadership quality', about his sports, his educational achievements (in matriculating and writing his exam papers in English so soon after arriving in Britain) about his efforts for reconciliation. 'His work also seeks to challenge prejudice in all its forms. At a time when understanding of the educational significance of the Holocaust was still in its infancy, Ben drew attention to [its] importance at every level. Ben was a robust voice in the struggle to secure the Holocaust on the English National curriculum.'

At a dinner in honour of Ben given in May 2016 by the '45s, partly to celebrate their 71st anniversary, he used a phrase not often found in the Helfgott vocabulary. He said he was 'humble' at the response he received from members and their families as they stood to cheer a man whose work for them had been anything but that.

For that dinner, the then Prime Minister David Cameron – which he signed 'David' – wrote a special message to Ben from 10 Downing Street in which he referred to his announcement on the previous Holocaust Memorial Day that 'a new, striking National memorial to the Holocaust was to be built in the iconic Victoria Tower Gardens next to the Houses of Parliament in Westminster'. He stressed that it 'will stand as a permanent statement of our values as a nation and form part of our national consciousness for generations to come.' As for Ben himself, he said 'I know there will be moments of sad reflection in which you remember all that was brutally taken away from you. But I also want you and your families to know how proud we are of you all and how inspired we are by your service to this country.'

It, in many ways, summed up the '45 philosophy and particularly Ben's belief, not in some kind of dual loyalty or joint citizenship, but of how the memories of a very un-British past have synthesised with an intense belief that they are part of a Britain they love. Perhaps more than anyone born here. It is amazingly similar to the stories of adopted children having a deeper love than usual for 'parents' who gave them homes and love that they could not have found in any institution. As they have demonstrated over all these years, this is Home (the capital is intentional).

In 1976, he had said: 'We have shown that the misery, cruelty, despair and injustice that were inflicted on us did not break our indomitable will. It did not consume us with hatred to the point of destroying our own and other people's lives. Instead we set out to create a new life.'

It is perhaps because Ben has stressed these things himself that his work has succeeded and his views have been so respected, Even those opinions which have not so easily been accepted, both among survivors and people in the general British Jewish community.

It is his views on twenty-first century Poland and Germany that spike what is undoubtedly the most controversial of all his thoughts and the activities in which he has been involved. How, I asked, and numerous friends ask, is he able to seek and maintain such good relations with those countries? He, of all people? He who lost most of his family to Nazi bullets? He who was beaten and starved in their concentration camps? He who was almost killed by Jew-baiting Poles?

His critics – and to be fair there are not many of them – find it difficult to understand. But, as remarkably, as with practically everything else he does and he thinks, they go along with it. Almost as if disagreeing with Ben Helfgott was a demonstration of disloyalty, a kind of treason to the memory of the six million.

People could never deny Ben's loyalty to the country of which he has been a proud citizen. Nor could they query the MBE granted to him by the Queen of whom he is more than just delighted to consider himself a subject. Leading members of the British Jewish community submitted recommendations that he should be given an honour. The retired judge and former President of the Board of Deputies, the late Israel Feinstein, wrote saying 'He is a universally respected leader and a gifted example in the conduct of Jewish public business.' He paid particular tribute to Helfgott's 'immense popularity, which reflects his dedication and his achievements in the welfare and educational bodies where his services have been so prominent.' The then Home Secretary, Jack Straw, sent a handwritten letter of congratulation: 'I am writing to say how delighted I am that you have been awarded an MBE in the Birthday honours. It is richly deserved.'

Israel remains high on his priority list. Let's use the word 'pride' again. The progress of the country established only three years after his liberation from the camps he watched both from near and afar. The fact that the '45 Aid Society still helps survivors in Israel, where most of those who suffered from the Nazis and are still living and have their homes speaks volumes. 'I keep saying Israel is a democratic country, more democratic than any other country in the region.'

Each of his speeches to the '45s reflects both his opinions and the amount of work he has put in. He has found time to write countless book reviews – on the Holocaust, but also on anti-Semitism and, perhaps betraying his enthusiasm for history as a child, the story of Polish independence with regard to Jews. He was equally eloquent with a review of a study of French anti-Semitism, now a subject more topical than at any other time since the Second World War. Of the Holocaust, he could write: 'As the "Final Solution" became official policy, the Jews found themselves in a trap...rendered helpless by the unwillingness of the allies to help and the determination of the Nazis to murder. The Nazis believed in Jewish power and influence which the Jews did not have.'

He, for years, went lecturing whenever the calls came – to other charities, to schools, even to the Police Staff College, talking to budding senior officers about his experiences. 'You made a considerable impact upon each and every person who spoke with you as a Holocaust survivor; it is something they will not forget and will be of great use to them both as police officers and as people', wrote the assistant commandant, John Townsend. It wasn't his only contact with the police. In 2001 he lectured to a meeting at Scotland Yard, organised by the race and violence task force.

As we have seen, he still follows sports as though he were still an Olympian, lifting weights heavier than he is himself; he still is as excited by any race that stretches human endeavour to an incredible extent, as if he were standing by the finishing line with a stopwatch in his hand.

And, yes, he still actually *feels* part of the action. Part of the Helfgott regimen is to get up at 7am every day – so that if he has a meeting to attend, he wants it sharp at 9am. How else would he find time to read *The Times*? He has certain problems brought on by old age, but he keeps incredibly fit – hence the barbells lying under one of the dozens of bookshelves in his Harrow home. Those weights, which look like something out of a torture chamber, don't stay on the floor for long. Every morning – before breakfast and while listening to the BBC Radio 4 News – he lifts what he calls 'light' weights, a mere 25 to 30 pounds. They are hauled up in his own unique way 20 times each day.

If you talk to him, sports can seem as important as his various politically related activities – the ones that have always had such a personal relevance. As if he had nothing else to do in 2000, he welcomed the new millennium and century by taking part in the Stockholm International Forum on the Holocaust held at the Richard Stockton College at Pomona in New Jersey. All in a day's work for him.

Polish ambassadors have presented him with medals and exaltations. They made speeches, praising his work for reconciliation as they pinned on awards like that of the Knight's Cross of the Order of Merit or the Commander's Cross of the same order. Investing him with the commander's cross at the Polish embassy in London, the Ambassador, Dr Stanislav Komorowski, commented: 'Rarely do we have the opportunity to welcome to the embassy a person as distinguished in the field of Polish-Jewish reconciliation and co-operation as Mr Helfgott. Mr Helfgott has always emphasised the importance of the study of the history of the Polish Jews as well as of their culture, language, lifestyle and art.' Ben spoke of his reaction to the praise rained down on him: 'Whatever I have done to deserve this recognition, I did for no other reason than for my abiding and profound conviction of the importance of reconciliation and understanding to my fellow human beings.' Of his experiences, he said in his speech, 'As a youngster I was repelled by this [the Nazi murder programme] evil. Like many of my friends, I did not think of revenge. But I dreamt of the day when I would once again be free and would be able to tell that man is capable of the worst and he is capable of the best, of madness and genius. That the unthinkable is, indeed, possible.'

The then Chief Rabbi, Jonathan Sacks, Lord Sacks of Aldgate, was unable to attend the ceremony, but he wrote warmly to the Ambassador of the new knight: 'Ben Helfgott is one of the heroes of our community. A survivor of the Holocaust, he has dedicated his life to helping fellow survivors. Having witnessed the Angel of death, he has become an angel of Life…Ben is used to carrying heavy weights – at an Olympic level – but the weight of the Holocaust is the heaviest of all, and he has carried it with a strong heart, a generous spirit and great courage.'

Ben spoke, too, at a one-day conference on Polish-Jewish Relations held under the auspices of another Polish ambassador, Ryszaard Stemplowski. He said then: 'The conference evinced that there is still ingrained prejudice among Poles and Jews, especially among the old, but it is essential to make the young generation aware of the causes that brought about these unhappy circumstances. We need courage to combat these irrationalities.'

His award was warmly welcomed by the Jewish philanthropist the late Sir Sigmund Sternberg, who received a papal knighthood for his work for Jewish-Catholic relations. He spoke of his notion that 'We live again in days when hate-crazed people deliberately set out to take the lives of those they despise and would terrorise into submission. Sometimes they succeed in killing people. They can never destroy the human spirit. Ben is living powerful testimony to that fact and your country does well to recognise it [with the award]'.

Then Sir 'Ziggy' said this: 'He won fame and worldwide acclaim as the British lightweight weightlifting record holder, representing Britain in two Olympic Games. If there is one thing you can say about Ben it is that he himself is no lightweight.'

When the deputy head of mission at the London Polish embassy, Witold Sobkow, retired he used the occasion to write to 'Mr Helfgott' – he like the other diplomats from Warsaw one of the few people not to use Ben's first name. 'Before I left', he wrote, 'I wanted to drop you a note to say how much I have appreciated the co-operation I have enjoyed with you. I am very grateful for the good relations we have had and the co-operative way in which we have tackled the many important bilateral and international issues on which we have worked over the past seven and a half years of my stay in Britain. I will always value highly your precious advice and your friendship.'

Then there was a letter from another country about which much has been said about collaboration with the Nazis – in putting the Holocaust into effect – Latvia. From Riga, the Foreign Minister, Dr Atis Pabriks, wrote about a conference both attended of the Task Force for International Co-operation in Holocaust Research and Education. 'I am truly grateful', the minister said, 'that together we could acknowledge the importance of passing on to the future generations a profound understanding of the consequences of the Holocaust and sense of responsibility to human community.'

Jeffrey Pinnick – who, bearing in mind the many tributes awarded to Ben, calls him 'Doctor, Doctor, Doctor' – understands the pleasure Ben gets from these. 'I don't think he is taken in by these; they don't make him love Poland more than he would otherwise – I think he delights in receiving an award as part of the recognition it brings to his cause. I have heard him speak so powerfully against those people who are critical both of the Polish government past and present and the Germans, too. He believes that reconciliation is the step forward, that bitterness and recrimination should play no part in the lives of those people who suffered in the Holocaust. He believes you have to build on those tragedies and make the future better. He is so genuine in his feelings and the way he puts it over so passionately and genuinely.'

To Aubrey Rose, Ben 'has that rare quality of not holding things from the past against people of new generations'.

There are those who think that Ben is obstinate in the way he maintains his points of view. Pinnick told me, 'I have never known him to be swayed by views of other people, views that he doesn't hold himself'.

Of course, everything comes down to the Holocaust. He constantly thinks of all that has been lost; that, had there been no Nazi mass murders, the world's Jewish population could, he estimates, now be something like 30 million strong – almost twice as big as the figure today.

To the '45s, he pleads that they follow his example and go back to Poland and the other countries from which they came. But, naturally, just for visits, to retrace their own and their loved ones' footsteps. He says it is important that they can recall their roots and also to meet Poles who are still around and could tell stories of Jewish neighbours in places like Piotrkow. I saw for myself how Ben put that into practice himself, staying in an hotel in the square which was once so Jewish, in the library which was once the synagogue and the place from which his mother and sister were dragged with hundreds of other Jews and taken to the forest to be murdered. We were, as recalled earlier in this book, in the cemetery where the men of the town were shot one by one. We walked through the streets to the old ghetto and into the apartment block where they lived. Was this some kind of pilgrimage? I think it probably was, although, once more, I was amazed at the apparent lack of emotion. I saw him speaking Polish to the inhabitants. All part of his links with his origins.

On the evening of our visit, having dinner in one of the open-air restaurants in that Piotrkow square, I asked what it felt like for him at that moment. I know I sensed there were ghosts walking around wearing armbands with the blue Star of David, not as a symbol of pride, but another attempt at humiliation and a ticket to the gas chambers and the killing fields. 'As for me,' he told me, 'I know the history of this place, I can speak the language. When I get into a car or a taxi and I talk to them in Polish, to them I *am* a Pole. I tell them I have lived in England for 70 years and they can't believe it. I have got friends here. I know a man who has told me he wishes he had been born a Jew – even after the history of this place. He has gone to Israel twice and loves the country. It's nice to have friends like that.' It is no surprise that he is chairman of the Institute of Polish-Jewish Studies at Oxford – studies you cannot make without knowing something about the intense anti-Semitism that many would think Poles learn with the first drops of their mothers' milk. 'Learn' has always been a watchword for him. Like language itself and history. History of the two countries where he has lived all these years.

Of course, history is about people and, over the years, not many people who have met him escape either his attention or his memory. But what is there about English history that appeals? It is not knowing what happened in 1066 – rather, not *just* what happened in 1066; not knowing the names of Henry VIII's six wives, though he probably does; not even the dates of the Civil War that led to Charles I losing his head – but about the governments and the *people* they governed.

He puts a gloss on Britain and its populations over the years that others from the same background as he might not. He compares it with Poland but the awards presented to him by his native land are testimony to the affection he feels for that country – inexplicable to many.

He puts that into an historical context, too. 'Britain's history is a marvellous history and a different history.' Different from Poland's, he explains. 'The [British] people didn't kill each other [not mentioning that Civil War or the barons whose ancestors came over with William the Conqueror, although he could say that the Normans were French, at least]'. On the whole, Britons didn't kill each other like they did in Poland. 'The Polish history is a terrible history. People always being killed and occupied. Britain is ahead of other countries and that is because they did things slowly.' Maybe that is why he became so enamoured of Britain. Ben Helfgott slowly calculates his every move and the results are generally what he intended them to be in the first place.

I often wondered whether a man who goes so often to his native land, travelling on a British passport, is ever considered to be a traitor by the Poles he meets. He says he never has been. He is plainly 'at' home in Poland, but not *in his* home. 'I do not regard Poland as home', he emphasises, 'but when I go there it isn't strange either. I am comfortable'.

That is him. He regards himself as 'comfortable' in what has been his homeland since 1945. Just over 70 years an Englishman. Although, not quite. The baggage he carried on arrival has long been stowed away. But there are, shall we say, a number of things still in his pocket. Most of them if he ever unloaded them, and he never will, could be filed under the heading 'Memories', most of them revealed in these pages. I would really love to know whether the slight accent in which he speaks English becomes an English accent when he talks in Polish on his visits to Piotrkow or to people in government – some of whom, like the assistant speaker of the Polish Parliament, hail from his old home town and are old friends.

He is unrepentant about his feelings for Poland and the Poles now – which still strikes other Jews as somewhat bizarre. He is not a man to spout cliches, but, to use one, he says he speaks as he finds – in the right language for the situation which, to him, means that he liked the people he played with as children and sees no reason to change his mind now. He knows that there was virulent anti-Semitism, but he was not affected by it himself. Not, that is, until that day in September 1939.

Occasionally, a total misuse of both language and thought will overtake well-meaning gentiles who have been known to tell friends or neighbours in a jocular way, 'As a Jew you are a great Christian'. If turning the other cheek could be said to apply here, he can appear to be the embodiment of that. As we have seen, even after the war, he experienced violence at the hands of Poles but even that doesn't influence him (and today refuses to see anything but good in Germans of the twenty-first century).

He liked the Poles as a child and, as he told me, 'I have no reason to think otherwise now. They are very affectionate to me. You see, it is always a question of how you want to look at something from your own point of view. And how you look at people. Most people have never come across Poles [even now when they supply the best plumbers around] but they have heard things. When I first came to Britain, I met young Jewish people who said they didn't like Poles. I said, "Have you ever been to Poland?" and they would reply "No, but my grandma came from there. She told me about it." I would ask when that was and they'd say something like "1902" and I'd tell them, yes, that was the worst time for the pogroms, but Poland didn't exist then.'

It would be difficult not to answer that that was playing with facts. Poland as an independent state did not exist, but the people living there regarded themselves as Poles and constantly talked – in Polish, not Russian – about Polish patriotism. The country may have been part of the Czar's Russian empire – a big slice of that empire – but it had its own culture and, very much, its own anti-Semtism.

'It is wrong to accept just what one person says.' He does not include himself as the 'one person'. Maybe his answer, in the face of so much to the contrary, is the right one. After all, he is talking about himself and his own experiences – and will not allow his childhood memories to cloud his view, which is plainly sincere. If, in so many people's eyes, bizarre. But he calls witnesses to strengthen his case – witnesses who exist in that memory bank. Such as the cashier at the local cinema which, as we shall see, he patronised even when he was living in the Piotrkow ghetto.

But he is open to the controversy. In a speech he said: 'Our experiences may have hardened us and made us more realistic about human nature, but they have also left us with a dream to live in a world of understanding, compassion, fraternity and love for our fellow man.'

He says his sons have entered, benignly, the controversy and ask why he is so keen on good relations with his former countrymen. 'I said I do not defend them', he told me. 'I tell them how it was. I tell them that before the war, our life was not bad in Poland in comparison to what happened afterwards. We went to school, we travelled and had the same problems of a lot of other people.'

The matter of their sharing the same problems, indeed the same history, is one that constantly comes up. His old friend Harry Spiro points to the good that the '45 society and the man who first thought of it has brought him and his fellow Boys. 'There was no such thing as counselling. People ask about that. I say that we never needed counselling – we had the '45 group and we had Ben.' There are, he said, perhaps 40 of the 730 Boys who came over in 1945 still living and in Britain. Those 40, he concedes, owe so much to the name Helfgott. 'I really admire the guy.'

People admired, too, the way he helped with their own lifestyles. For instance, the Maccabi Association installed new weightlifting equipment in their gym. For the ceremony of unveiling a plaque, they invited Ben to perform the honours – even though he had no direct connection with the supply of the equipment, bought as part of a legacy.

It wasn't a widely publicised event. Nor, surprisingly, was Ben's contribution to the debate over Prince Harry wearing a Nazi uniform for a fancy dress party, which threatened to cause serious problems for the Royal Family. A member of the Prince of Wales's staff who had just returned from a tour of Australia, New Zealand and Fiji thanked his friend Ben for helping to cool the row which he said was 'a stupid incident'. He said it had reached the south island of New Zealand when he was there 'and had dogged us since. It was thoughtless and ignorant and insensitive and he has acknowledged [it was] what being 20 is all about. He still feels apologetic and regrets it bitterly. So, of course, do we all.' Then, the courtier added: 'The furore reminded me of all the wonderful work that you have done to spread better understanding and acknowledgment of the Holocaust.'

In a way, this was an unusual kind of friendly society, the '45s. 'Very much', Spiro says. 'Whatever we have done, we did because we wanted to do it. Many times we didn't agree with Ben, but we nearly always came down to saying yes. The people we help, they were nearly all very genuine, in genuine need. None of this would have happened without Ben.'

It wouldn't be right to say or even think that all has been lovely in the '45 garden. 'There have been disputes, sometimes very hot disputes. They didn't like everything he did. They would say 'You go your way and we'll go ours.''

Ben told how he was taking students around Piotrkow and overheard some women talking about them being Jews. 'There were four or five Asian girls among the students. I asked if they looked Jewish and was told only Jews ever came there. The point is you can't expect anything from these persons unless you understand that people acquire things that they learned from their homes and surroundings. They are ignorant and are anti-Semitic. I have made many friends among people who are not ignorant and are also anti-Semitic. I have made friends who first had bad thoughts about Jews.'

Harry Spiro says he has come round to agreeing with Ben's feelings about the Poles and the Germans he has met. 'I am a great believer – and more so in recent years – that you have to educate and talk about problems with people. I know that Catholic organisations had a lot to do with helping the Germans to do the terrible things they did do. But it took 2,000 years and finally John Paul said that the Jews did not kill Jesus. I haven't got 2,000 years to wait [before making up]'.

Ruth-Anne Lenga has seen the Ben Helfgott who, while demanding – not asking – for the tragedy of the Holocaust never to be forgotten, shares his doubts about the way in which it is spoken of these days – particularly when two words are omitted from speeches and memorials – 'the Jews'. She told me: 'One of the things [that bother him] is the temptation to generalise the Holocaust, to refer to other persecuted groups. He is adamant you must maintain that it was the genocide of the Jewish people. There are in the field also among some Jewish organisations those who want to be inclusive and people tend to be generous with this boundary.'

He himself told me: 'It is not that I don't approve. We have had our own Holocaust. We mark it in Yom Hashoah, the day of the Holocaust. We treat it as a day to remember what happened to our people, to *us*. I am sure some people are learning from it. But a lot are not and it is an uphill battle.' But is it the unique status of the Holocaust that is damaged because it is linked with the other events in the world that, in non-Jewish minds, also need to be remembered? 'Yes and no', he says. 'It is a question of how you introduce the subject. But in so many cases, people make these events equal to the [murder of the six million].' That is why the construction of a new Holocaust memorial, open to the public gaze, is so important to him.

Ben took up the theme in perhaps a more general way. 'There are people who have not learnt the lessons of the Holocaust because we are fighting each other, we talk about togetherness; when it comes to it, we are attacking each other.' Was he talking about his fellow Jews? 'Yes'. Was he talking about Israel and the diaspora's attitude to it? 'Yes'. 'There are among us people who want to adapt ourselves to other [cultures] and if others can't, they [think those] can go to Israel. They are the people who don't realise that Israel only has to lose one battle and it is finished. That will be the end.'

His work extended beyond Britain's shores, and provided yet another spectrum to what was increasingly being called the Shoah. Letters proved that not all survivors left their native lands, despite all that had happened to them. A lot, of course, were locked behind the old Iron Curtain and couldn't get out – or, if they could, many were too old or too sick to do so. There was, for instance, this letter from Igor Kogan, from Kiev. He was president of the Ukranian Association of Jewish Former Prisoners of Ghettos and Nazi

Concentration Camps. Tellingly, it is also called 'Raus'. He wrote: 'You went through so many things in your life and now your kindness helps people like you, people who went through miseries, cold and hunger. Your support warms our hearts. We appreciate every single person who offers us the help you provide us. We pray for you and praise God that he let us know you.'

I asked his views about the Catholic Church, so often condemned as being the root of Polish anti-Semitism. He has not had many dealings with priests, he admits. But there was one priest, Stanislaw Mufia, who wrote books and articles calling for good relations with Jews. 'He died in his 60s and I cried for him then.' Then, there was a better known priest. 'You have got to remember they had a Pope who understood Jews, was brought up with Jews and did a lot to change the world.'

It drew me, finally, after months of talking to Ben to a closely related issue. Surprisingly – to me, at least – the Holocaust appears to bring out some sort of latent feeling about religion in his mind. Although he had a religious upbringing (short as it was) he is not a man for the rituals of his faith. He doesn't observe the dietary kosher rules – and nor do two of his sons. Michael is the one who keeps kosher and, indeed, is lay head of his local synagogue. Ben is not a synagogue goer. Shoah plays a much bigger part in his life than shul. And yet, when everything else has been said, God enters our conversations. He talks about the religious wars and then says: 'A lot of the killing was supposed to be in God's name. When you believe in a god, you have to make sure there's just one God. Every human being belongs to God and the difference is in how you pray. It is not anyone's business. It is God's business. No human being has the right to judge people. We have come so far, we have learnt so much, and yet there are those who want to take us back to the Middle Ages. Who has ever met God? What is wrong if people pray to God the way they want to pray? It shouldn't bother anyone. In the Jewish religion we have a lot of talking to God. And Jesus? He was a Jew. He was not a bad Jew. He was a good man who tried to help people and they made him out as something else. The final judgment will come in Haolam Haba (the world to come).'

Strange to hear such a classical Hebrew phrase from a distinctly secular Jew. But then that was part of the Holocaust truth: no-one was asked by the Nazis if they believed in God. No Nazi asked a Jew if he were Orthodox or Reform.

Ben's mantra has always been, he says, to inform but not to preach. As he said in a speech delivered at the Bevis Marks Synagogue in September 2011:

'My Holocaust experiences have hardened me, made me more realistic about human nature but I was repelled by the evil I witnessed.

I despaired but I did not let cruelty and injustice break my spirit. I refused to poison my life with revenge and hatred for hatred is corrosive. Instead I was left with a dream – to live in a world of understanding, compassion, fraternity and love for my fellow man.

In spite of the fact that I have diligently pursued my career, sporting activities as well as cultural and social engagements, I have always been conscious of my responsibility to preserve the memory of those who have perished in such a barbarous way.

It has always been my mantra to promote Holocaust education and remembrance and to encourage others to do the same. It is gratifying to see that in recent years many institutions throughout the world have been established with this as their goal.

I must emphasize that I have never been obsessed with the Holocaust. Had I been, I would have failed my parents and society.

All my adult life, I have striven to overcome bigotry and racial prejudice brought about by ignorance and intolerance. To this purpose, I spend most of my time promoting research, education and remembrance of the Holocaust in the hope that the lessons of the Holocaust may be learned and understood.

I believe the Holocaust which established the standard for absolute evil, is the universal heritage of all civilized people. The lessons of the Holocaust must form the cultural code for education toward humane values, democracy, human rights, tolerance and opposition to racism and totalitarian ideologies.'

The future for him is wrapped up in children – his own grandchildren and everyone else's. 'The most important thing in my life is the prayer that no child should ever have to go through the horrible childhood I experienced. I was a child, but had to live like a man.' A man deprived of everything decent.

A few pages back, I mentioned the details of Ruth Rosen's CD 'Speak the Unspeakable'. The subject of this book has been a man speaking the unspeakable for over 70 years. Unspeakable things might have been thought by other people and could have remained unspoken had not a little man called Ben been determined to make his still accented voice heard. So many words, so many thoughts, so many actions. Ben Helfgott, the great survivor. His greatest challenge is that there has been so much *to* survive. And he has.

# EXTRACTS FROM SPEECHES BY BEN HELFGOTT

———

## Reunion Celebrating the 10th Anniversary of the Liberation of The Boys, 1955

We have gathered together to celebrate the 10th anniversary of our liberation and although this is a momentous meeting to all of us it is inevitable from the nature of its function that I have to recall the past and thus unleash old wounds and memories.

Ten years ago, from the millions who perished at the hands of the barbaric Nazis, we were among the fortunate few who were rescued by the allied forces and once again became free human beings. Most of us, by then, had already lost our families and were completely in the dark as to what was going to happen to us and undecided about what to do. To return to our respective countries was like committing suicide. We had never cherished any love or devotion for these countries, the hatred, persecution and bitter anti Semitism that prevailed there before the war still lingered in our minds. Besides, we were very frightened. We were free but were still obsessed with fear – all kinds of fear.

The stabilising framework of the family pattern had long been broken and in most of our cases non-existent. That twin pillar of independence and security which plays such an important part in the mental development of young people was deplorably absent. True, our experiences in the camps and the early loss of our parents which meant that we had to fend for ourselves at an early age, has given us a more mature outlook. But at the end of the war we were still adolescents who were in great need of guidance and care.

It was in this mood of trial and tribulation, apprehension and anxiety that fortune smiled on us and supplied us with the answer to our problem of the day.

Due to the relentless efforts of a number of English Jews, some of whom we have the honour to have with us tonight, we were admitted to this country and given a chance to rehabilitate ourselves.

The process of our adjustment was not an easy one. The social workers had a most unenviable task as we were very difficult. But, then our background and experience was such that we could not have been ourselves had we behaved differently.

During the last ten years that have passed, great radical changes have taken place in our lives.

The ready co-operation of the English people in general and the Jewish community in particular has helped us to restore our confidence and stability. The British way of life based on the Rule of Law, Popular Government and on the spirit of tolerance and freedom has had a profound and salutary effect on us. It has helped us to modify our views on society and see things in a different light. It has given us a more balanced outlook and thus made us appreciate the responsibilities incumbent upon the individual in the community.

I should perhaps mention that well over half of our group have emigrated to other counties to join their relatives. Some went to fight for Israeli independence, something we should be very proud of, and may I here pay tribute to their courage.

In spite of the lapse of time and the distances that separate us, we still maintain contact with each other and are always very interested to learn about each other's progress. We are like a large family spread all over the world but united by a common bond that springs from our similar experiences in the past. We know that we can always rely on each other and that we are not alone and this is a most gratifying thought.

You will forgive me if I bring out an aspect of our past that is often overlooked which is Jewish pre-war life in Poland and in the other Eastern countries.

Who of us can forget the traditional ceremonies, customs, dress and intense religious fervour that was so pervading and that had remained unchanged throughout so many centuries. Anachronistic as it was, it had a charm and beauty that the very thought of it evokes in us a deep emotional feeling. Whether we come from orthodox or non-orthodox families, we cannot help having a feeling of nostalgia and sentiment about it which seems to grow stronger as we are getting older. I believe it is especially felt during the Jewish festivals. This makes our bond even closer.

Finally, may I express the hope that the best way of reciprocating our appreciation and gratitude to the community will be to serve it to the best of our ability by taking an active and responsible part in its affairs.

# Reunion of the '45 Aid Society, 1975

There have been anniversaries ever since the curtain went up at the end of the war on a Europe saturated with Jewish blood. We, ourselves, have commemorated our liberation first every five years and more recently annually. However, the theme of the 30th anniversary seems to be accentuated and has assumed greater significance. One would have thought that there is no need to be reminded that we come from the shattered remnants of the communities in Europe, survivors of the greatest agony in the history of man's inhumanity. But in vain so we delude ourselves. A whole new post-war generation has grown up both Jewish and non-Jewish without being aware that never in all recorded history had any family of the human race been overwhelmed by such a tidal wave of grief and havoc as that which engulfed the Jewish people in the Nazi decade. These stark and unique memories which we share together are completely incomprehensible to those who were born after the war in countries such as this where freedom is prevalent and the five giants of want, disease, ignorance, squalor and idleness, as Lord Beveridge referred to them, have largely been overcome. I would like to illustrate my point. Only recently I talked to a young newspaper reporter. In the course of conversation he unusually asked 'what was it like in the concentration camp?' I was dumbstruck for a minute, which he obviously noticed and apologetically said 'you know I was born after the war'. A few minutes later, when I told him that 732 of us were brought over by the CBF and a smaller number by Rabbi Schonfeld he remarked innocently 'a lot of you survived'.

I believe that he is very much the prototype of the post-war generation and reflects their thinking.

That is why anniversaries are so important and in particular this year. People need reminding, not only of man's inhumanity to man but also of the circumstances which gave birth to the State of Israel, the reason for her so-called obsession for security and the need for her self-preservation.

Furthermore we live in an age of terror and turmoil where the Rule of Law is being tested severely. There are very few communities in the world where Democracy and the Rule of Law still flourish. Inflation too is playing its part in destroying the fabric of Western Society.

Humbly I submit, we are a living memorial of what can happen to a people when civilisation breaks down for we are the youngest survivors of the Holocaust and thus the end of a line. We also serve as an example of what can happen where each and everyone is allowed to give expression to his abilities. For we have elevated ourselves from the abyss of destruction to the pinnacle of reconstruction and respectability. Of course, this transformation could not have been achieved without the help and kindness which we receive so profusely at a time when we needed it most.

We formed our Society about 12 years ago with the object of helping our brethren who were less fortunate than ourselves and to assist any other needy causes and to pass the lessons of the Holocaust on to the public at large. Over the years we have endeavoured to uphold these aims to the best of our ability, so our work is increasing in importance. The peril of Israel, the Arab boycott, the danger from the left and from the right demands that our story, our uniqueness, be constantly told and retold. There have been many crises in civilisation and somehow mankind has always emerged stronger, however not without convulsions and upheavals. We have to learn to weather the turbulent times in which we live. We have always felt a close bond of friendship to each other and have eagerly lavished hospitality on one another and now more and more of our members are beginning to take a greater interest in our activities and more and more are realising that the inner strength engendered by the common experiences arising from the ordeals of suffering and persecution will help to sustain us in these difficult and uncertain times.

....It is important that our children nurture on the security which comes from such deep friendship and it has been our cherished hope that as they grow up they will accept membership of the society as part of their heritage and become more deeply involved in our activities.

As always the pleasure of this occasion is heightened by the fact that we have as our guests people whose association with us has been very close, Many of them have watched us through the days of our rehabilitation and now like doting parents take pride in our achievements.

On behalf of our Society, may I extend a warm welcome to Mr Oscar Joseph, our President, Mrs Montefiore, Mrs Blond, Mrs Hahn Warburg, Miss Joan Steibel, Miss Goldberger, Sister Maria, Mr Friedman, Mr and Mrs Yogi Mayer, Mr and Mrs Solly Marcus and Joe and Hadassa Finkelstone. We are grateful to Lord and Lady Janner and to Lord Nathan for being with us here tonight. I know what a full schedule they had today and for this reason we are all the more appreciative of their presence.

# Address to the Piotrkow Society
# New York, 1992

I am grateful that my very close friend Ben Giladi has asked me to address you today.

Even if he did not ask me to address you, just to be here with my dear friend and landsman Krulik Wilder, and commemorate with you the 50th anniversary of the deportation to Treblinka of our nearest and dearest is for me a most moving experience. Those of us who have now have settled in England and who are more or less of the same age and who originate from different parts of Poland have, for years, been commemorating the memory of the six million once a year at he beginning of May, coinciding with our liberation when we share the memory of those whom we loved and knew so well so many years ago and permit our personal traumas to merge with those of our collective.

Whenever possible I have tried to attend the Hazkarah of our Landsleit in Israel, always looking, searching and recapturing a thread, a connection with a past that is deeply embedded in my consciousness. It is difficult to convey, to someone who has not gone through our experiences the meaning of such encounters, the depth of feeling that it evokes. We remember our friends, our neighbours as they were before they were taken away to the gas chambers – young, happy and smiling with great expectations and full of *joie de vivre*. We talk of a vanished world that had no chance to blossom and we cherish the thought that we are privileged to revere their memory for most of them have probably no-one to say Kaddish for them. To those who have lived a normal life and who do not begin to think about their deceased friends until late in their lifetime, this may sound rather morbid That is why it is so difficult to comprehend the enormity of the crime that was committed against our people.

I have also visited Piotrkow a few times drawn by a kind of nostalgia – a nostalgia that only persists in my mind when I am away from Piotrkow, for when I am there after a few hours I can't get away quickly enough. The buildings are the same as they were when we lived there. Outwardly, little had changed. When I walk on the streets that I walked as a boy, in my mind I am completely oblivious of those walking in the street. What I see are images of those with whom I walked and played all those years ago. I am conscious too of the close proximity of my family. I know that just being there is the most tangible contact I can have with my parents, sister, members of my family and all my friends and acquaintances who perished so tragically and prematurely. The majority who live there today are hardly aware of the kind of life that existed there before the war. The vibrancy and dynamism that was bursting at its seams. Apart from the cemetery, there is hardly a sign that Jews have ever live there.

As we meet here today 50 years after the selections and the deportations of 22,000 of our compatriots to the gas chambers of Treblinka, we are bound to acknowledge that the passage of time has not entirely healed our wounds. We do not have to search into the inner recesses of our minds, our anguish, our grief and trauma seem to be continuously lurking in the dark. In spite of the fact that most of us have lived a full and fruitful life, there is hardly a day or week that goes by without triggering off some association with those bleak and calamitous days. Our memory instead of fading with the years looms larger in our consciousness. Who of us can ever forget those frightful, frightening and traumatic seven days – 14th-21st October – and the butchery that followed in the aftermath.

How can one describe the feeling of a mother torn away from her children or a father torn away from his family, of the bedlam that reigned in the deportation square? Is it possible to imagine the disorientation, the feeling of isolation, the utter devastation that confronted those of us who returned to the small ghetto from our place of work where we were quartered during the time when the deportations took place?

Recalling these memories is by its very nature a painful experience, but we have no alternative but to live with the memory of lives gratuitously and viciously annihilated. They are an inescapable part of our collective memory, a part of our identity and means to our self understanding. Our common background also carries memories and echoes of the stirring world into which we were born. As the years go by the more insistent becomes the desire to recapture something of the elemental power that has harnessed this vibrant and exciting life. Who can forget the talent, the genius, the traditional ceremonies, customs ant the intense religious, Zionist and socialist fervour that was so pervasive? We also remember the cynical world in which we spent our childhood, a world of unemployment, virulent anti-Semitism and persecution. These stark and unique memories that we share together are completely incomprehensible, especially to those who were born after the war in countries where freedom and the Rule of Law is prevalent.

It is now generally accepted that the lessons of the Holocaust are of universal significance. The Holocaust offers mankind for their reflection, the acme, the culmination of the unprecedented spectre of man's inhumanity to man and the intolerable perversity of human nature. It points to the degradation, humiliation and cruelty to which man can be subjected when the Rule of Law is manipulated and abused.

However it is important to remember that constant mourning on its own is a futile exercise which can too easily become chronic morbidity; As the former Chief Rabbi of the U.K., Lord Immanuel Jacobowitz , put it 'we must beware against breeding a Holocaust mentality of morose despondency among our people especially the young'. The Holocaust must not be presented in a way that will encourage passivity, depression and even extremism. Nor must the Holocaust be relied upon as an essential incentive to Jewish activity. The Holocaust alone is not a symbol of Jewish identity and survival. It is the quality of the Jews who have perished which determines the notional tragedy of the Holocaust. The real and ultimate tragedy lies in the destruction of the great centres of Jewish learning in Europe. The milieu of indigenous Jewish living which for centuries has been the cradle of Jewish leadership was obliterated. The source from which Jewish life drew its nourishment was destroyed. We must invest all our energies and efforts in the revitalisation of our lifeline and spiritual revival that would to some extent soothe the wounds and heavy losses that were inflicted. We must not only analyse how they died but delve also into the way in which our unfortunate brothers and sisters lived. Jewish lessons of the Holocaust should motivate us to probe into the life of those who perished just as we examine their death.

All this needs emphasising as frightening errors are constantly repeated, lessons which are painfully learnt are forgotten in the space of a generation. The accumulated wisdom of the past is heedlessly ignored in every generation. Our vulnerability requires constant vigilance. Who would have imagined 47 years after the war controversies around the Holocaust would continue unabated. It is not just the denial and revision of the Holocaust, nor the tracking down of the criminals that fuel controversy and attract the attention of the world media, but many other aspects that are continuously catapulted into prominence to which we are inescapably bound to react. Despite the Holocaust and the crushing of Nazi power, anti Semitism has not vanished even from countries where the Jewish population has practically ceased to exist. The rise of Islamic fanaticism is accompanied with anti Semitism and virulent anti Israel sentiment. The collapse of communism and the dissolution of the Soviet Union has, if anything, exacerbated the underlying currents of anti-Semitism prevailing in these countries. It is an acknowledged fact that times of great change, while engendering hope and expectation, also bring great uncertainty and danger. Eastern Europe, intoxicated at regaining an opportunity for democracy but without practice for almost 45 years and the former Soviet Union (C.I.S.) hardly used to democracy, may yet fall prey to nationalism poisoned by racism and religious fundamentalism. Demagogic leaders driven to extremes by economic deterioration may exploit ethnic tensions involving minorities and old rivalries, as can e seen in what was Yugoslavia, Armenia, Azerbijan, Georgia and Abkhaiz and many others.

The Jewish community in the world is also watching with apprehension the rise of the far-right or neo-fascist political parties in Western Europe. The far right seems to feel little of the guilt that made anti-Semitism socially unacceptable for nearly two post-war generations. As Mrs Jean Kirkpatrick stated when she was the American Ambassador to the UN, 'Anti-Semitism is not a problem to be solved once and for all. It is not a battle won on a single battlefield in a single war. It is a struggle that must be continued day after day, week after week,, month after month, year after year.' There is, therefore, no room for complacency. Experience has shown again and again that eternal vigilance is of sublime importance.

Still anti-Semitism, however disturbing and pernicious, should be perceived differently today from that of the 1930s. Then, in the face of persecution the doors were closed for us, we stood alone, we were abandoned, helpless and facing extinction. Today as we have watched in awe. the great ingathering of hundreds of thousands of Russian Jews and from other countries where Jewish lives are jeopardised, we can't help reflecting what would have been the outcome had there been a State of Israel in the 1930s. How many Jews would have been saved? How many of our parents, brothers, sisters, uncles and aunts or cousins would have had the opportunity to live a full and happy life? Israel's existence has enriched our lives, enhanced our pride and identity and has served as a rallying point for culture and Jewish living. With the birth of the State of Israel the destiny of our people had entered the autonomy of its choice. We have become the agents of our history.

It is also important to remember that in addition to a Sovereign Jewish State, Western Jewry enjoys unprecedented prosperity and political influence and Eastern European Jews, Jews from the former Soviet Union, are emerging from a prolonged period of oppression and isolation. What is more, liberal democracy, with its political and legal defences against anti-Jewish doctrines in Western Culture, has firmly denounced anti-Semitism. Although racial ideology has been debunked and Christian theology repudiated it still casts a shadow but we must realise that they have lost their potency

It is necessary to remind ourselves of the positive aspects of contemporary Jewish life before we are overwhelmed by the depth of despondency. Those of us who live in the diaspora are fully integrated into the fabric of society. The political, social and economic problems that the world is at present experiencing is in the main a problem to which all the Nations in the world, us included, have to address themselves.

I would like to conclude with a statement made by Itzhak Rabin the Israeli Prime Minister in his inaugural speech in the Knesset:

'We have to see the new world as it is now – to discern its dangers, explore its prospects and do everything possible so the State of Israel will fit into this world whose face is changing. No longer are we necessarily a people that dwells alone, no longer is it true that the whole world is against us. We must overcome the sense of isolation that has held us in the thrall for almost half a century.'

# Ben Helfgott

| | |
|---|---|
| Since 1982 | Deputy to the Board of Deputies of British Jews |
| Since 1988 | Trustee of the Board of Management of the Holocaust Education Trust |
| Since 1994 | Chairman of Polin - Institute of Polish Jewish Studies |
| Since 1995 | Founding Patron and Member of the Advisory Group of the Permanent Holocaust Exhibition at the Imperial War Museum |
| Since 1995 | Member of the Executive of the Negotiating and Allocations Committees of the Claims Conference for Jewish Material Claims Against Germany |
| Since 1998 | Member of the Executive of the World Confederation of Holocaust Survivor Organisations |
| Since 1998 | Member of the International Task Force of International Co-operation in a variety of fields related to Holocaust Education, Memorialisation and Research(Now known as International Holocaust Remembrance Alliance (IHRA) |
| Since 2005 | President of the Yad Vashem - UK Foundation |
| Since 2009 | Member of the Assembly of Founders of the Foundation for the Preservation of Jewish Heritage in Poland |
| Since 2012 | President of the Holocaust Memorial Day Trust |
| Since 2013 | Member of the Prime Minister's Holocaust Commission |
| Since 2014 | Member of the Leadership Council of the Claims Conference for Jewish Material Claims |
| Since 2016 | President '45 Aid Society Holocaust Survivors |

## Positions Held in the Past:

| | |
|---|---|
| 1963-2016 | Chairman '45Aid Society Holocaust Survivors |
| 1965-1984 | Member of the Executive of the Central British Fund now known as World Jewish Relief |
| 1976-1984 | Joint Treasurer of the Central British Fund now known as World Jewish Relief |

| | |
|---|---|
| 1985-2005 | Chairman of Yad Vashem Committee of the Board of Deputies of British Jews |
| 1978-2014 | Member of the Executive of the Wiener Library |
| 2005-2008 | Treasurer of the Holocaust Memorial Day Trust |
| 2005-2011 | Trustee of the Holocaust Memorial Day Trust |

## Honours and Awards:

| | |
|---|---|
| 1994 | Polish Knights Cross of the Order of Merit for promoting friendly relations between Poles and Jews |
| 2000 | M.B.E. for services to the community |
| 2005 | Commanders Cross of the Order of Merit of the Republic of Poland |
| 2006 | Hon. Doctorate University of Southampton |
| 2011 | The Times Sternberg Active Life Award (Runner up ) |
| 2012 | Lifetime Achievement Award Jewish News |
| 2012 | Hon. Doctorate Lit University of London (Ed) |
| 2014 | British Prime Minister's UK Points of Light Award |
| 2014 | Fellow of the University of Cumbria |
| 2015 | Freeman of the City of London |

# Ben Helfgott
# Sports Record

| 1954 | British Champion | 11 Stone |
| 1955 | British Champion | Lightweight |
| 1956 | British Champion | Lightweight |
| 1958 | British Champion | Lightweight |

---

| 1956 | Olympic Game Melbourne | Captain British weightlifting team |
| 1960 | Olympic Games Rome | Captain British weightlifting team |

---

| 1958 | Commonwealth Games Cardiff | Bronze medallist |

---

| 1954 | World Championship Vienna | British team |
| 1955 | World Championship Munich | British team |
| 1958 | World Championship Stockholm | British team |
| 1959 | World Championship Warsaw | British team |

---

| 1955 | World Festival of Youth Warsaw | British team |
| 1957 | World Festival of Youth Moscow | British team |

| 1950 | World Maccabiah Games | Gold medal lightweight class |
| 1953 | World Maccabiah Games | Gold medal Lightweight class |
| 1957 | World Maccabiah Games | Gold medal Lightweight class |

---

BRITISH RECORDS HELD

| Lightweight class | Two hand press Right hand |
| 11stone division | Hand press 11 stone |
| Middleweight class | with dumbbells |
| 12 stone division | Left hand press 11 stone |

Ben Helfgott
was the only
Holocaust
Concentration
Camp
Survivor who
competed in 2
Olympic
Games.